SAM SHEPARD

SAM SHEPARD

Don Shewey

Updated Edition

DA CAPO PRESS

Library of Congress Cataloging-in-Publication Data

Shewey, Don.
    Sam Shepard / Don Shewey.—1st Da Capo Press pbk., up-
dated ed.
        p.   cm.
    Includes bibliographical references and index.
    ISBN 0-306-80770-X (alk. paper)
    1. Shepard, Sam, 1943–   . 2. Dramatists, American—20th
century—Biography. 3. Actors—United States—Biography. I. Title.
PS3569.H394Z88   1997
812′ .54—dc21
[B]   96-37920
                                                              CIP

Grateful acknowledgment is made for permission to reprint the
following copyrighted material:
Excerpt from *Contemporary Dramatists*, Second Edition, 1997. Re-
printed by permission of St. Martin's Press, Inc. and Macmillan
Press Limited, London and Basingstoke.
Excerpts from *Motel Chronicles* by Sam Shepard. Copyright ©
1982 by Sam Shepard. Reprinted by permission of City Lights
Books.
Excerpts from "Holy Ghostly" and "Unseen Hand" in *The Unseen
Hand and Other Plays*, copyright © 1972 by Sam Shepard, used
with permission of the publisher, The Bobbs-Merrill Company, Inc.
Excerpt from *A Book on the Open Theatre*, copyright © 1970 by
Robert Pasolli, used with permission of the publisher, The Bobbs-
Merrill Company, Inc.
Excerpt from "Rip It Up" in *Hawk Moon* by Sam Shepard. Copy-
right © 1981 by Performing Arts Journal Publications. Reprinted
with permission of the publishers.
Excerpts from *The Rolling Thunder Logbook* by Sam Shepard.
Copyright © 1977 by Sam Shepard. Reprinted by permission of
Viking Penguin Inc.
Excerpt from an article on Sam Shepard by Scott Christopher
Wren in *West Coast Plays 7*, 1980; published by the California
Theatre Council, 849 South Broadway, Suite 621, Los Angeles, CA
90014. By permission of West Coast Plays.
Excerpts from "Shepard" by David Thomson in *Film Comment*,
December 1983, © David Thomson.

13 12 11 10 9 8 7 6 5 4

First Da Capo Press edition 1997

This Da Capo Press paperback edition of *Sam Shepard* is an
updated edition of the one published in New York in 1985.
It is published by arrangement with the author.

Published by Da Capo Press
A Member of the Perseus Books Group
http://www.dacapopress.com

Manufactured in the United States of America

To SMSgt. Delbert Leroy Shewey, USAF (Retired)

Have you ever seen anything of double nature? When the sun's standing high at noon and the world seems to be going up in flames, I've heard a terrible voice talking to me.

—*Woyzeck*, Georg Büchner

Contents

Introduction:

THE ARTIST AS HERO

I believe in my mask—
The man I made up is me.

—"Crow's Song," *The Tooth of Crime*

There has never been anyone else in American culture like Sam Shepard. He has been called both "the greatest American playwright of his generation" and "the thinking woman's beefcake." He has spent over thirty years writing plays, and almost from the beginning he has been hailed as a major talent, an original voice, a genius of the theater. At the age of forty he surprised everyone, including himself, by becoming a celebrity as an actor in films. His movie stardom is both ironic and fitting. For Shepard has always peopled his plays with heroic figures from the myths of popular culture: cowboys and rock stars, detectives and jazzmen, killers and dreamers.

Growing up in the late forties and fifties, his imagination was shaped by Hollywood movies, comic books, television, and rock 'n' roll, the culture of junk and fun. Out of all that he created plays that bore little resemblance to the tradition of American dramatic literature, making up his own rules for theatrical action and a language that popped and crackled with the modern sounds of a society bedazzled by electronically generated images of itself. By chance—or destiny—he proved to be perfectly suited to film acting, as if a lifetime of movie memories had prepared him for stepping in front of a camera. So by 1984, at the age of forty, he had gone full circle from movie fan to movie star, just as his plays were beginning to reach beyond a coterie audience to a mass public.

Nineteen eighty-four turned out to be a peak year for Sam Shepard, in terms of both creative output and public recognition. He was wrapping up shooting on his latest movie, *Country*, co-starring Jessica Lange, when he learned that he had been nominated for an Academy award for his performance as Chuck Yeager, the pilot who first broke the sound barrier, in Phil Kaufman's *The Right Stuff*. For the first time ever, he had two hit plays running simultaneously in New York. One of them, *True West*, was shown on national television in January, and the other, *Fool for Love*, earned him his ninth Obie award in May as both author and director. Brandeis University awarded him its annual Creative Arts award for lifetime achievement in the theater. And *Paris, Texas*, a movie that Shepard wrote for German director Wim Wenders, won top prize—the award for best picture—at the Cannes Film Festival.

This concatenation of events helped solidify Shepard's status as an American cultural icon. Part of the attraction of Shepard's movie persona is the audience's knowledge that underneath those handsomely craggy features is the mind of an extraordinary playwright, and the audience for his plays has swelled with the ranks of those curious to know more about the man in the movies. He has become something unprecedented in American culture, an artist who straddles the seemingly opposed worlds of highbrow literature and mass-media entertainment. At first he seemed to dabble in acting as a sideline to his major work as a writer. Yet over time he has maintained his visibility and stature in both fields. He has few rivals as the most important and original American playwright to emerge since Tennessee Williams; one of his best plays, *Buried Child*, won the Pulitzer Prize for drama in 1979. On film he has cultivated a curious mystique as a modern-day cowboy who exudes an understated yet unmistakable erotic presence that women especially find both exciting and disturbing. His attraction stems not from the acting bravado of an Olivier or a Brando but from a kind of charismatic authenticity that harkens back to an earlier era, a mythic presence that makes such male movie idols as Robert Redford and Mel Gibson seem pale and manufactured by comparison. Then, too, he has the one thing such fine, earthy actors as Jack Nicholson and Robert Duvall lack: an undeniable, even romantic beauty. His reputation as a literary adventurer and his screen image as an archetypal American male make Sam Shepard a unique combination of Ernest Hemingway and Gary Cooper.

In movies Shepard frequently plays a type of man familiar from the history of American film: the strong, silent type, the lone figure, the modern-day cowboy. But it's a role he also plays in real life and in his writing, where it's not so easily accomplished or readily accepted. Athletes, sometimes politicians, certainly movie stars can be heroes in American society. But artists are rarely accorded that kind of esteem. And Shepard is genuinely an artist of the theater, exploring in his idiosyncratic, poetically charged language and theatrical gestures the complexities, difficulties, and quirky humor that lie beneath his rugged facade of American manhood.

A true American artist, Sam Shepard is always searching for roots. And like Americans in the past, he looks west, to the frontier, the wilderness, the territories, hoping to find in the midst of the unknown something he can recognize as home, something he can recognize as himself. *The New York Times* christened Shepard "the playwright laureate of the West consistently, ruthlessly true to his experience of a wilderness where America has always hidden its promise and its dream."

"There are areas like Wyoming, Texas, Montana, and places like that, where you really feel this ancient thing about the land. Ancient. That it's primordial," Shepard once said. "It has to do with the relationship between the land and the people—between the human being and the ground. I think that's typically Western and much more attractive than this tight little forest civilization that happened back East. It's much more physical and emotional to me. New England and the East Coast have always been an intellectual community. Also, I was raised out here, so I guess it's just an outcome of my background. I just feel like I'll never get over the fact of being from here."

While his public image is fascinating, Shepard also has an interesting private life. An army brat, he grew up in semirural California, and he still prefers country life to city life. He raises horses, drives a pickup, and doesn't travel by airplane. Although he does business in Los Angeles and New York, he spends as little time as possible in those metropolitan media centers. Almost from the beginning of his career he has sought to avoid publicity, rarely giving interviews and never appearing on television. It may be that Shepard shies away from the press out of bitterness at the derisive and misunderstanding reviews he received early in his career. His attitude also grows from a strong impulse to protect his loved ones: his ex-wife O-Lan and their son Jesse, movie star Jessica Lange and the three children he has raised with her. With his history of being smitten both with and by the media, he recognizes how the power of publicity can damage people's lives. "I prefer a life that isn't being eaten off of," he says. "It's very easy to be *fed* off of in a certain way that distorts and actually diminishes you completely, destroys you to the point where you don't have a life anymore."

Possibly the most important reason Shepard shuns publicity is that he recognizes of the elusive nature of personal identity. The very idea of playing different roles as an actor acknowledges the multiplicity of personalities that exist within an individual, and the theme of self-transformation turns up again and again in Shepard's writing—and his life.

Shepard's relative reclusiveness has largely served to cloud his artistic persona with a mystique that in our celebrity-conscious society is always perceived as glamorous, and that makes him even more sought after as a media figure. While he maintains an image of integrity by resisting the star-making machinery, he must also realize the subtle ironies involved in his situation. If he really wanted to be a recluse and "let the work speak for itself," would he expose himself to the world so readily on the movie screen? Repelled by the trivial and soul-smothering aspects of show business, he is still drawn into it and irresistibly fascinated by its power.

"Shepard has a real love for the popular myths of our culture and a genuine nostalgia for some lost age of innocence when life was simpler in America," one critic has written. "Shepard's greatest contribution to a new American mythology may well be his elaboration of a new myth of the modern artist."

His first major play was *The Tooth of Crime*, an eerie showdown between two futuristic rock stars written in a strange, made-up slang. Many critics still consider this Shepard's most original work. It certainly established his peculiar blend of imaginative language and pop-cultural debris.

"I'm interested in exploring the writing of plays through attitudes derived from other forms such as music, painting, sculpture, film, etc., all the time keeping in mind that I'm writing for the theater," Shepard once wrote. "I consider theater and writing to be a home where I bring the adventures of my life and sort them out, making sense or non-sense out of mysterious impressions. I like to start with as little information about where I'm going as possible. A nearly empty space which is the stage where a picture, a sound, a color sneaks in and tells a certain kind of story. I feel that language is a veil hiding demons and angels which the characters are always out of touch with. Their quest in the play is the same as ours in life—to find those forces, to meet them face to face and end the mystery. I'm pulled toward images that shine in the middle of junk. Like cracked headlights shining on a deer's eyes. I've been influenced by Jackson Pollock, Little Richard, Cajun fiddles, and the Southwest."

The Tooth of Crime was written in London, where Shepard had fled with his wife and son to escape the drug-ridden madness of New York. But this three-year stay in England made Shepard think a lot about what it meant to be an American. When he returned to the United States in 1974 and settled on a ranch in Marin County, California, perhaps inevitably his work gravitated toward the family—the great subject of American drama from Eugene O'Neill to Tennessee Williams—in plays like *Curse of the Starving Class*, *Buried Child*, *True West*, and *A Lie of the Mind*.

Around the same time, Sam Shepard was making his auspicious debut as a film actor. Though he had long been fascinated with movies and had tried his hand at writing screenplays (he worked on Michelangelo Antonioni's *Zabriskie Point*), he had little experience acting and no particular training. He turned out to be a natural, however, and suddenly people who had never heard of a playwright named Sam Shepard were paying attention to this handsome, snaggle-toothed, downright sexy movie actor with a charismatic combination of tenderness and virility that hadn't been seen since Gary Cooper in his prime. There was a mysterious moodiness that added to his charm, and it didn't hurt matters that you didn't see him on TV making small talk every time you turned around—he kept to himself.

"Sam Shepard is what a star is supposed to be—a ball of fire in a black sky. Brilliant, but very far away," says fellow playwright Marsha Norman. "Too many stars are just too close. They say too much. They smile too much. We know too much about them. Their desperate need for publicity destroys the privacy they need to keep working and clarifies what must remain mysterious if we are to keep fantasizing about them. Sam Shepard makes us guess."

After being a renegade in the theater for twenty years, in the 1980s Shepard entered the culture to the point where rock critics mentioned him in reviews of Bruce Springsteen and literary critics likened his plays to the fiction of Raymond Carver. (A California rock band even named itself after his play *True West*.) It wasn't the Pulitzer that made him famous, though, but the movies, and it's a sign of how undervalued theater is in this country that Sam Shepard with a couple of movie roles commanded the kind of attention and respect from the mass audience that nearly two decades of being the most important young American playwright never brought him. The nice part about that is that people who just discovered him as a playwright had a long, rich dramatic history to go back and explore. "If plays were put in time capsules," *Time* magazine once said, "future generations would get a sharp-toothed profile of life in the U.S. in the past decade and a half from the works of Sam Shepard."

After hitting a peak in the mid-'80s, Shepard's star went into decline. His 1985 magnum opus *A Lie of the Mind*, which he referred to as "a big-assed play," was the culmination of his string of family plays. A six-year silence ensued. His Oscar nomination for *The Right Stuff*, meanwhile, seemed in retrospect to be a fluke rather than a harbinger of things to come. While he continued to act in movies, he played character parts rather than starring roles, often in mediocre films that seemed like mercenary projects rather than artistic choices.

During this slow period of his productivity as a writer, of course, Shepard was raising two young children with Jessica Lange. In addition, he was trying his hand at independent filmmaking and learning about the tedious process of securing financial backing as well as the technical aspects of shooting, editing, and marketing low-budget films. His two efforts as a film director, *Far North* and *Silent Tongue*, were artistically ambitious and commercially unsuccessful. Shepard returned to the spotlight in the mid-1990s when he began once more to devote his creative energies to the theater. In particular, his personal involvement in major revivals of *Buried Child* and *The Tooth of Crime* instigated a reconsideration of his body of work as a playwright.

In the original version of this book, published in 1985, I surveyed Shepard's artistic career as a classic rags-to-riches success story. For this updated edition, I had to revise my overview. Incorporating the two substantial chapters I've added to this edition, I found myself composing something less glamorous, perhaps, but more intriguing: the chronicle of a life. Clearly, the myth of the artist as hero that Shepard embodies is not a one-way trajectory to triumph and glory. Like any mythical hero's adventure, Shepard's has been a journey replete with ups and downs, surprising opportunities and disappointing dead ends, stitched together with a handbul of dogged obsessions.

An extremely private person, Shepard tries whenever possible to avoid the press. He has over the years given a number of ex-

tensive and invariably revealing interviews, but even then he usually prefers to talk about his work and often refuses point-blank
to answer questions about his personal life. His plays tell us quite
a bit about his personal history, but as works of fiction they offer
clues, not a road map.

In his *Rolling Thunder Logbook,* Shepard called Bob Dylan "an
invention of his own mind. The point isn't to figure him out but
to take him in." This book, too, is an attempt not to analyze Sam
Shepard but to take him in. It is by no means a finished portrait
of the artist but a study of a man continually remaking himself,
not a final solution to the mystery but an introduction, one stop
on a journey that still has a long way to go.

Chapter One:

THE FINDING
OF FANG

You can't escape, that's the whole thing, you can't. You finally find yourself in a situation where, like, that's the way it is—you can't get out of it. But there is always that impulse towards another kind of world, something that doesn't necessarily confine you in that way. Like I've got a name, I speak English, I have gestures, wear a certain kind of clothes . . . but once upon a time I didn't have all that shit.

—Sam Shepard in an interview with *Theatre Quarterly*

Sam Shepard was born on November 5, 1943, in Fort Sheridan, Illinois, an army outpost situated on Lake Michigan. "They weren't kidding, it was a real fort, where army mothers had their babies. My father was in Italy, then, I think," Shepard once said— only back then he didn't have the name he has made famous. He was born Samuel Shepard Rogers III and called Steve, although if he were royalty his name would have been Samuel Shepard Rogers VII.

"My name came down through seven generations of men with the same name each naming the first son the same name as the father," he wrote, "then the mothers nicknaming the sons so as not to confuse them with the fathers when hearing their names called in the open air while working side by side in the waist-high wheat. The sons came to believe their names were the nicknames they heard floating across these fields and answered to these names building ideas of who they were around the sound never dreaming their real name was lying in wait for them written on some paper in Chicago and that name would be the name they'd prefix with 'Mr.' and that name would be the name they'd die with."

The Rogers family had deep roots in Illinois. Shepard's great-grandfather, Samuel Shepard Rogers IV, had been an editor on the Chicago *Daily News*. And his oldest son had married and settled down with Helen Dodge, granddaughter of Civil War hero Lemuel P. Dodge, in a small town some fifty miles outside of Chicago called Crystal Lake, which is where Shepard's father was born February 3, 1917.

As a playwright Shepard would later plumb his father's heritage for his mythical investigations into the American family, *Curse of the Starving Class* and *Buried Child*, but in his early plays he often served up autobiographical family history with only the thinnest veil of disguise. In a one-act play called *The Holy Ghostly*, the character Pop chides his son for changing his name from Stanley Hewitt Moss the seventh to Ice, from which we can probably assume that the ensuing monologue bears a strong resemblance to the saga of the Rogers family fortune, at least according to Pop. "Me, I never had no real breaks," he says.

My old man was a dairy farmer. Started hittin' the bottle and lost the whole farm. Things started goin' down hill from that point on. Next thing he got himself a job sellin' Hershey bars door to door. Never saw much a' Pa then. Travelin' all around. Chicago, Detroit, Des Moines, Tucumcari, Boise. Then we found out that Pa got his self so drunk in a hotel room that he fell asleep with a cigar burning in his hand. Burned the whole hotel right to the ground with him in it. So I had to go to work. Support the whole family.

Then my brother Jaimie comes home one day complainin' of a bad pain. Take him to the doctor and come to find out he's got himself a case a' polio and they're gonna have to take his leg off. The whole damn leg from the hip down. That was right around the time a' the great Depression. . . . So me, I'm workin' night and day in Macy's downtown Chicago and bringin' home the bacon once a week so Ma can buy the groceries. By the time Jaimie gets old enough to work I'm startin' to think on marrying yer mother. 'Course Jaimie was a cripple but strong as an ox from the waist up. . . . First thing ya' know he's out there in the real world drivin' a goddamn Bekins truck with a wooden leg. So me, I get myself hitched to yer mother and get all set to take off fer college and get myself a diploma so's I could make me a heap a' money, when lo and behold if old Uncle Sam don't decide it's come my time to serve my country. So off I goes to learn how to fly B-24's and B-17's and drop bombs and whatall. Italy, Holland, Germany, England, the whole shebang. Then I come back with nothin' to show for it but some Jap rifles and Kraut helmets and little red bombs cut on my leather jacket with a Gillette Blue Blade. Each one showing mission accomplished. Each one showin' I got back alive. But I was feelin' all right 'cause about that time I got myself something to look forward to stateside. I'm comin' home to my little woman in Rapid City, South Dakota, and she's got one hell of a package waiting fer me. She's got me a son. A son with my name and my eyes and my nose and my mouth. My own flesh and blood, boy.

Shepard's mother was born Jane Elaine Schook on July 16, 1917, in Lombard, another suburb of Chicago, to Frederick deForest Schook and Amy Victoria Byron. When her husband was called away on military duty shortly after their marriage, Jane Rogers stayed with her mother-in-law, who still lived in Crystal Lake, except for when the time came to deliver her firstborn child at Fort Sheridan. "The exact time of my birth, according to this Head Nurse, was three in the afternoon. . . . But I have verification from other sources (not my mother) that it was something like 2:47 a.m. which puts me in the wee hours of the freezing morning," Sam Shepard once wrote. As a writer, he has always sought to mythicize his own life, and what better place to begin than with the first moment? "There was no traffic on the streets below and the town was dark due to the wartime curfew. . . . Pale green light poured through [the windows], casting a double beam on my unconscious mother across the room. I watched her body. I knew I'd come from her body but I wasn't sure how. I knew I was away from her body now. Separate. . . . I felt a tremendous panic suddenly. I was between these two worlds. The world I'd left behind and this new one. I had no idea where to turn."

He didn't have to worry about that for a few years, at least. While his father was still in the service, his mother toted him around from one army installation to another—South Dakota for a few months, then off to Utah, and then Florida. Finally they got stationed someplace more exotic: Guam.

A tiny island due south of Japan, due east of the Philippines, and next to the deepest spot in the Pacific Ocean (the Mariana Trench), Guam is primarily known as an American military installation. "I remember the tin-roofed huts that we lived in, because it used to rain there a lot, and the rain would make this incredible sound on the tin roof," Shepard once said. "Also there were a lot of Japanese on the island, who had been forced back into living in the caves, and they would come down and steal clothes off the clothes-lines, and food and stuff. All the women were issued army Lugers, and I remember my mother shooting at them." His mother also drove a jeep, crashing through the jungle and brandishing her .45 just to get to the drive-in theater where she and her little boy in a cowboy hat watched Song of the South projected onto a bedsheet.

While he was in the Army Air Corps, Shepard's father was hardly ever home, but after Guam he got out of the service and settled down in California before his son started going to grade school. If Shepard has dim memories of his peripatetic infancy (sleeping in motel bathtubs in Idaho, his mother humming "Peg o' My Heart" while carrying him around in a brown army blanket), he was spared many of the harsher rituals familiar to that species of youngster known as the army brat: changing schools every year or two, constantly adjusting to new neighborhoods and baseball fields, learning very young the bittersweet chorus of "Make new friends but keep the old/One is silver and the other's gold." By the time he started school, the Rogers family had traded the rootlessness of army life for the more settled if still restless suburbs of California.

They first lived in South Pasadena, a little town of 23,000 people located in the San Gabriel Valley just east of Los Angeles, with one of Shepard's aunts (his mother's sister) who "had some money"; one time she took her nephew to the Farmers' Market in Los Angeles in her '45 Dodge to look at the myna birds. But eventually the family—which included not only Sam Rogers, Sr., his wife Jane, and Sam Jr. (called Steve), but also two daughters, Sandy and Roxanne—got their own house in the same community. It was a small but typical two-story building that Steve, who slept in a bunkbed underneath his kid sister, got to know so well he could walk through it with his eyes closed, "past the snarling Tiger painted on silk, brought back by my Dad from the Philippines; past the portrait of a train conductor painted by my Grandfather; past the pink Hibiscus flowers glowing in the light from the bathroom."

Although Pasadena is well-known as a prosperous orange grove town with its own "Millionaires' Row," South Pasadena is less grand, a mostly residential suburb, "one of these white, middle-class, insulated communities—not all that rich, but very proud of the municipal swimming plunge and the ice-skating rink, and all that small-town-America-type stuff." That's where young Steve Rogers began his education at Lincoln Elementary School. He was five years old when he started school because his birthday was in November, so during his childhood he was usually a year younger than most of the kids in his class.

He was always a fantasist. When he was seven years old he wrote a story called "The Finding of Fang" about two orphans taken care of by their grandparents; one was named Steve, after himself, and the other was a made-up brother named Spencer, as in Tracy. Young Steve always loved the movies. Years later he would doodle in his notebook, "I keep praying for a double bill of BAD DAY AT BLACK ROCK and VERA CRUZ." He was particularly fond of John Huston movies, any John Huston movies, but he especially liked *The Treasure of the Sierra Madre* (possibly because Sierra Madre was a real California town not ten miles from where he grew up) and has been known to impress his friends with a pretty good impersonation of Walter Huston in that movie. And one of his all-time favorites was *King Solomon's Mines* with Stewart Granger and Deborah Kerr, which came out in 1950. It was "the movie that most haunted me as a kid. I've never seen it since then but images from it still remain. Watusi warriors with red clay stripes down their noses. Raised black welts studding their chests. Teeth filed down to needle points. Lions ripping someone's arm off. Flies landing on someone's lip and the lip not moving. Torches in caves. Blue jewels surrounded by skulls. That English actor guy half scared to death. . . . I entered the world of the movie so completely that the theatre became a part of its landscape. . . . I was in the cave of King Solomon at the candy counter. The 'Ju-Ju-Bees' were jewels."

Looking back, he remembers himself as "an arrogant, horrible, asshole kid" being raised in a very straight environment. His mother was a schoolteacher, and his father was trying to finish his college degree by taking night classes on the G. I. Bill. "He was very strict, my father, very aware of the need for discipline, so-called, very into studying and all that kind of stuff. I couldn't stand it—the whole thing of writing in notebooks, it was really like being jailed." He was brought up in the Episcopalian Church, "but that was another kind of prison to get out of, you know. There's nothing worse than listening to a lot of people mumbling, and outside the sun is shining."

Once, when he was ten years old, Steve ditched school with two guys who were brothers. They stole bicycles and rode around all day near the Arroyo Seco, a dry gulch near South Pasadena that had a park for picnicking but also a few tin shacks in the dunes where teenagers had orgies. The three boys got picked up by the cops late at night, and Steve's mother had to come and retrieve him; his father wouldn't go because he was too pissed off.

It was the beginning of a stormy relationship between father and son. "My father had a real short fuse," Shepard recalls. "He had a really rough life—had to support his mother and brothers at a very young age when his dad's farm collapsed. You could see his suffering, his terrible suffering, living a life that was disappointing and looking for another one. It was past frustration; it was anger. My father was full of terrifying anger." Sam Sr. was quite old-fashioned in his ways. He listened to Dixieland music on 78 rpm records and played drums with a trad-jazz band; in fact, he taught Steve to play when he was thirteen. But the family didn't own a television set because Mr. Rogers said they didn't need one.

"It was hit and miss, always hit and miss," Shepard's sister Roxanne remembers, speaking about the relationship between her brother had with her father when they were growing up. "There was always a kind of facing off between them, and it was Sam who got the bad end of that. It was Dad who always set up if it was on or off. Dad was a tricky character. Because he was a charismatic guy when he wanted to be—warm, loving, kind of a hoot to be around. And the other side was like a snapping turtle. With him and Sam it was that male thing. You put two virile men in a room and they're going to test each other. It's like two pit bulls."

Steve started high school in South Pasadena, but when he was around twelve years old the family moved to a town called Duarte about fifteen miles to the east and a few notches lower on the social scale. "We moved to this avocado ranch," he said. "It was like a little greenhouse that had been converted into a house, and it had livestock and horses and chickens and stuff like that. Plus about 65 avocado trees. You can't depend on the rain in California, so we had to rig up an irrigation system which had to be operated every day. And we had this little Wisconsin tractor with a spring-tooth harrow and a disc, and I made some money driving that for other people in the neighborhood—there were a lot of citrus groves. I really liked being in contact with animals and the whole agricultural thing, but it was a bit of a shock leaving the friends I'd made."

Duarte was oddly stratified for such a small town; it had rich people, middle-class families, and the downright poor. "It was the first place where I understood what it meant to be born on the wrong side of the tracks, because the railroad tracks cut right down through the middle of this place: and below the tracks were the blacks and Mexicans." Dry and flat, the town was dominated by rock quarries, cement companies, and the City of Hope Medical Center, an institute devoted to cancer research.

Duarte is where Steve Rogers grew up and where Sam Shepard began to invent himself. The avocado ranch would become the setting for his award-winning play *Curse of the Starving Class*. And his 1969 drama *The Unseen Hand* takes place on the outskirts of Azusa, a little California town whose motto is "Everything from A to Z in the USA." It sounds ludicrous and made up, but Azusa is a real place, the next town over from Duarte. "These towns are obsessions of mine because of their accidentalness," Shepard once explained. "Nobody actually set out to start a town called AZUSA or DUARTE. They happened. They grew out of nothing and nowhere. Originally the valley was covered with citrus groves. The kind you see in Hollywood postcards from the thirties and forties. Rows of neat shining lemon trees and orange trees with smudge pots. These billowed out black smoke in the early morning to keep the frost off the trees. Eventually Los Angeles had a population kick-back. People who couldn't make it in the big city just drove away from it. They got so far and just quit the road. Maybe some just ran out of gas.

"Anyhow," he continued, "they began to nest in these little valleys. Lots of them lived in trailer camps. Weird government industries began to sprout up. Places where they make nose cones and satellite tape recorders. People had work. It was a temporary society that became permanent. Everybody still had the itch to get on to something better for themselves but found themselves stuck. It was a car culture for the young. For the old it was just a dead end."

In his plays Sam Shepard often returns imaginatively to his adolescence and recollects the Southern California of the fifties in the long verbal arias that are characteristic of his work. The character called Kid in *The Unseen Hand* extols the virtues of his hometown while a bunch of Wild West bandits sit around and laugh at him:

Shut up! Shut up! I'll kill you all! I'll kill you! This is my home! Don't make fun of my home. I was born and raised here and I'll die here! I love it! That's something you can't understand! I love Azusa! I love the foothills and the drive in movies and the bowling alleys and the football games and the drag races and the girls and the donut shop and the High School and the Junior College and the outdoor track meets and the parades and the Junior Chamber of Commerce and the Key Club and the Letterman's Club and the Kiwanis and the Safeway Shopping Center and the freeway and the pool hall and the Bank of America and the Post Office and the Presbyterian church and the Laundromat and the liquor store and the miniature golf course and Lookout Point and the YMCA and the Glee Club and the basketball games and the sock hop and graduation and the prom and the cafeteria and the principal's office and Chemistry class and the county fair and peanut butter and jelly sandwiches and the High School band and going steady and KFWB and white bucks and pegged pants and argyle socks and madras shorts and butch wax and Hobie boards and going to the beach and getting drunk and swearing and reading dirty books and smoking in the men's room and setting off cherry bombs and fixing up my car and my Mom, I love my Mom most of all. And you creeps aren't going to take that away from me.

Shepard pictured the same scene from an outsider's point of view when he had Hoss, the main character in *The Tooth of Crime*, reminisce about his high school days hanging out with two buddies, a mulatto named Moose and Cruise, a cat from Canada who dressed and wore his hair like Elvis Presley. In the incident that comes to mind, the three of them are cruising for burgers at Bob's Big Boy in Pasadena when a gang of eight crew-cut athletes from their school decides to pick a fight. A crowd of girls begins to form, and a rumble ensues. "Then I saw it," Hoss recalls.

This was a class war. These were rich white kids from Arcadia who got T-birds and deuce coups for Xmas from Mommy and Daddy. All them cardigan sweaters and chicks with ponytails and pedal pushers and bubble hairdo's. Soon as I saw that I flipped out. I found my strength. I started kickin' shit, man. Hard and fast. Three of 'em went down screamin' and holdin' their balls. Moose and Cruise went right into action. It was like John Wayne, Robert Mitchum and Kirk Douglas all in one movie.

Although Sam Shepard would like to pretend that he was always a bad-ass juvenile delinquent growing up, Steve Rogers was somewhere in between a glee-club cheerleader-type like the Kid of *The Unseen Hand* and *The Tooth of Crime*'s tough-talking scrapper precociously schooled in class analysis. Or more likely he was both things at the same time. He made the track team in school, and although the coaches were puzzled by his erratic performance in practice, they were delighted when he broke the league record in the 220-yard event. The secret was that he was on Benzedrine. He may have stolen a car once with his friend Tim Ford, "one of those early Austin Healeys with red leather tuck and roll and wire wheels," and driven to Mexico, getting a fake ID and drinking up a storm in San Diego. But to buy the first car he ever owned—"a '32 Ford Deuce Coup, metallic blue paint job, black tuck and roll, '48 Mercury flathead engine and three speeds on the floor"—he worked for two summers at a horse ranch in Chino, stripping the stalls down to the concrete floor, his eyes burning from horse piss, his hands scorched with lime.

Many of Steve's after-school and summer jobs related to his calling as a Future Farmer of America. He worked as a "hot walker" at the Santa Anita Race Track, a sheepshearer, herdsman, and orange picker. He was also a certified member of the 4-H Club, and he even had the grand champion yearling ram at the Los Angeles County Fair one year. Of course, 4-H Club wasn't all milk and cookies—it also allowed for plenty of opportunities for rolling in the hay, quite literally. One particular county fair was made memorable by his dalliance with a girl who was a participant in the Beef Project, which far outclassed even fancy sheep like Steve's, as she made sure to let him know. Even swine outclassed sheep; only poultry and potholders ranked lower. What won her heart, apparently, was his triumph the previous year in the pig scramble, a fairground event requiring firm and dextrous use of the hands.

He was apparently never shy when it came to sex. One reminiscence published years later has teenaged Steve taking a train trip across the country to visit his grandparents back in Illinois. On the same train was a fifteen-year-old Mormon girl who looked like Tuesday Weld, whom he considered "the Marlon Brando of women" because she had the guts to go on a TV talkshow in bare feet. They got to talking somewhere around Reno and ended up in her stateroom doing the horizontal bop all the way across the Great Salt Lake Desert. Her daddy met her at the station, and Steve went on to Chicago, hitching a ride out to his grandparents' farm. His grandfather, a redneck and staunch Harry Truman fan fond of writing letters to the editor signed "Plain Dirt Farmer," was an invalid who sat shriveled up in front of the television watching the baseball game; when it was over, his grandmother would drop whatever she was doing and snap the set off. At night Steve wandered around studying the pictures of his uncles on the wall: "The Uncle who died in a motel room on his wedding night. His wife who died with him. The Uncle who lost a leg at the age of ten. The Uncle who married into the Chicago Mafia. The Uncle who cut timber in the Great North Woods. The Uncle who drove for Bekins." (Presumably that's the same one who lost the leg.) "The Uncle who raised Springer Spaniels." He soaked up the scene for later use. (In *Buried Child*, young Vince visits just such a nest of colorful relatives.)

Steve felt close to his grandparents, at least partly because he didn't get along with his father. After graduating from high school, he wrote a friendly letter to his grandmother telling her his plans for the future. He was spending the summer working for a veterinarian in nearby West Covina—because he was so good with animals, it was sort of assumed in the family that Steve would be a vet when he got out of school—and he had enrolled for the fall semester at Mount San Antonio College, a two-year junior college in Walnut, a small, pretty town on the opposite side of the San Gabriel Valley from Duarte. His tentative major was education, he'd signed up for the golf team, and he was thinking of trying out as a high jumper for the track team. But he also confided his doubts about pursuing the logical sequence of events. He thought he might sell his entire flock of sheep and concentrate on raising German Shepherds; his prize dog had already collected a number of trophies and ribbons. He was even thinking of chucking the idea of school altogether and going up the Yukon to work as a lumberjack with a couple of friends, including a Canadian fellow named Dennis Crews (the one fictionalized as "Cruise" in *The Tooth of Crime*). But he admitted that the latter course of action would probably evaporate the minute his father got wind of it—as indeed it did.

He spent three semesters at Mt. SAC, as it was familiarly known. Bored with classes, unhappy at home, restless as only a lonely teenager in a small town can be, Steve found himself drifting into the theater, almost totally by chance. He acted in a campus production of *Harvey*, Mary Chase's comedy about an amiable drunk who sees a walking-talking rabbit. And when he was cast in Thornton Wilder's *The Skin of Our Teeth*, he recruited a guy he went to high school with, Charles Mingus, Jr., to fill the part of a black character. He even wrote a play for *MoSAiC*, the campus literary magazine, called *The Mildew*, which he remembers as a Tennessee Williams imitation about a girl who is raped and then taunted by her stepfather. But he always dates his real involvement with theater from his introduction to the Irish-born playwright Samuel Beckett.

"I hardly knew anything about the theater," he likes to say. "I remember once I went to this guy's house who was called a beatnik by everybody in the school because he had a beard and he wore sandals. And we were listening to some jazz or something and he sort of shuffled over to me and threw this book on my lap and said, 'Why don't you dig this,' you know. I started reading this play he gave me, and it was like nothing I'd ever read before—it was *Waiting for Godot*. And I thought, 'What's this guy talking about, what is this?' And I read it with a very keen interest, but I didn't know anything about what it was. I didn't really have any references for the theater, except for the few plays that I'd acted in."

Dazzled by Beckett's absurdist stage poetry and smitten with the acting bug himself, Steve Rogers somehow knew that theater offered him the chance to change his life. "I sort of used acting as a means to get out of my environment," he said. "In Duarte, nobody was doing anything except going to the Alpha Beta supermarket." In the Rogers household, nobody was doing anything except fighting. When Steve read in the newspaper that something called the Bishop's Company Repertory Players was holding auditions, he went in, and they snapped him up—not surprisingly. By this time he had grown to his full six-foot-one height, and even with his crooked teeth and Southwestern drawl his lanky frame and prominent cheekbones gave him an unmistakable presence. The next day they put him on a bus to Pennsylvania, and he spent the next eight months playing one night stands in churches. He later confessed to an interviewer, "The religious cover was a phoney. We were really a bunch of frustrated actors who couldn't find a niche." They performed everything from an adaptation of *Winnie the Pooh* to *A Sleep of Prisoners*, Christopher Fry's 1951 drama about four soldiers locked in a church who use the pulpit to express their boredom and general disgust, then go to sleep and dream of biblical battles (Cain and Abel, Abraham and Isaac, etc.).

"It was a great time," he said. "I really learned what it is to make theater. We'd go into churches, mostly in New England, set up lights, do makeup, do the play, tear it all down, and leave to go down the road the next day. It really gave you a sense of the makeshift quality of theater and the possibilities of doing it anywhere. That's what turned me on most of all. I realized suddenly that anybody can make theater. You don't need to be affiliated with anybody. You just make it with a bunch of people. That's still what I like about it."

What he liked about theater first, though, was that it got him out of one identity and into another. He could have stayed in Duarte and finished college, set up shop as a vet, and moved smoothly into middle-class suburbia. He could have stayed on the land and taken a job he was offered to run a herd of five hundred Sundowns at a sheep farm in Chino. Or he could have just dropped out and turned on like so many of his generation and either died young or ended up a balding burnout bagging groceries at the Alpha Beta.

Instead he answered the call of his restless spirit and hit the road like Jack Kerouac, only going in the opposite direction. And once he got to the East Coast and had his fill of playing in churches, it was easy enough to get the bus to stop and let him off at the one place that irresistibly attracts dreamers and schemers from all over the world—New York City.

It was while he was on the road with the Bishop's Company that Steve Rogers acquired a new name. One delightfully absurd story has it that he changed his name to Sam Shepard "because it was shorter." He was a little more forthcoming in a *New York* magazine interview with journalist Pete Hamill. "I always thought Rogers was a corny name," he said, "because of Roy Rogers and all the associations with that. But Samuel Shepard Rogers was kind of a long handle. So I just dropped the Rogers part of it. That had gone on for generations, that name, seven generations of it. It kind of shocked my grandparents more than anybody, I think, 'cause they kind of hoped I would carry it on. Then I called my kid Jesse, so that blew it entirely. Now in a way I kind of regret it. But it was, you know, one of those reactions to your background."

He laughed.

"Years later," he added, "I found out that Steve Rogers was the original name of Captain America in the comics."

Chapter Two:

DRAGONFLY FROM A HELICOPTER

I turned myself into an actor and came East in a red bus, acting all the way. I was dropped off in New York and teamed up with a painter kid that I knew before and had flown in while I was riding the bus all that time. I began experiments with various plants and growths that led to rhythm discoverings in space and time through packing up words and stretching them out along with their size and shape and sound. Once this got started lo and behold there came phantoms and ghosts speaking these words. At this point my acting stopped.... And things began to crackle.

—Shepard in program note for *Red Cross*

Imagine coming off an avocado farm in Rock Town and landing in NEW YORK CITY, the Big Apple, populated by eight million and bulging at the seams, screaming subways underneath, towering skyscrapers overhead, a different world on every block. It's 1963, Kennedy's in the White House (not for long . . .), the baby-boom generation is coming of age, the air is electric with jazz, hope, prosperity, energy, you're nineteen years old and just off the bus. Having changed his name on the road from the one he shared with an all-American comic-book hero to that of a famous wife murderer, Sam Shepard tucked his hometown good manners away in his suitcase (he might need them someday), free now to act out his wildest fantasies to his heart's content.

He had done his share of hell-raising, hot-rodding, and tail-chasing back in high school, but that was idyllic, small-town California, where you knew every face and every inch of the town in excruciatingly thorough detail. This was the big time, and to tell the truth, he found it almost overwhelming. "He was like a refugee," an old friend recalls. He started off looking for work as an actor, making the rounds with his picture and resume, but he wasn't having much luck.

"I was living in Spanish Harlem," Shepard remembers, "and I saw in a gossip column that this guy I went to high school with, who happened to be Charles Mingus's son, was busing tables at the Village Gate. I went down there and he got me a job as a busboy." Mingus also gave Shepard a place to live and, probably more important, a crash course in urban survival.

Mingus had had a somewhat more tempestuous childhood than Shepard. He came from a broken home—his father, the great jazz bassist and composer Charles Mingus, had left his wife and two sons behind in California when he moved to New York. And his mother in turn left Charles Jr. with her parents in Duarte while she took her younger child with her to nursing school. So Charlie was raised primarily by his grandfather and grew up somewhat alienated, a black kid in a white suburb, a jazzman's son in the land of the Beach Boys. He began painting and sculpting at an early age—also experimenting with drugs.

By the time he got out of high school and took off for New York, he already had a critical perspective on the world of which Sam Shepard was almost completely innocent, and Mingus set about repairing the situation. It would never have occurred to Shepard, for instance, to label his high school "fascist," as Mingus did, for firing a biology teacher who taught evolution. These little lessons in sociopolitical thinking didn't demolish Shepard's all-American-boy attitude so much as make him aware, possibly for the first time; of his unquestioning acceptance of the "Mother, God, and Country" principles with which he was brought up. Now, with Mingus as his guide, he was learning some of the alternatives.

One of the major alternatives to the straight-and-narrow lifestyle was chemical. If it could be smoked, sniffed, or swallowed, Shepard and Mingus tried it once. If they liked it, they did it again. "I never shot up," said Shepard, "but I mean I used everything on the street." Another playground was sexual. "I rode everything with hair," he said. "Charles had this knack of picking up these amazingly straight women—stewardesses and secretaries. Charlie was always splattered with paint, and I didn't take too many baths back then. And there were cockroaches all over the place. But these women would show up in their secretarial gear. It was wild. I couldn't believe it."

The two of them lived in a condemned apartment building on Avenue C, occupied primarily by artists, that became known throughout America and Europe as a place for young people to crash, a haven from the craziness of a world that didn't understand them. The East Village in the early sixties was the outer limits for fancy uptowners (even though large communities of working-class ethnic immigrants lived there) but it was also the hotbed of a burgeoning culture of bohemians who considered themselves pioneers for a new society. "The whole thing is like a romantic revival of the wild, wild West," wrote John Gruen in *The New Bohemia*. "Take its mode of dress: strictly boots and saddles. New Bohemia likes leather jackets, Levis, western boots, work shirts, long hair, beards, moustaches, and one concession to the twentieth-century movie-star complex: sunglasses. From the single vigilante to the hell-bent posse, they ride in search of something that used to be known as 'justice' and 'vengeance,' but which seems now to be a confrontation with LIFE, which is 'out there.' "

Shepard and Mingus fit right in with the misfits. "Charles and me used to run around the streets playing cowboys in New York," Shepard said. "We'd both had the experience of growing up in California, in that special kind of environment, and between the two of us there was a kind of camaraderie, in the midst of all these people who were into going to work and riding the buses."

Shepard was always attracted to the cowboy as a fantasy role model. "Cowboys are really interesting to me," he used to say, "these guys, most of them really young, about 16 or 17, who decided they didn't want to have anything to do with the East Coast, with that way of life, and took on this immense country, and didn't have any real rules. Just moving cattle, from Texas to Kansas City, from the North to the South, or wherever it was."

Never mind that Shepard had recently made his pilgrimage in the opposite direction with nary a Longhorn to present as credentials. He enjoyed playing the role of hick from the sticks, an urban cowboy long before the days of designer jeans. He liked the way his jangly Southwestern drawl clashed with honking Bronx accents and the flamboyant jive of Manhattan street blacks. Maybe in contrast to the placid suburbs of Southern California, New York City offered a stronger sense of the wilderness, where mere survival was a challenge.

In any case, the two of them behaved more like primitive creatures than cowboys. Partly because they were young kids from out west turned loose in this hyperurban environment, partly because they were often stoned out of their minds, they spent a lot of time mentally AWOL. They couldn't tell a dragonfly from a helicopter.

Probably the best education-by-exposure Mingus gave Shepard was musical. Sam had picked up a taste for music and a skill for drumming from his father, but in New York he really got into it. He practically idolized Dannie Richmond, the young drummer in Mingus Sr.'s band who shared the apartment on Avenue C for a while. Charlie Mingus's relationship with his father was cordial but not particularly close. One time after a gig at the Five Spot, Shepard and Mingus rode with Mingus's father up Third Avenue in a cab, stopping three times along the way to buy grapes. The elder Mingus asked the two boys if they needed a woman; they said no.

Since Shepard and Mingus Jr. worked at the Village Gate, a popular nightclub on Bleecker Street, they got to see the best shows around for free—jazzmen like Roland Kirk, Cannonball Adderley, and Eric Dolphy as well as comedians like Woody Allen and Flip Wilson. "I worked three nights a week," said Shepard, "and got about fifty bucks a week for doing hardly anything, except cleaning up dishes and bringing Nina Simone ice."

It turned out that most of the other guys who worked at the Village Gate were actors, musicians, or writers, and that gave Shepard the itch to be an artist. "The people that were most admirable to me were, first, musicians," he once told *Esquire* magazine. "They had an instrument, they could play alone, by themselves; that was their craft, you know, that was their thing. Next, I admired painters. I wanted something like that, something tangible that I could work on, something that I did by myself." Heavily influenced by Jack Kerouac, Lawrence Ferlinghetti, and other Beat poets, he had tried his hand at writing poetry, but he thought most of it was pretty bad. Writing plays appealed to him because "I always liked the idea that plays happened in three dimensions, that here was something that came to life in space rather than in a book. I never liked books, or read very much." He did study a few playscripts—by Edward Albee, Harold Pinter, Samuel Beckett—and went to see Albee's *The Zoo Story* as well as *The Dutchman* and *The Slave* by LeRoi Jones ("a beautiful writer and a great playwright"). But on the whole Shepard was more interested in writing plays than seeing them.

He was always a rather dramatic guy. One of the ways he used to make friends was to engage someone in crazy dialogue as if the two of them were in a play. Bill Hart, who was Shepard's roommate for several years after Charles Mingus, remembers that although they had been introduced to each other, one day Shepard came up while he was sitting on a curb in Washington Square Park and started talking to him as some kind of made-up character. Hart immediately responded with some bizarre repartee of his own, and the two became friends. Some found it disturbing the way Shepard could switch personalities from one minute to the next, and in fact he frequently popped tablets of niacin, a vitamin used to treat schizophrenics, saying, "This is my together drug." But the thing is, he simply liked *playing*, whether tennis-without-a-ball or overgrown cowboys-and-Indians, and writing was a good way to do it.

Fortuitously, the Village Gate's head waiter, Ralph Cook, was given the use of St. Mark's Church In-the-Bowery, which he decided to convert to a theater. He named the place Theater Genesis and announced it would be devoted to producing new plays, so Shepard spoke up and said he'd written one called—what else?—*Cowboys*. It opened October 10, 1964, the second production that Theater Genesis had ever done. The cast consisted of two Village Gate waiters (Robert F. Lyons and Kevin O'Connor, the latter of whom went on to become one of the enduring stars of off-off-Broadway theater), and it was directed by Ralph Cook. It was also the first time the former Steve Rogers used the name Sam Shepard in public. If people wanted to confuse him with the controversial Dr. Sam Sheppard, who spent ten years in jail for killing his wife until his conviction was overturned on appeal, why, Sam didn't mind at all—in fact, he rather enjoyed it.

The script for *Cowboys* no longer exists (Patti Smith later said in a poem that Shepard wrote it on the back of Tootsie Roll wrappers—a much-quoted assertion that Shepard disclaims). But the playwright rewrote it three years later and called it *Cowboys #2*. The best account of Shepard's first produced play is probably Jerry Tallmer's review of the Theater Genesis production in the *New York Post*: "Two young men ... are discovered in an unidentified space beside a blinking light and a roadside repair fence. They talk various dialects from Country Western to Walter Brennan to Haughty British to Plain American. They wait for rain. It rains. They grovel in the mud. They inspect the kingdoms around them of alfalfa and avocados and birds of paradise. They are attacked by Comanches and Apaches (on sound track) and fight them off. They describe loving, imaginary breakfasts. They have a falling out over an imaginary lost canteen. They dive away from police sirens. They practice baseball. Then they use the baseball bit to turn on the audience and attack it as a megalopolitan mass of morons.... The Indians return, the two young men whip out their rifles and blast away—at the spectators."

The critic didn't care much for the play. "Indeed," he sniffed, "in structure and psychic spleen it is a clear derivative of *The Zoo Story*, though it also owes its debts to such unlikely parentage as *Waiting for Godot* crossed with *Of Mice and Men*." Still, it's clear from his description that Shepard's first produced play included several elements that would pop up again and again in later plays: the central relationship of two guys (whether side-kicks or alter egos), cowboys, Indians, the use of different voices, direct address to the audience, the celebration of breakfast.

There was another one-act play on the bill with *Cowboys* at Theater Genesis called *The Rock Garden*, but Tallmer didn't even stay to see it. That play, which Shepard says is about leaving his family, takes place in three scenes. In the first, a boy and girl and their father sit wordlessly at a table until the girl spills a glass of milk. In the second, the boy fetches his mother glasses of water while she chatters on about the weather. In the third, the boy and his father sit around in their underwear. The father drones on about household chores, inducing such boredom that the boy falls out of his chair three times. Finally, the boy speaks:

When I come it's like a river. It's all over the bed and the sheets and everything. You know? I mean a short vagina gives me security. I can't help it. I like to feel like I'm really turning a girl on. It's a much better screw is what it amounts to. I mean if a girl has a really small vagina it's really better to go in from behind. You know? I mean she can sit with her legs together and you can sit facing her. You know? But that's different. It's a different kind of thing. You can do it standing, you know? Just by backing her up, you know? You just stand and she goes down and down until she's almost sitting on your dick. You know what I mean? She'll come a hundred times and you just stand there holding onto it. That way you don't even have to undress. You know?

After about five minutes of this, the play ends with the father falling out of his chair—and not out of boredom.

The critic from the *New York Herald Tribune* was apparently so outraged by *The Rock Garden* that the rector of St. Mark's, Michael Allen, had to defend the play in print, saying, "I believe this whole generation of young people is saying to us in effect, 'Look, you use beautiful words and do ugly things; we'll take ugly words and make beauty out of them.'" The irony of it all, of course, is that the final scene from *The Rock Garden* was subsequently included in Kenneth Tynan's long-running erotic revue *Oh! Calcutta!*—for many years the only work of Sam Shepard's that was ever performed in a Broadway theater, and the first to provide him with a steady income as a playwright ($68 a week).

Because the daily papers gave it such dismal reviews, the Shepard double-bill that opened in October of 1964 played to tiny audiences for the first two weeks. That changed—everything changed—when the *Village Voice* critic Michael Smith, the earliest and most ardent champion of off-off-Broadway theater, published his glowing review congratulating Theater Genesis for discovering a new talent. "The plays are difficult to categorize, and I'm not sure it would be valuable to try," wrote Smith. "Shepard is still feeling his way, working with an intuitive approach to language and dramatic structure and moving into an area between ritual and naturalism, where character transcends psychology, fantasy breaks down literalism, and the patterns of ordinariness have their own lives. His is a gestalt theater which evokes the existence behind behavior. Shepard clearly is aware of previous work in this mode, mostly by Europeans, but his voice is distinctly American and his own."

With these two tiny one-act plays, performed for three weeks in a church hall on Second Avenue twenty years ago, Sam Shepard's career as a playwright began. And if it weren't for the credence that a single critic gave to his talent, it might have ended there, too. "Jerry Tallmer from the *Post* and all these guys said it was a bunch of shit, imitated Beckett or something like that," Shepard said later, remembering the response to his debut as a playwright. "I was ready to pack it in and go back to California. Then Michael Smith from *The Village Voice* came up with this rave review, and people started coming to see it."

Once that happened, Shepard was hooked. He started churning out plays, almost literally by the dozen. He wrote constantly, night and day, standing up and sitting down, by himself and in a crowd. "He wrote plays like other people took drugs," a friend jokes. Shepard has said that he used to think of it like writing songs. After all, it was 1964, Beatlemania was sweeping the nation, British rock 'n' roll and Motown soul were dominating the airwaves, Bob Dylan was pricking consciences with his poetic protest anthems, and songs were very important to the youth of America. By the end of the decade Shepard would have written eighteen plays that got produced, uncounted others completed but not produced, and who knows how many begun but never finished. Actress Joyce Aaron, Shepard's first girlfriend in New York, says she has a whole suitcase full of manuscripts Shepard gave her that no one else has ever seen.

Not every play was a *Long Day's Journey Into Night* with every line dredged up from the soul and chiseled into place. They were tossed off, and many were completely forgettable. It didn't matter. Shepard and other young playwrights at the time weren't trying to prove anything. They had the bug, and instead of hoarding plays to protect their value as commercial properties, they put them on as fast as they could write them, rapidly blurring the distinctions between the life they were living and the life they were writing about. "I was very lucky to have arrived in New York at that time, because the whole off-off-Broadway theater was just starting," he said. "I had a place to just go and put something on without having to go through a producer or go through the commercial network. All of that was in response to the tightness of Broadway and off-Broadway, where you couldn't get a play done."

The time and place he was talking about—Greenwich Village and the Lower East Side of Manhattan in the early sixties—witnessed the convergence of many hip, hot art scenes. Frank O'Hara and LeRoi Jones were at the forefront of New York's answer to San Francisco's Beat poets. A new generation of painters like Robert Rauschenberg and Claes Oldenburg were making the transition from Abstract Expressionism to Pop art. Underground film was happening. Everyone from John Cage to the Fugs was making new music. These people were all a little bit older, though, and had a little more money (from selling their work, teaching, trust funds) than most of the kids who gravitated toward the theater. Shepard at this point was still living with Charles Mingus in a derelict apartment on Avenue C near Tompkins Square Park. Scrounging to pay the rent and eating in the kitchen of places where he worked busing tables, he couldn't afford East Village nightlife, swilling brews at the Dom or nursing cappuccinos at Cafe Le Metro, even if he wanted to. For him, off-off-Broadway offered, almost literally, a place to come in from the cold.

The phenomenon known as off-off-Broadway was a theatrical playground custom-built by and for media-fed baby-boomers coming of age in the cultural and political ferment of the early 1960s. Like the Pop art movement and rock 'n' roll, it was partially caused by the staidness of the artistic environment into which it exploded. "By the late 1950s the New York theater had reached an appalling economic state," wrote Albert Poland and Bruce Mailman in the introduction to their indispensable 1972 volume, *The Off-Off-Broadway Book*. "Broadway was going the route of the big Hollywood studios. It was producing fewer plays and each production was more expensive. The goal was superproductions with star-studded casts, equaling *safety*. Off Broadway, traditionally the home of the experimental, was finding itself in the same position. By 1960 it cost between twelve and fifteen thousand dollars to produce a straight (non-musical) play off Broadway. The audience that Off Broadway had developed, the intelligentsia, were interested in revivals: O'Neill, Ibsen, Chekhov, and the avant garde (Genet, Pinter, Beckett, Ionesco)—but they were not interested in unestablished new American playwrights."

The Caffe Cino, a minuscule sidestreet storefront generally credited as the birthplace of off-off-Broadway, opened in 1958 as a bohemian hangout where occasionally friends of the owner, Joe Cino, would put on poetry readings and scenes from plays. By 1961 the Cino had become a real theater, an anarchic, unpretentious, amazingly prolific collective of actors and writers ranging from Village eccentric H. M. Koutoukas to the now-famous Lanford Wilson, not to mention such gay-theater pioneers as Doric Wilson and Robert Patrick. In 1961 the Reverend Al Carmines of the Judson Memorial Church welcomed the new influx of Village artists into his congregation and founded the Judson Poets' Theater, which attracted new playwrights such as Maria Irene Fornes and Rosalyn Drexler and produced Carmines's own musical settings of plays by Gertrude Stein in the church's choir loft. The following year Ellen Stewart, a Chicago-born freelance fashion designer with a thick Creole accent, rented a tenement basement with two friends, and because one of them was a playwright, Paul Foster, they decided to put on plays. When the police started snooping around, assuming that a black woman entertaining so many male visitors could only be a prostitute, she started serving coffee, and the place became Cafe La Mama. Still in existence but no longer a coffeehouse, it is world-renowned as La Mama Experimental Theater Club.

Off-off-Broadway instigated a renaissance in new American playwriting that eschewed the rules of traditional commercial theater both in style and in substance. It became a nurturing ground for dozens of playwrights over the course of a very few years, including some who would go on to great success and es-

teem in the American theater, such as John Guare, Israel
Horovitz, Tom Eyen, Ed Bullins, John Ford Noonan, Harvey Fi-
erstein, and A. R. Gurney, Jr. It incorporated the voice of the
emerging black theater and gave gay artists a forum for the un-
selfconscious exploration in the theater of their own lifestyles. It
was the ultimate, uncensorious nesting ground for fledgling playwrights who could try whatever they wanted—ten-minute monologues or four-hour epics, comedies about suicide or camp
tragedies—without being told they were doing it wrong. It battered down the barriers of what could be presented onstage by
featuring nudity and four-letter words as facts of life rather than
titillating rarities, and it violently rejected polite drawing-room
chatter, to explore issues ranging from Vietnam and racism to the
latest edition of an *Archie* comic book. As Elenore Lester commented in *The New York Times*, "Most of the writers on the OOB
circuit write as though they were born into the world the day after
some metaphysical H-bomb exploded, and they accept this blasted
world as the natural environment and proceed to play around in
it with a great deal of gusto."

But off-off-Broadway didn't start out to be an institution, and
it was never an organized movement. It began by accident, spon-
taneously, among the unnumbered hordes of rambunctious kids
who fled small-town America in search of sex, drugs, and/or artistic expression and gravitated toward the bars, basements, coffeehouses, and grubby lofts of lower Manhattan. "On the Lower East
Side there *was* a special sort of culture developing," Shepard
would recall later. "You were so close to the people who were going to the plays, there was really no difference between you and
them—your own experience was their experience, so that you began to develop consciousness of what was happening . . . I mean,
nobody knew what was happening, but there was a sense that
something was going on. People were arriving from Texas and Ar-
kansas in the middle of New York City, and a community was being established. It was a very exciting time."

The important thing about all these off-off-Broadway pioneers
is that they didn't start theaters in order to make it big eventually
on Broadway, where the hits of the day were the likes of *Hello,
Dolly!* and *The Subject Was Roses*. They didn't do it for money,
because nobody got paid anything. And they didn't do it for the
glory, because none of these places seated more than a hundred
people, usually far less. They did it for themselves. Shepard was

no exception. "Writing was a kind of salvation for me," he said. "If I hadn't had that, I don't know what would have happened to me. I probably would have wound up a used-car salesman."

Chapter Three:

BOY GENIUS

First off let me tell you that I don't want to be a playwright, I want to be a rock and roll star. I want that understood right off. I got into writing plays because I had nothing else to do. So I started writing to keep from going off the deep end. That was back in '64. Writing has become a habit. I like to yodel and dance and fuck a lot. Writing is neat because you do it on a very physical level. Just like rock and roll. A lot of people think playwrights are some special brand of intellectual fruit cake with special answers to special problems that confront the world at large. I think that's a crock of shit. When you write a play you work out like a musician on a piece of music. You find all the rhythms and the melody and the harmonies and take them as they come.

So much for theory.

—Shepard in a 1971 biographical program note

Was it accident or ambition that landed Sam Shepard in all the right places at all the right times? His incarnation as the greenhorn busboy didn't last long because he was quickly clasped to the heart of the Village theater scene. He was lionized by LeRoi Jones and Edward Albee, introduced around the Caffe Cino by Michael Smith, just in general invited in. When the first group portrait of La Mama playwrights was taken for a fancy fashion magazine, featuring Lanford Wilson, Jean-Claude van Itallie, Leonard Melfi, Terrence McNally—all the bright young men—in coats and ties or collegiate sweaters, there was Sam, sleepy-eyed and thick-lipped, wearing an open-necked shirt and blue jeans, perched right next to La Mama herself. And only a little over a year after his first plays were produced in New York, Sam Shepard was already being hailed in *The New York Times*—in a December 1965 article entitled "The Pass-the-Hat Circuit" by Elenore Lester—as "the generally acknowledged 'genius' of the OOB circuit."

Like most of the other playwrights Shepard had quickly made the rounds and within a year had plays done at most of the theaters on the circuit. In February 1965 two one-acts were done at La Mama, *Dog* and *Rocking Chair*. At the same time, Edward Albee's Playwrights' Unit mounted Shepard's *Up to Thursday* at the Cherry Lane Theater along with Lanford Wilson's *Home Free* and Paul Foster's *Balls*. In September the Playwrights' Unit produced *4-H Club*, which was later broadcast on the radio drama series *Theater of the Ear*. *Icarus's Mother* was first performed in the fall of 1965 at the Caffe Cino, with the playwright himself stepping in for one of the actors during the last week of the run. And in January 1966 the Judson Poets' Theater gave the premiere of Shepard's *Red Cross*, on the bill with a new adaptation of *Antigone*.

Shepard was also gaining a reputation among theater people outside of New York. The Theater Company of Boston wanted to include Shepard in a festival of new American plays, so he went up to Boston in the fall of 1965 for a reading of his play *Three and Melons*. But he decided he didn't like that play, so the theater did *Icarus's Mother* instead, with young Blythe Danner playing one of the parts. Shepard was one of several experimental theater writers, including Megan Terry, Barbara Garson, Lanford Wilson, and John Guare, invited to the Yale Drama School in 1966 on fellowships that allowed them time and money to continue writing. Also in 1966 the Firehouse Theater in Minneapolis got a grant from the University of Minnesota's Office of Aid to Drama Research to produce Shepard's *Fourteen Hundred Thousand*, later broadcast coast to coast on educational television "so my mother got to see it."

But Shepard's headquarters, socially and artistically, was Theater Genesis, which unlike the Cino and La Mama focused on a small group of writers and was much more particular about the kind of work it presented. Among the writers produced there, besides Shepard, were Leonard Melfi, Murray Mednick, Tony Barsha, and Tom Sankey. Theater Genesis, according to its founder, Ralph Cook, "defined itself in terms of a deeply subjective kind of realism and, within the off-off-Broadway circuit, an almost conspicuous heterosexuality." Like the East Village counterculture around it, Genesis was heavily involved with politics and drugs. One of its most ambitious productions was Murray Mednick and Tony Barsha's *The Hawk*, a heavy play about the symbiotic relationship between junkies and drug dealers. The play was based on a poem by Mednick, directed by Barsha, and developed over a period of several months by a company of improvisational actors, including an English-born actress from California named Scarlett Johnson and her teenaged daughter O-Lan, who would soon become Sam Shepard's wife.

Theater Genesis first presented Shepard's play *Chicago* on a bill with Lawrence Ferlinghetti's *The Customs Inspector in Baggy Pants* in April 1965. Later remounted at La Mama and performed on tour in Europe, *Chicago* was one of the three plays for which Shepard received his first Obie award from *The Village Voice* in 1966 (the others were *Red Cross* and *Icarus's Mother*).

What were these plays like, and what made them so special? The main thing was that they dispensed with traditional character and plot, the two things most drama hinges on. In conventional plays the characters stay pretty much the same over the time span of the play, which could be two days or twenty years; that's how you recognize them. Shepard's early plays take place in real time—that is, continuously from beginning to end with no pretense of days or years passing, and in that short space of time the characters change a lot, play different roles (consciously and unconsciously), and go through different moods. As one critic notes, "They are abstract collages, consisting of lyrical monologues, stunning imagery, and a sense of paranoid despair." This approach conveys a truth about the nature of lived experience that conventional drama never could—that we don't really stay the same from moment to moment, even though to all outer appearances we're still the same person. "I preferred a character that was constantly unidentifiable, shifting through the actor," Shepard said, "so that the actor could almost play anything, and the audience was never expected to identify with the character." Instead, the audience reveled in . . . The Moment.

Shepard wrote these plays very quickly, on the inspiration of The Moment. He never rewrote them; if he didn't like a play when he was done with it, he started another. Instead of carefully working out plots and character motivations, Shepard expended his creative energy on the conceptual framework of each play, inventing purposely banal dialogue to stitch together images, actions, and comically/poetically extended monologues which puncture the surface of the theatrical event to release gusts of pure spirit. A good example is *Red Cross*, which combines these elements most schematically.

Jim and Carol are sitting in a cabin furnished with twin beds, two windows, and a screen door. Everything onstage is white—the sets, the costumes, the people. Carol wonders why she feels so sick, imagines skiing in the Rockies and having her head burst open in the middle of the slope, then runs out the door to do errands. Jim knows something she doesn't, because as soon as she's gone he takes off his pants and starts picking crabs off his skin. The maid comes in to change the sheets on the beds, and Jim shows her his crabs. Then he gives her a demonstration of how to swim, each of them lying on one of the beds while Jim spins out a verbal rhapsody on swimming. The maid responds with a vivid fantasy about drowning and turning into a fish. She leaves, and Carol rushes in to tell Jim about the crabs she's discovered crawling all over her, but Jim's mind has been blown by the maid's story. The play ends with him turning to Carol with a trickle of blood running down his forehead.

The dialogue in *Red Cross* is merely functional ("It's the maid, dear." "Come in, come in and have a bed or a seat. Whatever you want." "I want to change the beds is all." "Well, come in. The beds are here"), the story nonexistent, but the impact of the play comes from those dizzying monologues (on skiing, swimming, drowning), the sight of two people lying on beds "swimming," and that spot of red blood on an all-white set. "All Sam's plays," critic Michael Smith once wrote, "use the stage to project images: they do not relate to the spectator by reflecting outside reality (they are not psychological or political); rather they relate to reality by operating directly on the spectator's minds and nerves."

Chicago and *Icarus's Mother* are more elusive in terms of "story" and "meaning." In *Chicago*, Stu sits in a bathtub center stage while his girlfriend Joy rushes around preparing to leave for a job in Chicago; *Icarus's Mother* concerns five kids at a picnic on the beach waiting for fireworks to begin and trying to communicate with an airplane flying overhead. Both plays combine casual, disjointed, even random actions with dialogue that doesn't so much tell a story as create an image or cast a spell.

"The way that I think about that language is that it's happening inside all those people. That it just happened to be spoken because it's a play," Shepard once said. "Like you can be washing the dishes and [have] an apocalyptic nightmare going on inside you. People at a picnic, yet inside they're in turmoil. It's like as if it could be seen in this sort of way—that the play's silent and the dialogue just comes out of what's going on inside all those people. That's what's so neat about writing—you get to speak all that stuff that's going on in your head."

The fact of the matter is that Shepard's style of writing was largely determined by his style of living. Critics who scrutinize these early plays for deeper meaning usually miss the point. Shepard certainly didn't write *4-H Club*, a tiny one-act about three boys in a room making instant coffee, eating apples, and kicking trash around, to pay homage to "Beckett's reified metaphors and LeRoi Jones's urban cul-de-sacs," as one critic speculated. He was probably noting exactly what transpired the night before on Avenue C and, his stomach growling from a diet of apples and instant coffee, scribbling a theatrical snapshot of what it's like living hand-to-mouth in a crummy East Village apartment in the early sixties.

Friends of Shepard and Charles Mingus had no trouble recognizing *Cowboys* as a typical conversation between the two roommates; in fact, Mingus's father was so angry at Charles for letting Shepard steal his words that he refused to see any of his son's work for years. Both *Up to Thursday*, which the editor of *Best Plays of 1964–65* described as "about a sleepy youth who waits for clean underwear while two couples play games" and Shepard called "a bad exercise in absurdity," and *Three and Melons* were tangentially about dodging the draft—a popular sport among twenty-one-year-olds in 1965. (Shepard beat the draft by pretending to be a heroin addict.) And when Joyce Aaron, whom Shepard cast in *Up to Thursday*, became his girlfriend, she also became primary source material. They were constant companions for the next three years, and as one friend said, "Wherever they went, he got a play out of it."

"Perhaps because we were close during that period, I never knew where our life—where *my* life—was going to turn up on the page, or later on some stage, but inevitably there was always some aspect of our experience together that I would recognize," Aaron wrote in an essay on Shepard called "Clues in a Memory." "Yet I never felt exposed by Sam—he transformed whatever he drew on." A tiny, zaftig woman with long frizzy red hair, Aaron is a highly regarded performer and acting teacher; she divides her time between New York and Europe, living with her half-Dutch son and teaching (as a colleague puts it) *le Sam Shepard*. "I watched him write. I traveled with him. I knew where his plays came from, what their sources were. I saw how and where he didn't rewrite, and how and where he did." For instance, *Chicago*, which Shepard said he wrote in one day, came about because Joyce (thinly disguised in the play as "Joy") got a role in a Chicago production of *The Knack* directed by Brian Bedford; according to Aaron, the "Joe" her character talks to on the phone was based on Joe Chaikin, the experimental theater director whose Open Theater she belonged to.

The Open Theater was as much an influence on Shepard's early development as a playwright as his relationships with Mingus and Aaron. Although he would later be involved with the Open Theater as a writer, contributing material to their productions of *Terminal*, *Nightwalk*, and *Re-Arrangements*, at first he hung around with the group only because he was going out with Joyce. But he quickly became enamored of Joe Chaikin, both as a teacher and as a person. Chaikin, formerly an actor with the politically oriented Living Theater, started the Open Theater primarily as a workshop for actors to develop techniques for performing non-naturalistic material, the Brechtian plays and verse dramas that irresistibly attract the avant-garde. Chaikin's influence, direct or indirect, on off-off-Broadway playwrights—what they wrote and how it was performed—in the early sixties equaled the effect that Lee Strasberg's gospel of Method acting had a decade before on Broadway drama, to which the Open Theater was in part an innovative response.

Chaikin was as brilliant a teacher as he was an actor because he expressed his vision of acting as an almost spiritual quest with great eloquence and emotional directness. "We have to shake off the sophistication of our time, by which we close ourselves up, and to become vulnerable again," he told his actors. "We realize that life hasn't been too generous with us, and we've retreated. We've closed off a great deal of our total human response. But as actors we must open up again, become naive again, innocent, and cultivate our deeper climates—our dread, for example. Only then will we be able to find new ways to express the attitudes which we hold as uniquely our own."

Chaikin had tremendous influence on Shepard, not only as an artist but also as a person. The values he espoused—his steadfast faith in the priority of art over glamor, show business, wealth, and fame, the things that tantalize people in the theater all the time—made a deep impression on friends and colleagues. And Shepard's insistence on keeping tight control over his work and the hostility toward publicity that makes him so unusual among celebrities may be seen as his way of emulating the artistic integrity he first observed in Joe Chaikin.

"Making it in the theater is in one way or another irresistible to everyone. To me too," Chaikin would say. "But it's like the emperor's new clothes: it's something which you believe is valuable because everybody makes so much noise about it, but it really isn't valuable. For it doesn't make anybody more satisfied, nor does it elevate anybody. In order to make it, you have to groom yourself—you have to have an inoffensive personality; you have to modify yourself in many minor ways—but the ways become so many that the matter isn't minor anymore. Everybody has to do this anyway in life, but I really think that one should do the absolute minimum. The more you do—the more you try to get to the big ladder—the more you have to relinquish a certain element which our work requires. For example, when you go to parties which are profitable, you go, and you smile, and you make nice to people, and soon you don't know yourself in a sense. You lose a connection to your real responses." This sort of modesty and devotion to The Work, along with the refusal "to groom yourself . . . to have an inoffensive personality," characterizes Sam Shepard throughout his career, and it seems likely that Chaikin set the example.

Chaikin's training of actors must have rubbed off on Shepard, too. Based on the work of his teacher, Nola Chilton, Chaikin's workshops focused on sound-and-movement improvisations aimed at expressing the emotional undercurrents that accompany everyday behavior, finding a different theatrical language to distinguish the inside world from the outside. Critic Richard Gilman, who first met Shepard at the Open Theater in 1965 ("a James Dean-like youth with an un-Dean-like intellectual glint in his eyes"), suggests that the playwright picked up the technique of "transformations" from the Open Theater. "Briefly, a transformation exercise was an improvised scene—a birthday party, survivors in a lifeboat, etc.—in which after a while, and suddenly, the actors were asked to switch immediately to a new scene and therefore to wholly new characters. . . ." writes Gilman. "Shepard carried the idea of transformations much farther than the group had by actually writing them into his texts, in plays like *Angel City, Back Bog Beast Bait* and *The Tooth of Crime*, where characters become wholly different in abrupt movements within the course of the work, or speak suddenly as someone else, while the scene may remain the same."

It's no accident that Open Theater actors were prominently featured in early Shepard plays such as *Icarus's Mother*. Joyce Aaron performed in *Red Cross* and the television production of *Fourteen Hundred Thousand*, which also featured Kevin O'Connor and Chaikin himself. Aaron also appeared in *La Turista*, another play based on her adventures with Shepard, this time a notoriously disastrous trip to Mexico and Central America in the summer of 1965. Staying at the seedy Hotel Nacionale in Oaxaca, afflicted with horrible sunburns and dysentery, they hardly got any sleep, shitting and vomiting and somehow managing to find it all hilariously funny. The worst part was the plane trip. They hit terrible turbulence, Shepard became sick and frightened, and Aaron had to talk him out of completely freaking out. When they got back to the States and showed up at a theater festival in Pennsylvania, Shepard announced that he had taken his last plane ride, and thereafter did his traveling by train, bicycle, or pickup truck.

Shepard's first full-length play—i.e., two acts with intermission—*La Turista* was also Shepard's first play to be performed in an established New York theater outside the Village. During the production of *Red Cross*, Aaron had invited her acting teacher, Wynn Handman, to the play. Handman, who founded the American Place Theater in 1964 to develop plays as works-in-progress from staged readings to full productions, was encouraging to Shepard, so the playwright sent him *La Turista*. The play ran for two weeks at the American Place in March 1967, and was directed by Jacques Levy with Joyce Aaron (to whom the play is dedicated) and Sam Waterston in the cast.

Actually, the original script was in three acts, but when rehearsals began only one act was ready; Shepard had decided the second and third needed rewriting. Handman started to get worried when he kept seeing Shepard at the theater all day hanging around and beating bongo drums. Finally he said, "Aren't you supposed to be working on the play?" "I write at night," the playwright said placidly. "I work from midnight to five A.M." Eventually he came up with a single act drastically different from both the first act and the two he'd discarded.

La Turista opens in a Mexican hotel room painted bright yellow. Two young Americans named Kent and Salem with bright red sunburns lie on separate twin beds in their underwear reading *Life* and *Time* magazines. A Mexican shoeshine boy comes into the room, and they try to chase him off by yelling at him in pidgin Spanish and offering him money. The boy pulls the telephone out of the wall and spits on Kent. Kent runs into the bathroom, overtaken by diarrhea. After Salem tells a story about her childhood, the boy takes off his pants, climbs into Kent's bed, and describes a rich American he once worked for. Kent emerges from the bathroom to announce, "Well! I feel like a new man after all that!" His face is now painted white where he was previously sunburned and he's dressed exactly like the rich American the boy described: in linen shirt, handmade boots, Panama hat, and gunbelt but no pants (a detail the boy had left out). When he sees the boy in his bed, Kent screams and faints. Salem calls for a doctor, and a witch doctor arrives with his son to perform a weird ceremony in which live chickens are killed and their blood spilled on Kent's back, apparently to no avail. During the ceremony Salem is seized with diarrhea, and when she returns from the bathroom, also in whiteface, she puts on a poncho and tries to sell the Mexican boy to someone in the audience. The phone rings; it's the boy's father, who says he's coming to get him, and the first act ends with Salem saying, "You'll never make it alive!"

The second act takes place in an American hotel room decorated in tan and gray plastic. Kent is suffering from a mysterious sleeping sickness, and the doctor and son who arrive to treat him are dressed in Civil War costumes. The doctor makes Salem walk Kent around the room until he wakes up. When Kent does wake up, he babbles incoherently, engages Doc in a gunfight using his finger as an imaginary pistol, and starts doing a wild African dance. Then Kent jumps off the stage and, standing behind the audience, launches into a long, psychedelic monologue about a doctor and the Frankenstein-like monster he creates. The play ends with one of Sam Shepard's most amazing stage directions: "Salem and Sonny make a lunge for Kent, who grabs onto a rope and swings over their heads. He lands on the ramp behind Doc and runs straight toward the upstage wall of the set and leaps right through it, leaving a cutout silhouette of his body in the wall."

Shepard caused something of a stir at the time by specifically not inviting the critics, who were accustomed to reviewing all shows at the American Place Theater. He remembered what they'd had to say about *Cowboys* and *The Rock Garden*, and he'd learned he didn't really need the critics anyway. But some critics were interested enough to sneak in. Elizabeth Hardwick wrote a long, perceptive rave of *La Turista* in *The New York Review of Books* (among other things, she described the audience as "utterly depressing; middle-aged, middle class, and rather aggressively indifferent: a dead weight of alligators, dozing and grunting before muddily sliding away"), and *The Village Voice* gave the play a 1967 Obie award. When Bobbs-Merrill published the play the next year, the dust jacket featured a rather frightening photo of Shepard baring his gnarled teeth over "a random selection of critical comment on *La Turista*" by various friends (" 'Couldn't even skin it back'—Eddie Hicks," " 'But an artist is supposed to jerk off—Bill

Hart") and bewildered dignitaries (" 'Where do you come from'—
Robert Lowell," " 'How come we were banned'—Robert
Brustein").

It's probably just as well that the play wasn't widely reviewed,
because in a sense it defies critical analysis: criticism burdens plays
like *La Turista* with allegorical interpretations where only theatrical puns are intended. "Aha, I see—the Americans are full of shit!
And that south-of-the-border blood shed on the young American's
back, is that a reference to the Vietnam War?" *La Turista* is somewhat more ambitious than its predecessors, and it may indeed be
Shepard's crudely poetic rumination on being an American at a
time when Americans' popularity in foreign countries is on the
wane.

But the play is clearly of a piece with the early one-acts, demanding to be read not as a logical, linear narrative but as a
trippy theatrical experience defined by its shifting character-masks,
its time-stopping monologues, and its brilliant visual imagery (the
shockingly yellow hotel room, the eerie silhouette left at the end
of the play). These early Shepard plays are very much tied to the
time, the circumstances, and the specific performers involved in
their creation—the farther you get from those original considera-
tions, the more cryptic the plays seem. At best they seem like re-
peatable pieces of performance art, transcribed "happenings." At
worst they are quaint period pieces. The next set of plays based
on mythical figures from pop culture translate more readily to universal circumstances.

Shepard himself feels that the early plays were "kind of facile.
You get a certain spontaneous freaky thing if you write real fast.
You don't get anything heavy unless you spend real time," he told
The New York Times in 1969. "Now I'm dealing more with mythic
characters, a combination of science-fiction, Westerns, and television." After *La Turista*, Shepard, like his perfervid hero, took a
flying leap and transcended his persona altogether.

Chapter Four:

ROCK-AND-ROLL JESUS WITH A COWBOY MOUTH

In the old days people had Jesus and those guys to embrace
... they created a god with all their belief energies ... and
when they didn't dig themselves they could lose themselves
in the Lord. But it's too hard now. We're earthy people, and
the old saints just don't make it, and the old God is just too
far away. He don't represent our pain no more. His words
don't shake through us no more. Any great motherfucker
rock-'n'-roll song can raise me higher than all of Revelations.
We created rock-'n'-roll from our image, it's our child ... a
child that's gotta burst in the mouth of a savior. ... Mick Jagger would love to be that savior but it ain't him. It's like ...
the rock-'n'-roll star in his highest state of grace will be the
new savior ... rocking to Bethlehem to be born. Ya know
what I mean, Slim?

—Cavale in *Cowboy Mouth*

Rock 'n' roll was the heartbeat of American youth in the 1960s, and Sam Shepard felt the pulse. Beginning with *Melodrama Play*, which was first done at La Mama in May 1967 along with Leonard Melfi's *Times Square* (it was revived three times and toured Europe as well), Shepard started compiling a series of rock 'n' roll plays, continuing with *Forensic and the Navigators*, *Operation Sidewinder*, *Mad Dog Blues*, and his collaboration with Patti Smith *Cowboy Mouth*, culminating with one of his finest plays ever, *The Tooth of Crime*. Just the titles of these plays—and others like *Shaved Splits*, *The Unseen Hand*, *The Holy Ghostly*, *Back Bog Beast Bait*, *Blue Bitch*, *Killer's Head*—are a pleasure to recite in themselves. They also provide a key to Shepard's rock 'n' roll heart—the part that inspired him, when he got his first major playwriting grant from the Rockefeller Foundation in 1967, to spend the money on a Dodge Charger and a Stratocaster guitar.

Shepard's titles unmistakably recall the poetically evocative but inscrutable names of famous rock bands and albums from the sixties, especially the West Coast variety of acid rock. Squares made fun of them, but album titles like *Disraeli Gears*, *Between the Buttons*, *Axis: Bold as Love*, *Revolver*, and *Surrealistic Pillow* (not to be confused with Jefferson Airplane, the Grateful Dead, Moby Grape, Iron Butterfly, the Velvet Underground, and Quicksilver Messenger Service, as some of the best bands called themselves) gained mythical status within the sixties counterculture despite or because of having no literal meaning. Shepard was tuned into everything that was going on in the rock world, both as a fan and also as a member for several years of the Holy Modal Rounders, a folk-rock band with a cult following in New York whose motto was "If it doesn't make you feel horny it's not art."

Peter Stampfel, who started the Holy Modal Rounders in 1963 with Steve Weber, was retrieving his fiddle from a pawnshop on

Second Avenue one day when Sam Shepard struck up a conversation with him, and the two of them hit it off. Shepard had been playing drums behind a folksinger-guitarist who called himself the Heavy Metal Kid (after the William Burroughs character—no relation to what is now called heavy-metal rock), and they were looking for a bass player. The Rounders had broken up, and Stampfel was in the process of starting a new group, but he was also teaching himself bass. So he played in Shepard's group, and Shepard played drums in Stampfel's group, which was then called the Swamp Lillies. Meanwhile, Steve Weber had made a deal to record a Holy Modal Rounders album on the ESP-Disk label, so the Rounders regrouped, with Shepard now an official third member, to make the record in the summer of 1967. This was the period christened "the Summer of Love" by the hippies, whose long hair, flagrant pot-smoking, open sexuality, and antiwar politics outraged the "older generation" and kept the media supplied with colorful copy. Shepard took a dislike to all the "long-haired clones" in the Village and shocked his friends by getting a crewcut. The man who ran the record company was so horrified that he refused to put Shepard's picture on the Rounders' album jacket. You know, man, it was, like, not cool.

Shepard clearly had little use for the "flower power" side of the sixties counterculture, and he looks back on the heyday of hippies as something less than a love-in. "When this influx of essentially white middle-class kids hit the streets, the indigenous people—the Puerto Ricans, the blacks, the street junkies and all the people who were really a part of the scene—felt this great animosity toward these flip-outs running around the lower East side in beads and hair down to their asses. There was this upsurge of violence and weirdness, and everybody started carrying guns and knives," he told a college reporter for *Rolling Stone.* "I was using a lot of drugs then—amphetamines, smack. Drugs were a big part of the whole experience of that time. It was part of a feeling that you wanted to experience different aspects of reality." It wasn't, he quickly adds, just a field trip to get good material. "I didn't use drugs to write. I only used drugs to live," he said with a laugh. "But I was using heavy stuff, and I saw a lot of people go under from drugs, which is one of the main reasons I left the streets, because street life went hand in hand with that."

Rock 'n' roll wasn't exactly a refuge from the drug wars, but it kept Shepard off the streets. When the Rounders dissolved again,

Stampfel started another group called the Moray Eels with Shepard and a piano player named Richard Tyler. "The songs they were doing at that time were their own compositions—things with obscure titles like 'Black Leather Swamp Nazi,' " *Zigzag* magazine reported, "and they all lived in their Greenwich Village fantasy world." But the Rounders had such a strong following that when Stampfel and Weber reunited for a well-paying concert, a producer named Barry Friedman (who took to calling himself Frazier Mohawk) approached them to record another Holy Modal Rounders album. Stampfel insisted that it be a joint effort between the old band and his new band, so in March 1968 they all went out to Los Angeles where they recorded *The Moray Eels Eat the Holy Modal Rounders* for Elektra Records.

Jac Holzman, the president of Elektra who had discovered and first recorded such folksingers as Judy Collins and Tom Rush, seemed to be very taken with the group. "The Holy Modal Rounders might be akin to *Waiting for Godot*. It was an experiment with a kind of aural theater," he said. "The Rounders were a fascinating phenomenon, they were a lifestyle that not too much was known about, and musically they were very solid." You would never know it by listening to the record; whatever magic the Rounders produced in concert that earned them such a fanatical following never transpired in the studio. The Moray Eels album, which occasionally turns up in 29-cent bargain bins, is a perfect artifact of the whimsical druggy-rock of the time, clearly modeled after Van Dyke Parks's eccentric, James-Joyce-on-acid masterpiece *Song Cycle*, which had just been released to enormous critical acclaim. Stampfel considers the album an embarrassment——"a piece of shit," he cheerfully admits. "Weber wouldn't practice, and there was a lot of craziness going on because of all the drugs going around at the time. Sam wasn't taking too many drugs, but I was quite amphetamine-crazed at the time. It wasn't very pleasant."

Nonetheless, the band stayed in California and toured the West Coast for several months. Shepard had broken up with Joyce Aaron by the time he joined the Rounders in 1966. He had other girlfriends after that, including another Open Theater actress, Brenda Smiley, and when he went on the road with the Rounders he took along his new flame, an astrologer named Nancy. The band played at popular rock nightclubs in Los Angeles like the Kaleidoscope and the Cheetah, and they opened for Pink Floyd at the Avalon Ballroom in San Francisco. They even appeared on the hit TV show *Laugh-In,* playing "The Yo-Yo Song" for about fifteen seconds before Ruth Buzzi bumped into the band, pursued by a lecher.

Whenever possible, Shepard included the Rounders/Moray Eels in his rock plays. They weren't involved, however, with the first one, *Melodrama Play.* Along with rock music, *Melodrama Play* introduced a plot—of sorts—into Sam Shepard's work for the first time. Duke Durgens has written a song that is "the number one hit tune in the world," and now his manager Floyd has him cooped up in a room decorated with posters of Bob Dylan and Robert Goulet (with their eyes scratched out) under strict orders to write a follow-up. To get into the right mood for a new song, Duke has his girlfriend Dana cut his very long hair until it's very short (not unlike Shepard's protest crewcut). Duke's brother Drake and his partner Cisco arrive, and under duress Duke admits that it was Drake who wrote his hit song, "Prisoners, Get Up Out a' Your Homemade Beds." When Duke's manager Floyd hears this, he tries to force Drake and Cisco to write a new song.

At this point the plot peters out and the play drifts into random violence and claustrophobic chatter until it ends with pounding at the door, mayhem about to occur, and the radio blaring Duke's hit with Shepard's best Dylanesque lyrics:

So prisoners, get up out a' your homemade beds
Oh prisoners, get up out a' your homemade heads.

Melodrama Play is quite dated—a stage direction has Duke and Dana doing the frug—and only interesting really as a warm-up for later plays. The use of an onstage rock band, the transference of identities, and the "Awright-no-one-leaves-this-room"-type showdown (right out of The *Maltese Falcon*) foreshadow *The Tooth of Crime,* and Shepard would update the story of a visionary being held captive until he repeats a previous success with *Geography of a Horse Dreamer* in 1973. Nonetheless, Tom O'Horgan, the brilliant director who brought his off-off-Broadway theatrics to Broadway with *Hair, Lenny,* and *Jesus Christ Superstar,* staged the original production of *Melodrama Play* at La Mama, and it was sensational enough to inspire *Village Voice* critic Ross Wetzsteon to declare, "There is not the slightest doubt in my mind that Sam Shepard is the most important living American playwright."

Shepard found such praise excessive, at least while Tennessee Williams was still alive.

Underneath its pop-culture veneer, *Melodrama Play* does show Shepard beginning to explore age-old theater traditions for his own ends. "Neither this play nor any of the many others in Shepard's oeuvre which use similar material, is conventional melodrama," critic James Leverett points out. "But they all use melodramatic forms, particularly those with strong claims on the American imagination—the mystery thriller, science fiction, the western. . . . Aggression, paranoia, infantilism, narcissism are all parts of their melodramatic soul. They are also the very aspects of our society which Shepard repeatedly explores."

Aggression, paranoia, infantilism, narcissism—they were as crucial to sixties rock 'n' roll as John, Paul, George, and Ringo. They also played a big part in Shepard's next play, *Forensic and the Navigators*. (Not the Beatles, of course; the house band for Forensic was the Moray Eels, making their theatrical debut, although it was more like what Peter Stampfel calls "a musical non sequitur.") The play features two bumbling, long-haired revolutionaries named Emmet and Forensic—one of Shepard's many buddy-buddy pairs extending from Chet and Stu in *Cowboys* to Lee and Austin in *True West*—who use their housegirl Oolan as bait to ambush two sinister exterminators.

Forensic and the Navigators was first performed at Theater Genesis at the very end of December 1968. According to the director, Ralph Cook, Shepard started rehearsals with only a five-page scenario, which expanded night by night as he saw what the actors could do with it. One of the cast members was O-Lan Johnson, who had been quite mystified to audition for a play and discover a character in it bearing her name and saying things that she herself had said. It finally dawned on her that the author was this "crazy, skinny guy" she'd seen hanging around Theater Genesis. She'd be seeing a lot more of him before long.

Forensic is another play that critics like to mine for deeper meaning: "It is a critique both of the subservient bureaucrat and the timidly confused revolutionary—a comic-strip version of social conflict which sees the eschatological results of organized ineptitude." (To which Shepard might reply, "Eschato-huh?") The play has some thematic connection to other Shepard plays about young revolutionaries (*Shaved Splits, Operation Sidewinder, The Unseen Hand*), but like the previous one-acts it remains remarkable less for its dialogue or intellectual content than for its visual images and physical effects.

Most people who saw *Forensic* came away talking about nothing but O-Lan's hilarious demonstration of the best way to eat Rice Krispies; anyone who has seen this baby-faced but worldly-wise-looking actress onstage or in her movie roles in *The Right Stuff* or *Natural Born Killers* can imagine how delightful she was. And at the end of the play, as colored smoke started filling up the theater until the stage was invisible, the band came on and started to play very loudly, literally driving the audience from the theater. "I don't think it works either," the director told a disgruntled reporter from *The New York Times*, "but he wanted it that way." Shepard started off playing drums with the band, but midway through the run he left for Rome to work on the screenplay of the new Antonioni film *Zabriskie Point*.

After the international success of his first English-language picture, *Blow-Up*, Michelangelo Antonioni drove across the United States in the spring of 1967 and decided to make his next movie in America. He went back to Rome and with his assistant, Tonino Guerra, wrote the outline of a story about a semi-committed student activist and his apolitical girlfriend, who undergoes some sort of political enlightenment when he is killed by policemen. Antonioni returned to New York in the fall, met Shepard, and asked him to work on the script—mainly to render the director's ideas into contemporary American dialogue. "He took a look at me—it was like an actor's interview—and said you'll do fine. Be in Rome next week," said Shepard. "Because my play *Icarus's Mother* involved an airplane, and his movie also involved an airplane, he thought there was common grounds for us to write a script."

Shepard spent two months in Italy working with Antonioni and came back with him—presumably by boat, since you can't get to Europe and back in a pickup truck—to Los Angeles, where casting for the film began. (That's when he hooked up with Peter Stampfel again and recorded the *Moray Eels Eat the Holy Modal Rounders* album.) Shepard didn't stay with the picture to its completion. "I didn't know how to continue with what Antonioni wanted. He wanted political repartee and I just didn't know how. Plus I was twenty-four and just wasted by the experience. It was like a nightmare. I was surrounded by MGM and all that stuff," said Shepard. "I like Michelangelo a lot—he is incredible—but to submerge yourself in that world of limousines and hotels and re-hashing and pleasing Carlo Ponti is just . . . forget it."

Antonioni replaced him with a writer named Fred Gardner, started shooting in September, and finished in May of 1969. When the film came out in 1970, the credit for the screenplay went to Antonioni, Gardner, Shepard, Tonino Guerra, and Clare Peplo. During the filming of *Zabriskie Point*, Shepard managed to get work for his friends in the Open Theater, who appeared collectively in the movie's famous "orgy scene" featuring dozens of half-naked youths making love on the dunes in Death Valley. This scene caused an enormous ruckus among the locals, who tried to halt the film by invoking the Mann Act prohibiting the transportation of women across the state lines for "immoral purposes."

On the road with the Holy Modal Rounders the summer of 1968, Shepard wrote *Operation Sidewinder*, undoubtedly inspired, as the dedication indicates, by his experience working on *Zabriskie Point*:

DEDICATED TO THE FOLLOWING
FOR THEIR KEEN INSPIRATION:

MICHELANGELO ANTONIONI
DAPPER TOMMY THOMPSON
CRAZY HORSE
THE STONES
THE HOLY MODAL ROUNDERS
THE HOPI
NANCY
GABBY HAYES
OLD ORAIBI
MICKEY FREE
1968
O-LAN

Shepard's most sprawling and heavily plotted play—it has thirty-six characters, twelve scenes in two acts, and eleven songs—*Operation Sidewinder* is a movie written for the stage. The plot centers on a highly developed U.S. Air Force computer disguised as a giant sidewinder snake which has escaped from the lab into the desert. Military men race to retrieve the sidewinder before it can fall into the hands of some black revolutionaries plotting to take over the country by putting LSD in the water supply. In the play's first scene, however, the snake is spotted by a couple of tourists (a married couple on their way to a Las Vegas divorce) who stop to take a picture; when the woman gets too close, the snake grabs her, and when her husband goes for help, he gets shot by a wild-eyed young man who wants to capture the sidewinder-computer for an Indian tribe trying to contact extraterrestrials.

The play resembles an apocalyptic comic strip, since the characters are purposely drawn as stereotypes, starting with their names. The tourists are called Dukie and Honey, the military officials are drunken bozos with names like Captain Bovine and Doctor Vector (a German-accented Dr. Strangelove), and the black revolutionaries Blood, Blade, and Dude are first seen sitting in a '57 Chevy at a hamburger stand, where they're served by a miniskirted white carhop whose burbling solidarity rap ("You people have such a groovy thing going. I mean all this shit about the pigs, man. I mean fuck the pigs. Forget all those gray people") elicits the response, "Pass the french fries." The only noble characters in the play are the Indians, especially the charismatic half-breed Mickey Free. The play ends with an elaborate Hopi ritual in which the sidewinder makes contact with a UFO that zooms off into the sky with the Indians, Honey, and the Young Man.

The Young Man (clearly the author's stand-in) is an ambiguous character, impassioned and confused, a radical activist and a junkie. (In the play's most pathetic action, he tries to tie off with the snake's massive coil before shooting up.) Like the main character in Antonioni's *Zabriskie Point*, he identifies with his generation's political unrest but isn't totally committed to its tactics. And he shares Shepard's own intuitive, untutored politics, which put more credence in the American Indian movement's ancient spirituality than in the trendy ideals of the "Age of Aquarius." The Young Man perfectly demonstrates critic Bonnie Marranca's observation that "side by side with Shepard's glorification of the frontier ethic, and its concomitant isolationism, oppressive view of women, retreat from group concerns, is his sixties-style radical politics with its dread of the 'system,' its pastoral ideals, and persistent criticism of the American way of life."

Operation Sidewinder isn't terribly profound or hardheaded as political drama, but it manages to express a generation's legitimate agitation in theatrically effective terms, especially in the monologues, which had by now become a Shepard trademark. The Young Man's monologue that closes the first act uncannily associates patriotism and self-hatred ("I am truly an American. I was made in America. Born, bred and raised. I have American scars on my brain. Red white and blue. I bleed American blood. I dream American dreams. I fuck American girls. I devour the planet. I'm an earth eater. . . ."), while another stoned rap reads like a primer on the political despair and metaphysical agony of sixties American youth:

> This is how it begins, I see. We become so depressed we don't fight anymore. We're only losing a little, we say. It could be so much worse. The soldiers are dying, the blacks are dying, the children are dying. It could be so much worse. . . . Let's wait till four years from now when we can take over the Democratic Party. Teddy Kennedy is still alive. Let's not do anything at all. It can only get worse. Let's give up. . . . You can't win all the time. You can't always have everything your own way. You'll be arrested. You'll be arrested, accosted, molested, tested and re-tested. You'll be beaten, you'll be jailed, you'll be thrown out of school. You'll be spanked, you'll be whipped and chained. But I am whipped. I am chained. I am prisoner to all your oppression. I am depressed, deranged, decapitated, dehumanized, defoliated, demented, and damned. I can't get out. You can get out. You can smile and laugh and kiss and cry. I am! I am! I am! I am! I am! I am! I am! I am! I am! I am! I am! Tonight. In this desert. In this space. I am.

It's not hard to imagine what a better movie *Zabriskie Point* would have been if it had had that kind of passionate lyricism rather than Antonioni's glum European detachment.

Operation Sidewinder's production history is a saga in itself, complicated by the immensity of its technical demands. It was not the sort of thing that could just be flung onstage at *La Mama* on a twenty-dollar budget. The play was first optioned (for $500) by the Yale Repertory Theater to be produced in January 1969, but it kicked off a full-blown campus crisis when a committee of the six black students at the Yale Drama School demanded it be canceled because "the play is full of stereotypes about black men." (The original version of the play, published in *Esquire* in May

1969, had the black revolutionaries sitting in an orange Cadillac watching a black-power speech by Stokely Carmichael on TV.) Playwright Arnold Weinstein, a Yale professor who supported the black demands, gave Shepard's phone number in New York to the students, who appeared on his doorstep asking him to withdraw the play, which he did—not because he agreed with their assessment but because he declined to have his play become the scapegoat for grievances between the black students and the university faculty.

The play was optioned for a commercial production by Alvin Ferleger, who had produced Bruce Jay Friedman's off-Broadway hit *Scuba Duba*, and he in turn leased the rights to the Repertory Theater of Lincoln Center, which wanted *Operation Sidewinder* to fill the new-play slot in its season of American plays. The Lincoln Center experience was a big disappointment to Shepard, who was unhappy with the casting, particularly of the Young Man (Jon Voight was approached but turned it down), as well as director Michael Schultz's choice to cut down the play and concentrate on the spectacle. "The first time he came to rehearsal, he hated it so much he left," said Peter Stampfel, whose Holy Modal Rounders played their original songs between scenes. "When he came back a few days later, he hated it even more, so he never came back."

The Lincoln Center production also gave the mainstream critics a chance to have at Shepard, and they were almost uniformly scathing. Walter Kerr's review in *The New York Times* was typical: "There is only one thing wrong with Sam Shepard's deliberately non-rational, surreal, fancifully pictorial, carefully mythic, conventionally angry, heavily overproduced and rock-group-interrupted *Operation Sidewinder* now at the Vivian Beaumont. It isn't interesting." A television critic opined, "Not only would I not walk across the street to see it again, I wouldn't allow myself to be carried across the street to see it again, even if four girls looking like Raquel Welch offered to carry me in a silken sedan chair." (No wonder playwrights despair at the state of drama criticism.) As usual, it remained to *The Village Voice* to defend Shepard. John Lahr, who as literary manager for Lincoln Center had instigated the production in the first place, championed the play as "a grotesque spectacle of our psychic death and the possibility of rebirth."

For most playwrights, having a major production at Lincoln Center would be a full-time job for at least a year. Arthur Kopit spent three years just writing his Wild West extravaganza *Indians*, which opened around the same time as *Operation Sidewinder*, and when it failed on Broadway he went into hibernation for almost nine years. Not so for Shepard. Between the time he wrote Sidewinder and the time it closed at the end of April 1970, he had three new plays produced, he attended Open Theater workshops and contributed material to their production of *Terminal*, he got married, and he quit the Holy Modal Rounders for a more pressing engagement with the Rolling Stones. As Antonia Duren, Peter Stampfel's "old lady" and erstwhile member of the Rounders, put it, Sam Shepard was "a sworn enemy of terminal stasis."

The Rolling Stones adventure came about by happy chance. When Shepard went to Europe to work with Antonioni, one of the first people he met was Keith Richard, the rakish guitarist with the Stones, and they became hanging-out buddies. The Stones had had their tangential encounter with the cinema when Jean-Luc Godard used scenes showing them recording "Sympathy for the Devil" in his film *One Plus One*, and Mick Jagger—a natural movie star if there ever was one—would go on to star in *Performance* and *Ned Kelly*. But Shepard quickly became involved in writing a movie for the whole group called *Maxagasm*, "a distorted Western for the Soul and Psyche." The screenplay, with dialogue by Shepard based on a story by Anthony Foutz, featured characters with recognizably Shepardian names like Cowboy, Child, Princess, Feelgood, Speed, Peach, and the Mercenaries. Nothing ultimately became of the movie, but Shepard spent two years pursuing it on and off.

In the process he conceived intimate friendships with the Rolling Stones. He was so loyal to them that when he went to see a production in New York of *AC/DC*, Heathcote Williams's play about a couple of schizophrenic hippies, he stormed out halfway through the first act, yelling at the actors, "You can't talk that way about Mick Jagger!" And O-Lan confessed to friends that she used to be a Rolling Stones groupie. "Just think," she would sigh, "I used to chase Mick Jagger's car, and now I have tea with him."

During the time of his expedition with the Stones, two minor one-acts debuted. When a troupe led by Tom O'Horgan revived *Melodrama Play* for a 1969 college tour, they asked Shepard for a companion piece, and he gave them *The Holy Ghostly*, a sort of ghost story cum Indian ritual about a father and son sitting around a campfire. The play was perfectly suited to the environmental theatrics of O'Horgan's troupe (which featured future song-and-dance man Ben Vereen), but it is most interesting now for the autobiographical implications of the father-son relationship, particularly Pop's monologue on family history and his dissertation on drumming techniques, which have the air of bedtime stories lovingly remembered from Shepard's childhood.

Shaved Splits, given four midnight performances at La Mama in 1970, is a rather silly, cartoonish play about a pampered woman named Miss Cherry who sits around eating chocolates, reading porno novels, and insulting her servants until her boudoir is invaded by a revolutionary on the lam named Geez. The play opens with a pornographic voice-over ostensibly copied out of a smutty paperback ("His mighty cock glistened in the half white light of the moon.... The lips of Cherry's moist cunt throbbed with the anticipation of its entry") and ends with Geez fantasizing playing lead guitar with (who else?) the Rolling Stones.

His next play, *The Unseen Hand*, first produced at La Mama in December 1969, was much more substantial—in fact, it was something of a breakthrough for Shepard. Instead of creating cartoon characters with cliche dialogue, he was beginning to conjure up the mythical essence of familiar pop-culture figures in language flavored with his own distinctive lyricism.

Blue Morphan, a 120-year-old derelict camped out in the remains of a '51 Chevy on the outskirts of Azusa, California, is visited by Willie the Space Freak from far Nogoland. Though branded with the Unseen Hand, which punishes subversive thoughts by squeezing his brain until he collapses in a fit, Willie restores Blue's youth and brings back to life his brothers Cisco and Sycamore, Wild West gunfighters from the 1880s, to enlist their aid in overthrowing the High Commission that has enslaved his people. "If you came into Nogoland blazing your six-guns they wouldn't have any idea how to deal with you," Willie reasons. "You would be too real for their experience."

While plotting to overthrow the High Commission, they are overheard by Kid, a drunken high school cheerleader who has been de-pantsed by local jocks. Caught eavesdropping, Kid pretends to be on their side and offers advice for guerrilla warfare, but then he grabs Sycamore's gun and turns it on them, revealing his true colors in a long rhapsodic defense of Mom and apple pie. Suddenly, Willie goes into a trance and starts speaking a strange language. It turns out to be the Kid's speech backwards, and when it's over Willie is free of the Unseen Hand. He's cracked the code, and Day-Glo Ping-Pong balls fall from the sky. But for all that effort, nothing much changes. Willie goes back to his people, Blue and Cisco move on, Sycamore stays behind to inhabit Blue's Chevy, and presumably it all begins again.

The Unseen Hand is theatrically sensational with Shepard's by-now obligatory dazzling speeches, bizarre imagery (those Ping-Pong balls!), and actor transformations. The actor playing Blue gets to regress in age from 120 to 30, a feat outdone only by the cheap but satisfying sci-fi fits of Willie the Space Freak (an especially juicy role for Lee Kissman, who had appeared in the original productions of *The Rock Garden*, *Chicago*, *Red Cross*, *Shaved Splits*, and *Forensic*). But it also shows Shepard for the first time nudging himself away from simple, mundane dialogue; he creates separate vocabularies and ways of speaking for the Old West gang, the Kid, and Willie. Of course, Willie's trance raps—"Beam to head on sunset. Systol reading ace in. Dystol balance. Treble boost. All systems baffled"—are the most fun, even though they owe something to Lucky's speech in *Waiting for Godot*, and they suggest a trial run for the newspeak that runs through *The Tooth of Crime*.

The La Mama production of *The Unseen Hand* was revived a few months later with *Forensic and the Navigators*, an interesting double bill. Examined together, these plays reveal Shepard's fatalistic attitude (conscious or unconscious) toward politics. They basically say that it's pointless to try to change the world because it either goes on as usual (as in Unseen Hand) or destroys itself (as in *Forensic* and *Operation Sidewinder*) despite the best efforts of the right or the left, the young or the old, the square or the hip. Change is only possible from within.

Shepard's attitude may have been influenced by the teachings of G. I. Gurdjieff, a Russian-born spiritual master whose books outline a quest for self-knowledge through distinguishing the "real" (inner) world from the "illusory" (outside) world, whose values people tend to accept without questioning. Or it could be that Shepard was increasingly drawn to the Gurdjieff work because he already believed in the ultimate futility of overt political activity. "If the experience of being confronted by a theater event brings some shock to your reality, brings you in some kind of new touch with yourself—then it's important," he said in a *Village Voice* interview. "But if you leave the theater with a lot of theories about how to approach the world . . . well, that just lasts for a while."

The Unseen Hand and *Forensic* were produced off-Broadway by a young producer named Albert Poland at the urging of Toby Cole, who was then Shepard's agent. "When I went down to meet him for the first time at his basement apartment on Sixth Avenue, I walked in, and there was Sam Shepard with Levi's and no shirt on, which made me very nervous," Poland recalls. "He could see I was nervous, so he put a black leather vest on over his skin. We started talking about the music for the show, and I asked what he liked. He said, 'Oh, you know, Dr. John and the Night Trippers— of course, you've never heard of them.' I said, 'I have the record.' He had an image of what a producer was before I arrived, which we dispensed with in about five minutes. He told me he'd had awards and he'd had La Mama and all these things, and now what he really honestly wanted was a commercial hit."

Everybody associated with the production thought they had a smash. They sold popcorn, Abba Zaba bars, and Moxie in the lobby, and a rock band called Lothar and the Hand People played before the show and during intermission. But coming on the heels of the disastrously reviewed *Operation Sidewinder*, the double bill was treated by critics as a joke, "an evening of total immersion in camp." It limped to a close after four weeks of performances. Shepard was crushed, then furious, especially when Clive Barnes wrote in *The New York Times* that he wrote plays that were as disposable as Kleenex.

"I felt terrible for causing the playwright I thought was the best in America to have a flop," said Albert Poland, "but Sam was very kind to me. I was broke, producing shows out of a daybed and having lunch at the Russian Tea Room to raise money. Once it was getting very cold, and I was just wearing a raincoat, and Sam said, 'We've got to get you a coat, Al.' And he bought me a coat. He was very, very kind."

Although *The Unseen Hand* was not the commercial hit Shepard hoped for, it attracted the attention of numerous celebrities. Andy Warhol and Abbie Hoffman raved, and Robert Redford liked it so much he wanted to make a movie of it. This was right after *Butch Cassidy and the Sundance Kid*, and Redford, whom Shepard referred to as "Sundance," gave the playwright five thousand dollars to write the screenplay (he never finished it). If nothing else, Shepard got a kick out of sitting in on drums with

Lothar and the Hand People. And *Forensic and the Navigators* again featured the show-stopping performance of the Rice Krispies girl, now extremely pregnant and with a new name: O-Lan Johnson-Shepard.

O-Lan, who shares her first name with the heroine of Pearl S. Buck's *The Good Earth* (it is the name of a small red flower that grows wild in China), grew up in the Ingleside section of Los Angeles. When her father walked out on the family, O-Lan, her younger sister, Kristy, and her actress mother, Scarlett, left L. A. and made their way across the country, taking in laundry and scrubbing floors to support themselves. They finally ended up in New York, but there was a time in Chicago when they were so broke that O-Lan had to come home from school early because Scarlett needed her boots to go to work in. O-Lan quit school when she was fourteen, and both she and her mother got involved with off-off-Broadway theater.

Scarlett and O-Lan Johnson both acted in *The Hawk* at Theater Genesis, and that's where Scarlett met a young guy from Jersey City named Johnny Dark, whom she eventually married. O-Lan had met Sam Shepard in 1967 through Theater Genesis too—he had seen enough of her to create the character of Oolan in *Forensic and the Navigators* for her—but oddly enough they didn't become a couple for more than a year. Sam was still going with his astrologer girlfriend, Nancy, and besides, O-Lan was practically jailbait when they met.

She was still only nineteen, and he was twenty-five, when Sam and O-Lan got married on November 9, 1969, in a double ceremony with actors Walter Hadler and Georgia Lee Phillips at St. Mark's Church In-the-Bowery. Bill Hart was the best man, and O-Lan's sister, Kristy, was her maid of honor. The Reverend Michael Allen began by saying, "In a broken world and a polluted land, nothing could be more beautiful than a marriage." After poetry and folk songs were performed, the minister asked, "Who gives these people to be married to each other?" The congregation, dressed in antique finery, roared, "We do!"

"The wedding was incredible," reports Albert Poland. "Everybody was wearing country lace, and on the way in the Holy Modal Rounders passed out purple tabs of acid, which everyone took. And Sam—if you saw the wedding scene in *Days of Heaven*, that's the way he looked at his own wedding. He had a special look that

I'd never seen him have. He was like a beacon, there was light coming out of him. It was magic!"

The newlyweds lived in an apartment on Sixth Avenue downstairs from the one Sam had shared with Bill Hart, and the following May O-Lan had their baby. If it had been a girl, they were going to name her Kachina, after the Hopi Indian spirit, but it was a boy so they called him Jesse (as in Jesse James) Mojo (a Cajun good luck charm). Domestic bliss didn't come easily, however, to someone so notorious for his taste in women and chemicals, "a sworn enemy of terminal stasis." No sooner had Shepard become a husband and father than he embarked on what would become his famous Patti Smith period.

It all began when he sat in with the Holy Modal Rounders during a gig they had that summer at the Cafe au Go Go on Bleecker Street. "Sam had just written this amazing song called 'Blind Rage,' which was a sort of power-punkish number with lines like 'I'm gonna get my gun/Shoot 'em and run,' " Peter Stampfel recalls. "He would sing it and play drums at the same time. Well, Patti Smith was down there to write an article on the Rounders for some rock magazine, but as soon as she saw Sam she forgot all about the article. They took up with each other right off the bat."

Patti Smith was a skinny, intense, raven-haired poet from New Jersey drawn to everything exciting, dangerous, and fashionable—from Andy Warhol to rock 'n' roll, Rimbaud to William Burroughs. She dressed in black all the time, cut her hair like Keith Richard's, imitated Bob Dylan's walk in *Don't Look Back*, and wrote love poems about Marianne Faithfull and Warhol superstar Edie Sedgwick. By day she worked at the Scribner Book Store on Fifth Avenue, by night she hung out at the hip rock clubs like Max's Kansas City, where she met, made friends with, and had affairs with people she idolized—photographer Robert Mapplethorpe, Dylan cohort Bobby Neuwirth, musicians Todd Rundgren and Tom Verlaine. She wanted to be a star, she *was* a star, and it didn't take long before everybody knew it. Her first reading at St. Mark's Church, in February 1971, attracted the hottest people in rock, poetry, and fashion, and her incantatory performances—first with just toy piano, then a guitar, then a whole band—led to a record contract. She wasn't a great singer, but as a performer she was brilliant: brave, funny, relentlessly self-revealing. She reigned as a punk goddess for five years before retiring from the scene to get married and raise a kid.

In 1970 when she was still an imaginary saint, nothing attracted her like star power, and it zeroed in on Sam Shepard—tall, skinny (almost scrawny), pimply-faced but fire-eyed and charismatic. He moved into her loft on Twenty-third Street, and they later moved next door, to the Chelsea Hotel, a famous rock 'n' roll hangout in the sixties. Though their affair looms large in legend, it actually only lasted a matter of months, and Shepard frequently went back to visit his wife and newborn son. If O-Lan was not exactly delighted about having a come-and-go husband, she wasn't surprised, either, and she took a feisty attitude toward the situation. "If he's gonna have an affair," she told a friend, "I'm gonna have one too."

The affair between Sam and Patti, however, was flamboyant and the subject of much gossip around town, befitting their twin mystiques. Not that they were often seen together in public. "You never saw Sam out as a couple with a woman," said someone who knew him then. "He usually went places with a bunch of guys, mostly from the Theater Genesis crowd." He and Patti entertained each other and friends in the party-all-night atmosphere of the Chelsea. They got tattoos from a Mexican gypsy—a hawk moon for him, a lightning bolt for her. She turned him on to the French surrealist poets (Rimbaud, Villon, Nerval, Baudelaire), and he tried his hand at writing prose poems, some of which he published a couple of years later in a book called *Hawk Moon*, dedicated to "Patti Lee." But he never quit writing plays.

Mad Dog Blues was his most self-conscious recycling of pop mythology. Rock star Kosmo, a country boy who aches for the West, and his sidekick Yahoodi, a city slicker strung out on dope, conjure up images of Marlene Dietrich and Mae West (though a Mae West who sings like Janis Joplin) and set off on an adventure. Yahoodi and Marlene join Captain Kidd in his search for buried treasure, and Kosmo and Mae secretly follow them along with an old-timer they've picked up named Waco Texas. After Marlene leaves him for Paul Bunyan, Yahoodi shoots himself and Captain Kidd, so Kosmo and Mae steal the treasure. Jesse James holds them up and runs off with both Mae and the treasure, which turns out to be a bunch of bottle caps—like those Ping-Pong balls in *The Unseen Hand*, a worthless prize that suggests the game wasn't worth playing.

A meandering, drug-drenched meditation on the rock deaths of the period, *Mad Dog Blues* was another warm-up for *The Tooth of Crime*. The original production at Theater Genesis in March 1971 featured both Shepard and his wife; she played a dazzling Mae-West-as-Joplin and he led the three-piece band playing electric guitar, tambourine, and sound effects. He was still shacking up with Patti Smith at the Chelsea Hotel, and no doubt it was a sign of the strain on their marriage that her name appeared on the program as only "O-Lan" and he called himself "Slim Shadow."

"Slim" and "Shadow" were characters hired to track down a two-headed, fire-breathing swamp monster in Shepard's next play, *Back Bog Beast Bait*. Although it contains many fascinating ideas and images that turn up in later plays, *Back Bog Beast Bait* is dense and nearly impenetrable itself, another quasi-Indian ritual in three scenes about a group of people who seek to kill an evil beast; but when they find it, they all turn into animals themselves. (Many cryptic references in the play suggest it may be an allegory about drug addiction.) The play included songs written by Shepard, Antonia Duren, and Steve Weber of the Holy Modal Rounders, and Lou Reed from the Velvet Underground, and it was produced only a month after *Mad Dog Blues* at the American Place Theater with O-Lan in the cast playing a voodoo woman named Gris Gris. An uncomfortable situation arose when Shepard approached American Place producer Wynn Handman during rehearsals and said that he'd written a new play with Patti Smith and that they both wanted to perform it on a double bill with *Back Bog Beast Bait*.

Cowboy Mouth, his collaboration with Smith, remains one of the rawest and most exciting works Shepard has produced. "I'd never written a play with somebody before, and we literally shoved the typewriter back and forth across the table," said Shepard. "We wrote the whole thing like that, in two nights."

Allowing for some poetic exaggeration, the play provides a documentary account of their life together. From their self-characterizations—"Cavale: a chick who looks like a crow, dressed in raggedy black. Slim: a cat who looks like a coyote, dressed in scruffy red. They are both beat to shit"—to the detailed description of their room, you can practically hear the sound of that typewriter sliding across the table. "Scene: A fucked-up bed center stage. Raymond, a dead crow, on the floor. Scattered all around on the floor is miscellaneous debris: hubcaps, an old tire, raggedy costumes, a boxful of ribbons, lots of letters, a pink telephone, a bottle of Nescafé, a hot plate. Seedy wallpaper with pictures of cowboys peeling off the wall. Photographs of Hank Williams and Jimmie Rodgers. Stuffed dolls, crucifixes. License plates from southern states nailed to the wall. Travel poster of Panama. A funky set of drums to one side of the stage. An electric guitar and amplifier on the other side. Rum, beer, white lightning, Sears catalogue."

Cowboy Mouth is an exuberantly infantile game played by these two. Cavale has kidnapped Slim off the streets and wants to turn him into a modern-day savior, "a rock-and-roll Jesus with a cowboy mouth." They order up food from the Lobster Man, they fight, scream, roll around on the floor, make up characters, bang on their instruments, and tell childhood stories. Finally, Slim wants to go back to his wife and child, and he coaxes the Lobster Man out of his shell to become the "rock-and-roll savior" Cavale so desperately desires.

Friends of Shepard invariably confirm that *Cowboy Mouth* was one of the most exciting performances they've ever seen—the few that got to see it. Shepard performed for the dress rehearsal and a couple of previews for the American Place Theater's subscription audience, but the heat, both onstage and off, became too intense. "It didn't work out because the thing was too emotionally packed," said Shepard. "I suddenly realized I didn't want to exhibit myself like that, playing my life onstage. It was like being in an aquarium."

He smashed the fishbowl and left town without a word to anyone. He showed up in Vermont, where the Holy Modal Rounders were playing a college gig, and hung out with them until things cooled down. *Back Bog Beast Bait* played out its scheduled run, but Sam's disappearance marked the end of *Cowboy Mouth*. "O-Lan didn't know where Sam was," remembers Wynn Handman, "and Patti kept coming to the theater every night hoping he would show up. It was very sad."

By May 1971 Sam Shepard had been in New York slightly less than eight years. He'd gotten about as much out of it as a twenty-seven-year-old playwriting college dropout from small-town California could ever have dreamed, and it had him spinning. "I was living high," as *Mad Dog Blues*'s Kosmo says. "I was living in wall-to-wall carpets with color TVs and all the dope I could want and girls climbing all over me and my name in all the papers." The tension between the cowboy and the genius, his city life and his country roots, his marriage to O-Lan and his fling with Patti Smith was tearing Shepard up. Anyone who glanced at the program for *Cowboy Mouth*—one of the wildest bits of autobiography he ever produced—could tell it was written by someone who was clearly out of control:

> I'm listening to ole Bobby Dylan and trying to write something about me that might be of interest to folks out there. Maybe a few of my favorite words would do it. Here's a few of my favorite words: Slipstream, Tahachapi, Wichita, Choctaw, Apache, Switchblade, Bootleg, Fox, Vixen, Feather, Coyote, Crow, Rip tide, Flash Flood, Appaloosa, Pachooko, Cajun, Creole, Gris Gris, Mojo, Shadow, Cheyenne, Eucalyptus, Sycamore, Birch Bark, Creasote, Asphalt, Ghost, Saint, Aztec, Quaxaca, Messiah, Tootsie Roll, Abazaba, Cantalope, Antelope, Python, Yucca, Sapling, Waxing, Waning, Moxie, Hooch, Wolf, Pine, Pistol, Abalone, Cowboy, Stranger.

This is where he announced "I don't want to be a playwright, I want to be a rock and roll star" and how "Writing is neat because you do it on a very physical level. Just like rock and roll." He continued with a recap of his bad-boy past—part boast, part confession of various explosions of teenage aggression—before concluding his life story with a bravura list of his loves:

> I love horse racing and stock cars. I love the Rolling Stones. I love Bridgette Bardot. I love Marlon Brando and James Dean and Stan Laurel and Otis Redding and Wilson Pickett and Jimmie Rodgers and Bob Dylan and The Who and Jesse James and Crazy Horse and The Big Bopper and Nina Simone and Jackson Pollock and Muhammud Ali and Emile Griffith and My wife O-Lan and my Kid, Jesse and Patti Smith.

Then, like waking up from a dream, Shepard came to his senses. He realized, among other things, that he was killing himself with drugs and that he had to get out of New York. New York is a bastard. New York is a bitch. New York is poison. New York values competition over community. New York is about making money, not making friends. In New York everybody lives in an unreal world where you are a star and no one else exists. New York, Shepard concluded, is no place to live. He went back and patched things up with O-Lan, and they split for England with one-year-old Jesse, probably thinking the same thing Ellen Burstyn tells her son in the Martin Scorsese movie, *Alice Doesn't Live Here Anymore*: "Don't look back, kid, or you'll turn into a pillar of shit."

Chapter Five:

EXILE FROM MAIN STREET

Rock and Roll is definitely a motherfucker and always will be Rock and Roll made movies theatre books painting and art go out the window none of it stands a chance against The Who The Stones and old Yardbirds Credence Traffic The Velvet Underground Janis and Jimi and on and on the constant frustration of the other artists to keep up to the music of our time Rock and Roll will never die but what about the novel the theatre and all that culture stuff Norman Mailer insisting on being a man Edward Albee working from dawn to dusk for Broadway Peter Townsend says Rock and Roll is the perfect medium for self destruction and he don't mean suicide.

—Sam Shepard, "Rip It Up" from *Hawk Moon*

After leaving New York, Shepard spent three years in England detoxifying his system of the real and imaginary poisons it had absorbed in the last few years. A longtime racetrack habitue, he adapted himself to the local sport—dogs instead of horses. And like many an expatriate writer before him, he did his best work so far. Two of the five plays he wrote in England, *The Tooth of Crime* and *Action*, still stand among the best works by Shepard or any other playwright of his generation. "It wasn't until I came to England that I found out what it means to be an American," he said. "Nothing really makes sense when you're there, but the more distant you are from it, the more the implications of what you grew up with start to emerge."

England wasn't the only possible destination when Shepard decided to flee America, or even the most obvious one. He bought a fifty-acre farm in Nova Scotia, where he grew wheat and alfalfa, and he seriously considered becoming a Canadian citizen. So when he settled in London, he was frequently asked why, and he became good at flippant answers like "Because you speak English." But in a long, revealing interview with director Kenneth Chubb in the British magazine *Theatre Quarterly*, he explained the move more forthrightly:

"When I first got to New York, it was wide open, you were like a kid in a fun park," he said, "but then as it developed, as more and more elements came into it, things got more and more insane—you know, the difference between living in New York and working in New York became wider and wider, so that you were doing this thing called *theatre* in these little places and you were bringing your so-called experience to it, and then going back and living in this kind of tight, insular, protective way, where you were defending yourself. And also I was into a lot of drugs then—it became very difficult you know, everything seemed to be sort of shattering. I didn't feel like going back to California, so I thought I'd come here—really to get into music, you know. I was in a band in New York, and I'd heard that this was the rock 'n' roll center of the world—so I came here with that kind of idea. . . . My favorite bands are The Who, groups like that, so I had this fantasy that I'd come over here and somehow fall into a rock 'n' roll band." What could he have been thinking? That the Stones would fire Charlie Watts the way they did Brian Jones and install the author of *Maxagasm* on drums? That Keith Moon would fall over at the drum set and he could inherit the throne? Like his fantasy of becoming an actor when he first hit New York in the early sixties, "it didn't work." Shepard had to settle for being the star playwright of the London scene.

With its distinguished literary history and its long tradition of government subsidy, British theater offered a much more pleasant and nurturing environment than the theater world Shepard knew in New York. After the renaissance in British playwriting had begun in the late fifties, led by John Osborne's classic "angry young man" drama *Look Back in Anger*, a community of like-minded writers, directors, and actors had evolved untainted by the monolithic commercial-theater pressure that Broadway exerts on American playwrights. What's more, the steady market for quality television and radio scripts allowed writers to make a living at their trade. The London theater community quickly took Shepard to its heart, both as a person and as a playwright. They were delighted by his drawling, down-to-earth James Dean persona, so unlike the longhaired hippies they imagined young Americans to be, and they were fascinated by his plays with their mixture of poetic originality and classic Americana. In just the three years he lived in England, there were local productions of *La Turista*, *Icarus's Mother*, *Cowboy Mouth*, and *The Unseen Hand* as well as two productions of *The Tooth of Crime* and the world premieres of *Geography of a Horse Dreamer* and his feminist revue *Little Ocean*.

Shepard and his family first lived in a tiny apartment in the working-class neighborhood of Shepherds Bush. He and O-Lan had trouble finding someplace more comfortable because of their baby, and early in 1972 Shepard finally appealed to the American-born experimental theater director Charles Marowitz, who helped them secure an apartment in his North London neighborhood of

Hampstead, just across from the Central Park-like Hampstead Heath.

Naseem Khan, a writer for the weekly magazine *Time Out* who visited the Shepards at home, described the apartment as "one of those transit basement furnished flats dotted with personal paraphernalia—nappies, kid's toys, a guitar, a notice on the wall that reads, 'Race 8, Witches City, Sand Twist, Leemoss Daddy, Spitfire, Simons Rocket, Keywall Spectre.' On the divan Keywall Spectre dozes sloppily. He's a very large black greyhound that forms part of the Shepard stable of $2^{1}/_{2}$ dogs (the other half belongs to actor Tony Milner) and was bought for 200 pounds. 'This here dawg,' drawled Sam deliberately, 'is a real champ. Comes from Ireland, comes from the North of Ireland. The Bogside.' He paused while we all laughed and lit up cigarettes."

When he was settled, Shepard told Marowitz that he had just finished a new play and asked him if he wanted to read it. "My first instinct was to beg off as I was no true champion of his earlier work," Marowitz, who was the artistic director of the Open Space in London, wrote in *The Village Voice,* "but if you've ever met Shepard, you will realize that he is the personification of that conquering charm that is sometimes bred in the southern and western sections of America. Despite his 28 years, his febrile hassles with Antonioni and the jet set, and his Lincoln Center tribulations, he remains Huckleberry Finn minus the fishing-rod. (In time I was to learn he was also something of a Peter Lorre and a Bela Lugosi, but at the time the Huck Finn facade obliterated all other persona.)"

The new script was *The Tooth of Crime*, Shepard's first major play and the one still considered by many to be his best. "It was written in a nutty, juvenile scrawl in a series of lined notebooks," reported Marowitz. "It utilized an invented language derived from several American idioms which included pop, underworld slang, sports jargon, and that ever-changing vernacular that musicians continually keep alive amongst themselves and which gradually filters into the national tongue." Shepard said he originally wrote a three-act play with the same title that took place in a prison. "At the end it was a complete piece of shit, so I put it in the sink and burnt it, and then an hour later I started to write this one that's been performed."

The Tooth of Crime takes place on a bare stage equipped with only a silver-studded, "evil-looking" black chair. It stars Hoss, a leather-clad rocker who is a leading player in "the game." He's within shooting distance of a gold record, he's ready for a kill, and he has his girlfriend-assistant Becky Lou lay out his gear—two black satchels full of pearl-handled revolvers, pistols, derringers, and shotguns. But Hoss is worried; he fears he's falling behind. His astrologer tells him the stars don't augur well, he gets the news that his rival Mojo Root Force has invaded his territory and knocked off Vegas, the DJ Galactic Jack warns him about a Gypsy killer coming his way, and Becky Lou informs him that his favorite driver has been found in New Haven slumped over the wheel, his own gun in his mouth.

"There's no sense of tradition in the game no more," Hoss complains. "There's no game. It's just back to how it was. Rolling night clubs, strip joints. Bustin' up poker games. Zip guns in the junk yard. Rock fights, dirt clods, bustin' windows. Vandals, juvies, West Side Story. Can't they see where they're goin'! Without a code it's just crime." He calls for the Doc, who shoots him up with speed, and proposes to forget the rules of the game, to move outside. But Becky Lou chillingly reminds him of the lay of the land—that he's a domesticated animal now who would be easy prey on the street. "The only way to be an individual is in the game," she tells him. "You're it. You're on top. You're free."

Hoss is dubious, but with a snootful of cocaine he's ready to face his challenger, whose name is Crow and who "looks just like Keith Richard."

The entire second act consists of the showdown between Hoss and Crow, only they're slinging words instead of guns in a refereed match of images, poses, and virtuosic self-projection. It's a style war. New-styled Crow, the creepy challenger, throws Hoss off by learning to imitate his moves. They go three rounds, trading abusive verbal licks while a band grinds out a Stones-like musical backdrop. Hoss figures he can rely on the black rhythms and country roots of his music, but Crow scorns the very idea of roots and simply attacks with anything that comes into his head. He takes the first round, the second is a draw, and when Crow is proclaimed winner of the third round and the game, Hoss goes crazy and kills the ref. Having really gone outside the game, he tries to strike up a partnership with Crow, offering all his turf if Crow will teach him his ways. Hoss tries on Crow's mannerisms "like a suit a' clothes," but he finds he can't do it, slip in and out of styles with the new generation's conviction, so he gives up. He decides to leave Crow behind with a farewell gesture, an example of true style. "It's mine. An original. It's my life and my death in one clean shot." The shot goes through his head.

The Tooth of Crime almost completely breaks with Shepard's earlier work. There are clear-cut characters and a forward-driven story, elements he was formerly quite cavalier about, and there is no sign of the bold visual imagery or real-time onstage actions of the early one-acts. The only theatrical action is the duel between Hoss and Crow. But what's extraordinary about the play is its language—recognizably Shepardian in its pop-drenched references and its monological flights that can only be called musical. Yet the language is wholly invented for the purposes of the play, a sinister American rock-talk corollary to Lewis Carroll's "Jabberwocky" or the tongue of the droogs in Anthony Burgess's *A Clockwork Orange* (the film of which was released in 1971). Hoss speaks the jargon of "the game," which is never explained (you have to guess what "Markers" and "Gypsies" are in terms of the game, not to mention the function of "the code" or "the charts"), while Crow has his own vocabulary that's cryptic even to Hoss. "Very razor," he mutters, analyzing Hoss's style the first time his rival leaves the room, trying to copy his walk:

> Meshing patterns. Easy mistakes here. Suss the bounce. Too heavy on the toe. Maybe work the shoulders down. Here's a mode. Three-four cut time copped from Keith Moon. Early. Very early. Now. Where's that pattern. Gotta be in the "Happy Jack" album. Right around there. Triplets. Six-eight. Here it comes. Battery. Double bass talk. Fresh Cream influence. Where's that? Which track. Yeah. The old Skip James tune. Question there. Right there. (*Sings it*) "I'm so glad, I'm so glad, I'm glad, I'm glad, I'm glad."

Anyone can see that the speech contains words that belong to various idioms: British slang ("suss"), computer talk ("mode"), rock lore ("I'm So Glad" is a song from the British superstar trio Cream's first album *Fresh Cream*)—and it resembles, for instance, the trance-cries of Willie the Space Freak in *The Unseen Hand*. Similarly, the play must in some way be Shepard's response to Altamont, to Charles Manson, to the relentless litany of assassinated leaders, overdosed rock stars, picked-off Black Panthers, and all the other end-of-the-sixties death scenes that run together into one bloody blur. But the amazing—and disturbing—thing about *The Tooth of Crime* is that Shepard flips through these modern jargons and topical references without settling on any one, theatricalizing through sheer language the kind of dislocation he's dramatizing, a dread that we all recognize but cannot name. The title comes from French symbolist Stéphane Mallarmé's poem "Anguish," which goes in part:

> I ask of your bed the deep sleep with no dreams
> Which you, after your dark deceits, can enjoy,
> You who know more about oblivion than a corpse:
>
> For gnawing at my ingrained morality, Vice
> Has marked its sterility in me as in you;
> But while there exists in your breast of stone
>
> A heart which the tooth of no crime can wound,
> I flee,
> In terror of dying while sleeping alone.

The Tooth of Crime also picks up where *Cowboy Mouth* left off in its exploration of the implications of "stardom" as it was held out to Shepard by his New York experience in general and his encounter with Patti Smith in particular. For all his love of role-playing, Shepard took the game of stardom seriously. Weaned on the mythology of Western films, he viewed fame as valuable only insofar as it recognized heroism, authenticity, mastery, or accomplishment—traditional American values. Without something crucially important at stake, any conquest was meaningless. What he must have found frightening and alien in someone like Patti Smith was the pop notion of stardom as pure fantasy, the self-hype of Andy Warhol superstardom, a game played with nobody keeping score. For Shepard, that kind of stardom—based on a nebulous, self-projected image, as easily put on or removed as a bit of glittery makeup—is worthless. Yet it's so ingrained in contemporary culture that it's practically irresistible.

"The idea was like a gang-warfare situation, where the gangs had been split up into individual mobile warriors that fought from Maseratis and Lamborghinis with all kinds of fancy aluminum weapons," Shepard said in *Time Out* about his conception of *The Tooth of Crime*. "And using those people in a rock 'n' roll context. They're all killers, but they treat their situation like a rock musician—this whole 'macho' thing, y'know, this masculinity trip. And I was real interested in that, 'cause there seems to be a lot of that going on in every aspect of American life, from pimps up to Nixon. People competing in life and death situations with their images of who they are.

"And the other thing I was thinking of was what happens when people get so carried away with death, to really craving that. Because death has become really hip in New York. The more self-destructive you can become, the hipper it is. The more against yourself, like junkies. It's like a code, a badge. It's very hard to put your finger on it, but it's very strange what's happening. It's like the thing that used to be in high school, like who's the baddest dude and testing it by holding matches in their hand or something. It's developed into something much more frightening now, into people really putting themselves out with the heaviest kind of things that they can do. And that's what I was interested in in the play."

The Tooth of Crime premiered at the Open Space in a production directed by Charles Marowitz; Michael Weller, the American playwright (*Moonchildren*) and screenwriter (*Ragtime*) played the small part of Star-Man. But it was by no means an overnight sensation. "The play has been largely uncomprehended in London," Marowitz wrote in a dispatch to *The Village Voice*. "But the play is as American as rolled joints or faded Levis. It not only belongs in America, it actually looks exotic and unreal in England." Actually, the play should look exotic and unreal anywhere; what Shepard wasn't crazy about was the music, played in Marowitz's production by a band called Blunderpuss.

This has been a recurring problem in the history of the play. The first American production at Princeton University's McCarter Theater in November 1972 starred Frank Langella as Hoss, a wonderful actor but no rocker. "He has no idea what to do with the rock songs that Mr. Shepard has given him," one critic pointed out. "He just puts on a country accent and hopes for the best." After a lengthy exchange of letters with director Richard Schechner, Shepard allowed the avant-garde Performance Group to present the New York premiere of *The Tooth of Crime,* despite many misgivings about Schechner's plans to stage the play environmentally and to have the actors create music without instruments. "All the music is written down and fits each section of the play according to the emotional line that's going down," Shepard argued. "It's gotta be electric! No other way for it to work." Shepard saw a little bit of the Performance Group's production when they were rehearsing in Vancouver, British Columbia, and actively hated it; when it opened, many critics did too. Still, the play deservedly won an Obie award in 1973. In Schechner's production, Hoss was played by Spalding Gray, a Performance Group actor who went on to become a celebrated monologuist (best-known for *Swimming to Cambodia*, which was made into a film by Jonathan Demme). Starman was played by Elizabeth LeCompte, who later became the internationally admired director of the Wooster Group and recipient of a MacArthur Foundation "genius" grant.

The Tooth of Crime received a major New York revival at La Mama in 1983 that restored the original music, but that merely clarified the real problem, which is that the music Shepard wrote for the play isn't very good. It's all in basically the same style, a dated sort of late-sixties blues-rock that fails to distinguish characters or attitudes. It's the weak link in an otherwise perfect play.

Despite its flaws the initial London production acquired plenty of ardent admirers, particularly among younger theater people who were also rock fans, like Jim Sharman, an Australian-born stage director. Through a mutual friend who was a rock drummer, Sharman met Shepard to talk about a film project. "We never did talk about the film," Sharman said, "but we did talk about New York, the fifties, sci-fi, greyhound racing, John Huston movies, how rock 'n' roll changed the world and how the Velvet Underground was the best band ever, and wouldn't Lou Reed (their ex-lead singer) have been great in *The Tooth of Crime*, etc., etc."

When Sharman expressed interest in directing one of his plays at the Royal Court, Shepard suggested *The Unseen Hand*. "He constantly remarked that he wrote his plays like songs," Sharman wrote in *Plays and Players*,

> and I took this cue to treat several of the longer speeches in this style, including the Kid's "I love Azusa" speech—this was backed by the Morphons' fifties harmonizing of key phrases ("basketball-ball-ball," "dirty books-books-books")....
> All of this Sam loved, but his own favorite moment was the Nogoland map sequence, played by Willie as a "Mission Impossible"-type commander addressing his squad. We added some "Nice point there, Sycamore"-type lines to extend the

parody. I suspect Sam liked this scene because it was totally real yet at the same time inexplicable.

Sharman's production of *The Unseen Hand* went so well—it's still talked about as a memorable occasion in London theater—that he remounted *The Tooth of Crime* at the Royal Court less than two years after its original production at the Open Space. (In the roles of Willie the Space Freak in *Unseen Hand* and Crow in *Tooth of Crime,* Sharman cast Richard O'Brien, who wrote *The Rocky Horror Show* and appears as Riff Raff in the movie.)

By coincidence, during rehearsals for the revival of *Tooth of Crime* Shepard went to see the Who at a giant outdoor concert and it brought up again all his feelings about rock versus theater versus the rest of the world. "I'm thirty years old," he brooded, "and I'm at a rock concert in the middle of nowhere? Everyone's covered in red dust and chugging on wine bottles and the Who are cranking out 'Summertime Blues' like nobody's business. They'll always be this great. They were great then and they're great now but what the fuck time is it? Didn't I do this in '68?" he brooded. "The sun goes down and they whip into the first three notes of 'Pinball Wizard.' I counted them. The first three notes and everybody in the joint knows what song it is. Not only that but they all know the words! A hundred thousand people singing in unison some very tricky lyrics. I was stunned. Now this here is an audience to beat all. It took me a long time to give up the fantasy that a play could ever have the same unanimous impact as a piece of music, but this really drove it home."

For a while Shepard found domestic tranquillity in England. He and O-Lan savored the opportunity to raise their son in a civilized neighborhood, away from the omnipresent racial tension and drug dealing they remembered from the streets of New York. They enjoyed leading a "real life" and didn't just socialize with theater people, or if they did it was with theater people who shared other interests, like rock 'n' roll. "I often had the impression that if you know a lot about his work, it makes him uncomfortable," said a journalist who once took Sam and O-Lan to see a Zulu production of *Macbeth* in London. "He'd prefer to be around people who don't give a shit about his work." Shepard and family spent their summers on the farm in Nova Scotia, and at home in London the heath was handy for strolling with the baby and exercising the dogs.

Always the dogs! "Greyhound racing is great because you can breed your own dog, raise it, take it to the track, and race it, which is unheard of in horse racing because it's too expensive," said Shepard. "I had a dog that people at Hackney Wick will remember—a big, black, spotted dog called Keywall Spectre, the son of a great Irish dog called Spectre. Sprinting three hundred yards on the sand at Hackney, he'd win all the time.

"The Irish greyhound I think is the epitome of the greyhound," he enthused. "The great thing about them is they're cat-like. You can put them in the house and they'll lay down and sleep for hours. Take them out, and they'll just go! The Irish are great animal people. They're great horsemen and they know dogs, too. I was walking the dog with these Irish guys on Hampstead Heath, and one looked at the greyhound taking a leak against a tree and he says, 'See dat, boys! It's gotta be just like champagne. Clear, bright, it's gotta have a little glisten to it.' He's talking about the dog's piss! The condition of the dog's piss was indicative of its fitness to run."

Inevitably, the dog showed up in Shepard's plays. *Blue Bitch* was more or less a domestic comedy about two expatriate Americans, Dixie and Cody, trying to sell their greyhound Breeze so they can go back to Wyoming. A potential buyer keeps calling from Scotland, but Cody can't quite decipher his thick, gruff voice. A milkman arrives who miraculously speaks the Scotsman's dog-talk and settles the deal for them. The play was shown on BBC television, and in January 1973 it was staged by Shepard's old buddy Murray Mednick at Theater Genesis in New York with, ironically, Patti Smith playing Dixie.

Blue Bitch was more or less a sketch leading up to Shepard's next major play, *Geography of a Horse Dreamer*, "a mystery in two acts." One of several plays from this middle period that dwell on the artist-as-visionary and the exploitation he's subject to by people who can make money off his talents, *Horse Dreamer* concerns Cody, a young man from Wyoming with a gift for dreaming the winners of horse races. He's been kidnapped by gangsters and locked in a London hotel room. Under captivity he seems to lose his powers, but then he suddenly starts dreaming the winners of dog races—until he goes completely around the bend and starts talking first like an Irish dog trainer and then like a dog. A sinister-looking doctor called in to investigate Cody's problem is just about to remove the "dream bone" containing Cody's magic powers from the back of his neck when his two cowboy brothers burst in the door with shotguns and take Cody home to Wyoming.

The play was produced at the Royal Court in February 1974 with a cast that included the superb British character actor Bob Hoskins, and for the first time ever, Shepard decided to try his hand at directing. He considered it a relatively easy play to start with—he never would have undertaken *The Tooth of Crime*—but he was still nervous and called up several directors he knew for pointers. Directing proved to be an extremely educational and in a way humbling experience for Shepard, who had had many bitter fights with directors of his plays. "I used to think that a production was a miracle act," he said, "that actors very suddenly came to the play and it was realized in a matter of days"—that is, the same way he *wrote* his plays. "But that's not true; it takes a great deal of time. I've learned that it's important to have patience, and that things can't be rushed."

Shepard played poker with the actors and dragged them down to White City and Hackney Wick to watch him race Keywall Sceptre. Along with the camaraderie, he picked up from them a different attitude toward the discipline of making theater. "With English actors and directors, even in the alternative theatre, there's a craftsman thing at work. In London I ran into a ton of people who were passionate and at the same time workmanlike," he said. "In America you threw a lotta shit on the wall and hoped some of it stuck."

Directing had a lasting effect on his subsequent writing. "I've found I think I'm often too flippant about what I write—it's too easy to dash something off and say, okay, now act it: because when it comes down to the flesh-and-blood thing of making it work, it's a different world," Shepard admitted. "One of the things I've found is that it's too much to expect an actor to do a vocal aria, standing there in the middle of the stage and have the thing work in space, without actually having him physically involved in what he's talking about.... I don't go in for long speeches anymore."

By 1974, as both *Horse Dreamer* and *Blue Bitch* seem to indicate, Shepard's initial love affair with England was over. He'd let off some of the poison New York had left in his system, and he'd begun to get homesick. Like Cody, he was beginning to feel out of touch with the source of his powers. The new British rock music—David Bowie, Roxy Music, glitter rock—interested him far less than the Stones and the Who had, and he'd started listening again to traditional blues and jazz. He'd used records by Sidney Bechet, Ornette Coleman, and Clifton Chenier in his production of *Horse Dreamer*, and he'd even written a review for *The Village Voice* of two albums by avant-garde jazzman Coleman and Chicago bluesman Little Brother Montgomery, saying, "It's no good to read about New Orleans or Chicago or Arizona. All you get is facts. These guys give us the feeling of America, then and now."

O-Lan, too, was getting frustrated because as an American citizen she couldn't get work as an actress in England. She did write two musicals in London, though, one of which was performed at the Royal Court's Theatre Upstairs. And she appeared at the Hampstead Theater Club in a late-night show that Shepard wrote just for her and two friends, Caroline Hutchinson and Dinah Stabb, to perform. *Little Ocean* was a forty-five-minute fantasia on childbirth featuring a very pregnant woman (Dinah), a young mother (O-Lan), and a woman who's never been pregnant (Caroline).

It began with O-Lan tuning her guitar and Caroline blowing smoke rings—"Where did the habit come of handing out cigars?" "It's a tradition. Musta come from Cuba"—and proceeded through O-Lan's hymn to the masculinity of General Motors, Caroline's dream of a tadpole swimming through the little ocean of the womb, and Dinah's fantasy of the Garden of Eden (she wonders if Adam was a sissy and Eve had to get it on with a very sexy snake to start the human race). At the end, threatened in the park by stone-throwing hoodlums, the three women chase off their attackers with a soft-shoe and a song.

Little Ocean is a real curiosity for Shepard, the only play he's ever written for an all-woman cast. People often complain about the scarcity of roles for women in Shepard's plays, and the subsidiary, if not subservient, nature of the ones there are. So it would be delightful if *Little Ocean* were better known. Unfortunately, whether because it was written for a specific occasion or because it doesn't fit in with his manly image as a playwright, Shepard refuses to publish it or allow further performances. A British reporter once asked him why country and western music is so sad, and he replied, "Because more than any other art form I know of in America, country music speaks of the true relationship between the American male and the American female." And what is that? "Terrible and impossible."

By spring it was pretty clear that it was time to say good-bye to England. The question was where to go next. Not back to New York, that's for sure. Canada was still a possibility, and there was always the West. Wyoming? The home turf, California? It was partly out of this deliberation over the best place to settle down again in America, and partly the influence of German playwright Peter Handke's metaphysically restless *The Ride Across Lake Constance*, that Shepard wrote his most exquisitely condensed play, *Action*, which opens with the line "I'm looking forward to my life. I'm looking forward to uh—me. The way I picture me."

Action takes place in an undetermined locale. Onstage are a plain table with four settings for a holiday dinner and a Christmas tree blinking in the background. The sense is of a cabin deep in the woods, far away from everything else, in the dead of winter. The two men, Jeep and Shooter, are dressed in lumberjack attire and have shaved heads; Liza wears a forties-style dress, Lupe looks like a Mexican housewife. The title of the play is ambiguous because nothing happens in terms of a plot, yet the play is full of strong actions that—in the best Shepard tradition—have a particularly theatrical power because they are performed in front of the audience in real time with no faking. Jeep picks up his chair and smashes it to pieces three times; each time Liza brings in a new one and sweeps up the old one. Shooter pulls his overcoat over his head and imitates a dancing bear; Lupe does a soft-shoe sitting down. They all eat a turkey dinner. Jeep stands for a long time dipping his cup into a bucket of water and pouring it back until he suddenly pulls a dead fish out of the bucket, takes out his knife, cuts it open, and cleans it on the dinner table. Shooter sits on the floor and pulls an arm-chair over him like a turtle's shell so he can't be seen. The women bring out a basket of wet laundry and hang it on a clothesline that crosses the entire stage.

Shepard uses the generic title *Action* the same way choreographer Lucinda Childs calls a piece *Dance* or composer Steve Reich names a percussion piece *Drumming*. It is an expression of pure action without motivation. In another type of play, someone would make Jeep mad and he would smash chairs—then they'd talk about it for the rest of the play. In Shepard's work (*Action* and other plays), there's no motivation and often no consequence; these actions become characterization, the bits of information that would normally be slipped into dialogue or serve as character development. Shepard wants to bypass the thinking part of the brain that guards against new thoughts and go straight for the senses: smell the fish! hear the water pouring! feel the shock waves of smashing chairs! He's not spelling out a moral, he's making something happen. "Ideas emerge from plays, not the other way," said Shepard once.

In the context of Shepard's personal life, *Action* seems to express a yearning to reenter American life after a period of estrangement, his feeling a bit rusty at social customs that once were second nature. That feeling is both funny and scary, as this memorable passage suggests:

> Lupe: . . . I once was very active in the community.
> Jeep: What's a community?
> Lupe: (looking up) A sense of—A sense um—What's a community, Shooter?
> Shooter: Oh uh—You know. You were on the right track.
> Lupe: Something uh—
> Jeep: I know.
> Lupe: Yeah. You know. It doesn't need words.
> Jeep: I know what you mean.
> Lupe: Just a kind of feeling.
> Jeep: Yeah, I know what you mean.

But the ominous isolation of the characters and their impaired ability to articulate their thoughts also suggest the atmosphere of a drug rehabilitation center as well as a politically traumatized, if not postapocalyptic, society. Critic Bonnie Marranca calls *Action* "Shepard's most moving portrait of the American experience. . . . The triumph of *Action* is that it defines Nixonian America in a jagged, constrained structure that mirrors the very difficulty of finding a language of social communication and a means to express feeling: on a very basic level *Action* is about loss of language. The vision of Walt Whitman's America is brutally contrasted with what America had become."

The play transcends any narrow personal or political interpretations, though, to become a virtuosically self-contained theatrical event. As in concrete poetry, Shepard uses individual lines and actions not as building blocks in a narrative but almost as brushstrokes painting a picture on, in this case, the ephemeral contemplative canvas of the stage. His most Beckett-like play, *Action* resembles *Endgame* in that the entire play is a metaphor for itself as a vehicle for thinking about the world.

Action had its world premiere at the Royal Court in September 1974. It was directed by Nancy Meckler, a young American whose production of *Icarus's Mother* Shepard had admired and whose British husband ran the Hampstead Theater Club, where *Little Ocean premiered.*

Shepard wasn't around to help, though. He had long since sailed back to America.

Chapter Six:

DRAWING THE WAGONS IN A CIRCLE

Any move is possible. I've seen it. You go outside. The world's quiet. White. Everything resounding. Not a sound of a motor. Not a light. You see into the house. You see the candles. You watch the people. You can see what it's like inside. The candles draw you. You get a cold feeling being outside. Separated. You have an idea that being inside it's cosier. Friendlier. Warmth. People. Conversation. Everyone using a language. Then you go inside. It's a shock. It's not like how you expected. You lose what you had outside. You forget that there even is an outside. The inside is all you know. You hunt for a way of being with everyone. A way of finding how to behave. You find out what's expected of you. You act yourself out.

—Shooter in *Action*

"I feel like I've never had a home," Sam Shepard said in a 1979 interview, "you know? I feel related to the country, to this country, and yet at the same time I don't know exactly where I fit in. And the same thing applies to the theater. I don't know exactly how well I fit into the scheme of things. Maybe that's good, you know, that I'm not in a niche. But there's always this kind of nostalgia for a place, a place where you can reckon with yourself. Now I've found that what's most valuable about that place is not the place itself but the other people; that through other people you can find a recognition of each other. I think that's where the real home is."

After his expeditions in New York and London, Shepard's return to California was definitely about other people—a return, especially, to the family. And for Shepard, family became as much an experiment as drugs, jazz, theater, and rock 'n' roll had been: the search for a perfect world. It meant reestablishing close (but not too close) contact with his long-separated parents—his mother still lived on the outskirts of Los Angeles, while his father had settled himself in Santa Fe—as well as his sisters, who both lived in northern California. It meant surrounding himself with a family of other people created by choice rather than tradition; he, O-Lan, and their son Jesse moved into a house just north of San Francisco in Marin County which they shared with O-Lan's mother, Scarlett, and Scarlett's husband, Johnny Dark. And it meant seeking out the kind of artistic home he found before long at the Magic Theater in San Francisco.

Although he continued to explore pop mythology and abstract theatricality, thoughts of home and America inevitably pointed Shepard's writing in the direction of the family. In fact, as early as August 1974, during his annual summer visit to the farm in Nova Scotia after sailing from England for good on the ocean

liner *France,* Shepard began work on a three-act family play drawing on his own heritage. Until it trailed off early into the third act,
The Last American Gas Station featured characters named Dodge
and Halie, their sons Tate and Eamon (the latter an amputee who
wore a wooden leg), and Eamon's son Cody sitting around bloated
from eating Hershey bars on a set meant to resemble an Edward
Hopper painting. It was the first of several studies leading up to
the writing of *Buried Child*.

When the Shepard family first arrived in California from Nova
Scotia, they stayed with the Darks at their place in Mill Valley for
a couple of months until they found their own place in Corte
Madera, a nearby prefab suburb. The following year Shepard
leased a twenty-acre horse ranch in Mill Valley called the Flying
Y and started fixing it up for the whole gang to move into. "I
came out here because of my family and the weather," he told the
press, "and because there's very little original theater being produced out here. New York and London are polluted with theater,
and everyone goes to the theater with ready-made assumptions.
Out here, there's a possibility of getting something going."

Considering Shepard's growing reputation both in America and
abroad (in London, as critic John Lahr pointed out rather snidely,
the fringe theaters were "marketing him like Corn Flakes"), you
might imagine theaters would be crawling all over each other to
"get something going" with him. After all, just as the explosion of
new playwriting in the early sixties had created off-off-Broadway,
the increasing number of professional theater institutions around
the country had given birth to a new regional theater movement
as a nationwide alternative to Broadway, and one of the most
prestigious regional theaters was San Francisco's own American
Conservatory Theater.

But when Shepard approached ACT with his recent plays, such
as *Action,* he wasn't exactly treated like a homecoming hero.
"They told me I could maybe do them in the ACT basement or
wherever—you know, with no public audience invited. They were
totally unenthusiastic. It's like they're asleep, lobotomized over
there." Not that the general public was totally with-it: "Sam who?"
was still a typical response, and many people still confused the
playwright with the controversial Ohio doctor who spent ten years
in prison for killing his wife. In November 1975, after the *San
Francisco Chronicle* covered a local production of *The Tooth of
Crime,* a reader wrote in to say, "I enjoyed your review of Dr.

Sam Shepard's play, 'Tooth of Crime.' I was especially glad to hear that Dr. Shepard is accepted as a writer and is a useful citizen of the community again, something I didn't even know until I read your review"—probably because Dr. Sam Sheppard had died in 1970. "I really never did believe that he killed his wife," this hilarious letter went on to say before concluding, "This country always gives a man a second chance."

Fortunately, Shepard gave San Francisco theater a second chance. Not long after being rebuffed by the ACT, he met John Lion, director of the Magic Theater, at the home of poet and playwright Michael McClure. Lion and a few other graduate students at the University of California at Berkeley had founded the Magic in 1967 by staging avant-garde European plays in the back room of a bar. Located in the hotbed of sixties campus politics, they avoided the most feverish ideological battles by adopting a casual anarchy. "Our position was not to judge what was going on but to reflect; for this we took a lot of flack," said Lion. "Basically, we were a bunch of people who got together and tried to work out possibilities for living through theater." Before long the theater became known primarily for producing the wild, cartoonish plays of McClure (whose most famous play, *The Beard*, is an erotic showdown between Jean Harlow and Billy the Kid), although it also did Shepard's *La Turista* in 1970. Shepard liked Lion's easygoing attitude, and Lion admired Shepard's plays, so without a lot of to-do they launched a working relationship that continued for more than ten years.

Another reason for Shepard's interest in the Magic was probably its resemblance to Theater Genesis in that, among San Francisco theater groups, it was—as Ralph Cook had put it—"conspicuous in its heterosexuality." Particularly once Shepard was established as playwright-in-residence there, the Magic became even more of a clubhouse for the hipster version of good ol' boys. Although the Bay Area has for some time been noted for its prominent feminist, gay, and political theater companies, the masculine ethos was unquestionably championed at the Magic by Shepard and Lion, their pals Murray Mednick and Robert Woodruff, and all the young actors and directors who looked up to them.

You can't help noticing from his plays how machismo exerts an irresistible thrill for Shepard. Homosexuals are nowhere to be seen, though they are referred to as "fags" and "faggots," and even when women have leading roles they are always outnumbered and usually abused or humiliated. This is a continuing sore point even among feminists who admire Shepard's talent. One prominent woman director in New York, told that Shepard had taken up the sport of Indian polo, drily suggested that he probably used women as mallets.

Indeed, Shepard's machismo is hardly limited to his work. When he taught a playwriting course at the University of California at Davis in 1975, he insisted that the class meet in the stage shop where the sets were built—an ordinary classroom, it seems, was not masculine enough. And instead of using the men's room, in the middle of class he sometimes ambled over to a corner and relieved himself in a prop toilet that happened to be handy. It was a very butch gesture, showing what a down-home guy he was. But since the prop toilet wasn't connected to any plumbing, it meant that some poor student would have to come along and empty out Mr. Shepard's piss.

For his first official Shepard production at the Magic Theater, John Lion really wanted to do *The Tooth of Crime*, but the playwright talked him into producing *Action* along with a tiny play he'd recently finished called *Killer's Head*, in which a guy about to be electrocuted delivers a monologue about buying a new pickup and the problems of raising racehorses. The double bill opened at the Magic a couple of weeks after its New York premiere at the American Place (with an unknown actor named Richard Gere performing *Killer's Head*), where it made few fans among critics ("two of the most pretentious and tedious plays performed on the professional stage," said one, and most others agreed). The production at the Magic was directed by Shepard himself, and it was much better received by the critics, who welcomed the new star in their midst. A visitor from New York who observed a rehearsal marveled at the relaxed working atmosphere Shepard was able to maintain and asked how he did it. "Oh, you know," said Shepard, who could frequently be seen off in a corner giggling and smooching with one of the actresses in the show. "I don't know how O-Lan put up with it," sighs a woman who worked at the Magic then.

Shepard was also beginning to work on new stuff. The first go was a play called *California Heart Attack*, a sort of gee-it's-great-to-be-back exercise full of exclamation points, rhapsodic celebrations of things Californian (from cheeseburgers to Chicanos), and salutes to the lure of the West. The play was never finished, but it contained seeds of later work. Also around this time (early 1975), the Mark Taper Forum in Los Angeles gave Shepard a thousand-dollar commission to write a new adaptation of Christopher Marlowe's *Doctor Faustus*. The result was *Manfly*, a two-act play with music that owed a lot to the work of Michael McClure with its anthropomorphized animal characters and hipster versions of figures from legend (Skeetz for Faust, Mustafo for Mephistopheles, etc.).

The Taper ultimately declined to stage the play—in fact, *Manfly* remains unproduced—so after directing *Action* at the Magic, Shepard spent most of the summer reading Pablo Neruda and Robinson Jeffers while trying to figure out how to make the Flying Y ranch habitable. "I'm filled with a mixture of the past and all this new life happening to me now. Installing wood-burning stoves, roofing, fencing, foaling corrals, getting ready for the rains."

A week before the big move to the new house, Shepard got a phone call out of the blue. Bob Dylan was planning a "secret" tour of the Northeast with a show called the Rolling Thunder Revue, they wanted to film it as they went along, and would Shepard come along and write dialogue for the movie? Oh, and could he leave yesterday? Standing in a house full of packed-up boxes of toys, books, and kitchen things, Shepard had to think. For two minutes. The next day he got on a train back to his favorite city, New York.

As it turned out, Shepard got taken for a ride in both senses. The Rolling Thunder Revue was running on the adrenaline of chaos and last-minute changes; the logistics of getting dozens of musicians, technicians, family members, and friends to an ever-changing number of small-town concerts by bus and truck took precedence over the movie throughout the tour. At first Shepard was pissed off, because he hadn't just come along for his health. "They made some assurances to me in terms of money that they didn't follow through on," he complained to Larry Sloman, a Dylan groupie who was covering the tour for *Rolling Stone*. "There's like this reverse Dylan generosity syndrome here. They say that because Bob is so generous and this tour is making a sort of antimoney, antiestablishment position in terms of money and large halls, therefore they can rip you off and it's all right."

Before long Shepard relaxed into the craziness, cooked up scenes for the movie whenever he was asked to, and furiously scribbled in a tiny three-by-five-inch notebook the impressions that would later be published as his *Rolling Thunder Logbook.* Riding the bus through New England towns in the snow reminded him pleasantly of his days with the Bishop's Repertory Company, and he appreciated traveling with legendary musicians like Joan Baez, Joni Mitchell, Roger McGuinn, Bobby Neuwirth, and Ramblin' Jack Elliot. Ever the ladies' man, he worshiped Baez from a distance and got tight with Joni Mitchell, whom he admired because she had mingled quirky lyrics and rhythms with jazz structures "and even managed to bite the masses in the ear with it." (Perhaps it was Shepard who inspired Mitchell to make her adventurous *Mingus* album, a collaboration with his former roommate's father Charles Mingus.)

On top of that, he was fascinated to observe first-hand the way Bob Dylan made use of the personal mythology that surrounded him. "Dylan says he's 'just a musician,' and in his boots he needs that kind of protection from intellectual probes, which are a constant threat to any artist," Shepard mused. "Myth is a powerful medium because it talks to the emotions and not the head. It moves us into an area of mystery. Some myths are poisonous to believe in, but others have the capacity for changing something inside us, even if it's only for a minute or two. Dylan creates a mythic atmosphere out of the land around us. The land we walk on every day and never see until someone shows it to us." And he identified with the artistic and spiritual restlessness that lay behind Rolling Thunder, because it resembled the relationship between his own travels and work. "It's not just another concert tour but more like a pilgrimage. We're looking for ourselves in everything. Everywhere we stop. Even when we're moving. Trying to locate ourselves on the map."

The charm inevitably began to wear off. After one too many nights on the road, he wrote: "I'm cracking up behind this. My body quakes from it. This is truly being transported back to the midsixties when crystal meth was a three-square diet with 'yellow jackets' and 'black beauties' for chasers. Not just the sixties of the imagination but the actual body-and-mind sixties. The shattered feeling. I DON'T WANT TO GET BACK TO THE SIXTIES! THE SIXTIES SUCKED DOGS!" Were the seventies a big improvement, though? When he ducked out of the Rolling Thunder concert to check out the Tubes, who were playing down the street, he wound up bewildered and depressed. "What are all these kids doing watching this shit when they could be hearing good music?" he wondered. "They wanna see brains dripping from the ceiling. Is this the generation stuff that you hear about all the time? . . . Am I a part of the old folks now? Is Dylan?"

The thing that really bothered Shepard, and cured him forever of his fascination with rock stars as the contemporary manifestation of Wild West heroes, was the sheer arrogance that travels with celebrities, encasing them in an artificial world and holding them up as automatically superior to regular people, which went against the grain of Shepard's jes-folks temperament. "Even ordering food in a restaurant takes on a different tone from usual, because you're in the company of something that's so public that even the waiters know about it. You find yourself expanding to the smell of arrogant power or deflating to total depression. You begin wishing you could just go back into the kitchen with the waiter and wash a few dishes or even go back home with him and watch color TV with his grandmother. Anything just to get the taste back of 'normal everyday life.'"

The Rolling Thunder tour ended up back in New York City for a benefit concert in Madison Square Garden for Rubin Carter. (A former middleweight boxer languishing in a New Jersey jail convicted of murder even though key witnesses had recanted their testimony, Carter eventually won a new trial—and was acquitted—with the help of celebrities like Muhammad Ali and Dylan, who addressed his cause in the song "Hurricane.") Once it was over, Shepard couldn't wait to split for California. But he hung around long enough to see the New York opening of *Geography of a Horse Dreamer*, which his old colleague Jacques Levy directed at the Manhattan Theater Club. Dylan showed up for the opening night, too, noticeably drunk, and caused a disturbance by talking back during the climactic scene of the play and alarming the critics dozing with overcoats in their laps. In a way, Shepard dug Dylan's eccentric behavior, but on another level its out-of-control disrespect for other people epitomized everything Shepard disliked about "stardom." It was, at any rate, a perfectly absurd ending to the whole Rolling Thunder experience.

The movie that was made during the tour finally came out in 1978, a spectacular four-hour mess called *Renaldo and Clara*. The scripted scenes were cryptically interspersed with concert footage and more close-ups of Bob Dylan than even his most ardent fans really needed. Shepard appears in one scene saying to Dylan's wife Sara, "I need you to perform certain magical things. Because I'm afraid if I go out there on a boat without that, I'm gonna die." He used his experience as a hired gun on that and several other movies in his next major play, *Angel City*.

A lot of familiar Shepard material is recycled in *Angel City*, which could be called *The Tooth of Crime Goes to the Movies*. Like *Melodrama Play* and *Geography of a Horse Dreamer*, it concerns an artist under pressure to create a masterpiece; as in *Manfly*, he's asked to sell his soul to the devil, in this case disguised as Angel City—i.e., Hollywood. Rabbit Brown, a cross between a gumshoe and an Indian-style medicine man "geared in the old forms," is summoned down from his northern California retreat by an eccentric executive named Lanx (he keeps a drummer on salary in hopes of discovering a rhythm guaranteed to put mass audiences into a trance) to salvage a big-budget disaster movie. Wheeler, the mild-mannered but clearly insane director, blithely requisitions "not simply an act of terror but something which will in fact drive people right off the deep end.... Penetrating every layer of their dark subconscious and leaving them totally unrecognizable to themselves. Something which not only mirrors their own sense of doom but actually creates the possibility of it right there in front of them. That's what the people are crying out for and that's what we must give them. It's our duty."

Rabbit ought to know better, but like Lanx's starstruck secretary Miss Scoons, like the salaried drummer Tympani, like any good American, he's smitten with the silver screen. Both as fan and as manufacturer he can't resist "the vision of a celluloid tape with a series of moving images telling a story to millions.... Effecting their dreams and actions. Replacing their books. Replacing their families. Replacing religion, politics, art, conversation. Replacing their minds. And I ask myself, how can I stay immune?" And like all Shepard heroes who try to adapt their ancient wisdom to the modern world, he pays a terrible price: he becomes the kind of person he despises and his magic powers dissolve into green slime. "I give you the diamonds, you give me the disease," as the Rolling Stones song goes.

Angel City isn't one of Shepard's best scripts. Its verbal density and multilayered theatricality labor in service of a fairly conventional tale of how Hollywood creates mass-market dreams by crushing personal visions. But it was the first new play that

Shepard directed himself at the Magic Theater, and he used the production as a laboratory for two experiments. One involved using jazz onstage in the form of a nonspeaking saxophonist to underscore the play. (Rolling Thunder apparently cured Shepard of his devotion to rock—it virtually disappears in the plays after *Tooth of Crime*.) *Angel City* was also an opportunity for Shepard to articulate for actors a technique for performing his rather fluid characters. "Instead of the idea of a 'whole character' with logical motives behind his behavior which the actor submerges himself into, he should consider instead a fractured whole with bits and pieces of character flying off the central theme," he told the cast. "In other words, more in terms of collage construction or jazz improvisation." Many of the actors who worked on this production— including his wife O-Lan, John Nesci, Ebbe Roe Smith, and James (J.A.) Deane—formed the basis of a loose repertory company for Shepard's subsequent work at the Magic Theater.

He kept writing like crazy all this time. Besides *Angel City,* which opened in July 1976 and played through the summer, he composed with Catherine Stone a tiny "cowboy operetta" called *The Sad Lament of Pecos Bill on the Eve of Killing His Wife*, commissioned as part of San Francisco's bicentennial project. It was produced in the first annual Bay Area Playwrights Festival and launched an ongoing relationship with both the festival and its director, Robert Woodruff. And one of Shepard's most enigmatic plays, *Suicide in B-flat*, had its premiere in October at the Yale Repertory Theatre.

Two detectives, Pablo and Louis, are called in to investigate the mysterious death of Niles, a jazz pianist whose body is outlined on the floor of his apartment. They suspect foul play, act out various murder scenarios, and closely question Petrone and Laureen, the sax player and bassist who show up to rehearse Niles's brand of "visual" music (so high it can't be heard by humans). Niles himself appears, invisible to the others, accompanied by Paullette, a sort of spiritual guide from "the other side" who helps him say good-bye to his life by dressing up in different costumes (cowboy, tuxedo, etc.) and killing off that aspect of his personality. Apparently he committed suicide to escape his fame (like Hoss in *The Tooth of Crime*). Petrone senses his presence and—despite Paullette's frantic warnings—brings him back "inside," where he is handcuffed by the cops and taken off.

Suicide in B-flat is a transitional play for Shepard, combining numerous motifs from earlier plays (that outline on the floor, for starters, so similar to *La Turista*'s final image of self-escape) with ideas that would be more completely developed in the plays that followed. It belongs to the group of artist-as-visionary plays, which for Shepard were a sort of rite of passage, a function of growing up and facing the mean old world. After all, the Role of the Artist wasn't just an abstract theme in his plays, it was a burning issue in his life as well. No longer the carefree, rangy street kid who oh-by-the-way writes plays, he was struggling to deal with the new and tricky role of most-promising-young-award-winning-soon-to-be-a-major-American-talented-playwright-as-commodity. But even the most insightful and self-deprecating plays about the Role of the Artist smack of self-indulgence, if not self-righteousness, and Shepard's are no exception.

Still, everything you can criticize the play for—its obscurity, its recycling of other plays—also makes it fascinating, if only because you marvel at how, with every step ahead in his mastery of dramatic craft, Shepard tries to recreate his vision of the world. The crucial speeches in *Suicide in B-flat* vividly reimagine an entire life from birth to death, and the play rips the skin off the necessity for self-transformation that artists both fear and desire:

Niles: That's the reason I invented music. It filled me up. I got so filled up that I couldn't go on. Now I gotta start over.

Paullette: You gotta start from scratch.

Niles: But they showed me their music too. I borrowed from them. They showed me everything I know.

Paullette: But now you can't get to anything new. It's always the same. You're repeating yourself.

Niles: I'm repeating myself, again and again. It's not even myself I'm repeating. I'm repeating them. Over and over. They talk to me all the time. *(suddenly screaming)* THERE'S VOICES COMING AT ME!

After *Suicide in B-flat*, Shepard's next play was indeed a total departure—a three-act family drama written in a style much closer to the American realism of Eugene O'Neill and Arthur Miller than anything he'd done before. *Curse of the Starving Class* became the first in a series of family plays, but it was instigated not so much by autobiographical impulse as financial need. It all started during his Rolling Thunder escapade, when he got a phone call from Joseph Papp. The flamboyant and enterprising producer of the New York Shakespeare Festival, Papp had become famous for nurturing young playwrights and for mounting such award-winning plays as David Rabe's *Sticks and Bones,* Jason Miller's *That Championship Season,* and Charles Gordone's *No Place to Be Somebody* at the Public Theater, his downtown headquarters. He'd just achieved his greatest success by providing workshop space for the original production of Michael Bennett's smash-hit musical *A Chorus Line* when he decided to call the most promising young yaddayadda.

"I said hi, why don't you ever do any of my plays—in ten years he's never done one of my plays," Shepard recalled. "And he said I'd like to do one of your plays. Why don't you write one for me? And I said, how much money will you give me? And he said two hundred dollars. Two hundred dollars, sheeeee! I got him up to five hundred dollars. So I asked Joe, what kind of play do you like? And he said, oh, a family, two sons, one stays home, one goes off to Vietnam or anyway to war and gets fucked up." Never mind that that's the same story as *Sticks and Bones*—Shepard took the assignment, and the money, and went to work.

"*Curse* is the first time I've ever tried to deal with my family. Not really my family, just the—what do you call it—nuclear family. I've always been kind of scared of that. Because if you could really understand that, understand the chemistry and the reactions that are going on there, I've had the feeling that you'd understand a lot."

Shepard clearly had family on the brain anyway, what with setting up house at the Flying Y Ranch with his son, his wife, and O-Lan's mother and stepfather. All the traditional names for the relationships seemed awkward, if not ridiculous: O-Lan's mother, Scarlett, was youngish and bohemian enough to be more like an older sister, and Johnny Dark was only three years older than Shepard—Jesse called him Uncle Johnny. Living together, they were less like a traditional three-generation extended family than a community of Quaker Friends or pioneers. Especially with the dogs, the cats, the canary named Bing, and the horses, it was one big happy household, though it kept Shepard busy filling note-

books full of figures for supply costs, ranch work, chimney installation, and animal feed.

He also had his father to think about. "My Dad lives alone on
the desert," Shepard once wrote. "He says he doesn't fit with people." Throughout the winter of 1976 Sam Sr. wrote a few "Hi,
Steve" letters to his son full of paternal pride and personal misery,
asking for money and then apologizing for not writing sooner to
express his gratitude. Drinking too much and eating too little, he'd
hurt his elbow, gotten an infection, and couldn't afford to go to
the doctor. He'd had company for a while—a young construction
worker he'd taken in like a stray cat, his daughters Sandy and
Roxanne who came to visit—but after they were gone, he felt
more miserable than he had before. He was so proud of his son's
accomplishments and so ashamed that all he could think of was
now he knew where he could get a loan.

It was out of this experience, building a family of his own and
thinking about the one that produced him, that Shepard started
writing a play set on a dried-up avocado ranch in southern California. A play that opens with a woman frying bacon at a stove
while her son stacks wood in a wheelbarrow and goes into a reverie about the night before, lying on his back, smelling the avocado blossoms, listening to coyotes, staring at the model airplanes
hung over his bed, and hearing his father drive up drunk and get
out of his Packard.

> Feet coming. Feet walking toward the door. Feet stopping.
> Heart pounding. Sound of door not opening. Foot kicking
> door. Man's voice. Dad's voice. Dad calling Mom. No an-
> swer. Foot kicking. Foot kicking harder. Wood splitting.
> Man's voice. In the night. Foot kicking hard through door.
> One foot right through door. Bottle crashing. Glass break-
> ing. Fist through door. Man cursing. Man going insane. Feet
> and hands tearing. Head smashing. Man yelling. Shoulder
> smashing. Whole body crashing. Woman screaming. Mom
> screaming. Mom screaming for police. Man throwing wood.
> Man throwing up. Mom calling cops. Dad crashing away.
> Back down driveway. Car door slamming. Ignition grinding.
> Wheels screaming. First gear grinding. Wheels screaming off
> down hill. Packard disappearing. Sound disappearing. No
> sound. No sight. Planes still hanging. Heart still pounding.
> No sound. Mom crying soft. Soft crying. Then no sound.

Then softly crying. Then moving around through house.
Then no moving. Then crying softly. Then stopping. Then,
far off the freeway could be heard.

Only in a Sam Shepard play could this speech stand alone as ex-
position. You don't even realize you're listening to words—
Shepard's extraordinary language puts you inside the pounding
chest of that boy who's so familiar with the sounds of domestic
violence he can recognize every nuance.

Curse of the Starving Class mates all the trademark features of
a Shepard play (long, loopy monologues, strong visual images,
concrete onstage actions, the all-important breakfast) with a traditional plot and characters: "*Tobacco Road* done in the style of
an R. Crumb comic," as one critic wrote. Weston is the come-and-
go father, Ella the put-upon mother, Emma the pubescent tomboy, and Wesley the day-dreaming farm boy. Emma rides a horse,
Wesley raises lambs, and they'd just as soon stay on the farm, but
both their parents have independently made deals to sell the
property—Ella has a contract with a shady real estate speculator
(who takes her out for an all-night "business lunch"), while
Weston sells the deed to a bartender to pay off some gambling
debts. So the children fantasize about going away, she to Mexico
("Just like that guy. . . . That guy who wrote *Treasure of Sierra Madre*"), he to Alaska (the last frontier), leaving this country to "the
invisible zombies" who rape the land and stomp on anybody who
tries to get in their way. Out of these simple means Shepard
makes a drama with the inexorable build of a Greek play or an
episode of *The Honeymooners*. The overall sweep of the play is
tragic, taking in as it does the disintegration of the American family and the ascendancy of a consumer society efficiently condi-
tioned to value material goods over land and people. But
underneath its grand scheme the play concerns itself with mundane and often absurdly comic incidents: Emma has been preparing a lecture-demonstration on how to fry a chicken for her 4-H
Club, but Ella absentmindedly cooks the chicken and Wesley purposely pisses on her charts; Weston comes home drunk with a bag
full of artichokes, puts them in a pot to boil, and passes out on
the floor. There are patterns of action as rhythmical as music—
most notably, the slamming of the refrigerator door, as one member of the family after another idly looks in, stares for a while,
then drifts away empty-handed—and fables delivered off-handedly

as family stories, such as Weston's memory of castrating lambs, Ella's hilarious advice about "the curse" to Emma (who's just started menstruating), and the story that closes the play about an eagle who snatches a tomcat off the roof of the shed:

> They fight like crazy in the middle of the sky. The cat's tear-ing his chest out, and the eagle's trying to drop him, but the cat won't let go because he knows if he falls he'll die. . . . And the eagle's being torn apart in midair. The eagle's try-ing to free himself from the cat, and the cat won't let go. . . . And they come crashing down to the earth. Both of them crashing down. Like one whole thing.

With its recurring verbal and visual images, its biblical allusions, and its larger implications about American society, *Curse of the Starving Class* contains plenty of red meat for lit-crit analysis. "The play as a whole makes us want to gather together its ciphers and arrange them in their proper pattern and then explain them," critic John Glore observed. "No previous Shepard play has cre-ated that need, and more importantly, none has satisfied that need the way *Curse* does. *Curse* reaches for classical dimensions by giving us something—a Meaning—that will resound long after its theatrical sensation has faded. If Shepard's early plays were firecrackers—short, dazzling, potent, abrupt—*Curse* strives to give a deeper, more penetrating and lasting rumble of power."

Shepard knew this was a big play and wanted it done right. Joe Papp, who had commissioned it, definitely wanted to produce the play at the Vivian Beaumont Theater at Lincoln Center—the scene of the *Operation Sidewinder* debacle—in the fall of 1976. But Shepard was unhappy with the terms of the contract Papp of-fered, and while they went back and forth about money, schedul-ing, and choice of director, the production kept getting pushed back. Ultimately, it wasn't produced in New York until March 1978 at the Public Theater.

In the meantime, another script of Shepard's went into rehears-al under the auspices of Joe Papp. Shepard had written *Jackson's Dance* in England and sent it to Murray Mednick to direct at Theater Genesis. When the Genesis production failed to tran-spire, Shepard passed the play along to Jacques Levy, who started working on the play with a group of actors at the Public Theater. The play concerned the painter Jackson Pollock, whose "action painting" was a big inspiration to Shepard. "He came from Cody,

Wyoming, one of my favorite places," the playwright said. "He was influenced by Indian sand paintings, and that was where the notion of drip paintings came from. What really intrigued me was the evolution from those early figurative drawings into this other world. I could see how something moved from one territory into another. He discovered this explosion inside himself." As the production of *Jackson's Dance* progressed, Levy found it difficult to extract from Pollock's widow, the painter Lee Krasner, the necessary legal clearances. Rather than wrangle with an artist he admired, Levy chose to let the play go.

Curse of the Starving Class had its world premiere in April 1977—not in New York but at the Royal Court in London. Only a few weeks later, in an unprecedented move, *The Village Voice*'s Obie Award committee declared it the best new play of 1977 on the basis of the published edition alone. The award was controversial; several of the judges publicly denounced the practice of bestowing such an honor without first seeing the play onstage. Shepard, however, was very moved by the award. "I'm very happy to receive this award since it marks the first time that a play of mine has been recognized for itself," he wrote back.

Undoubtedly, he also appreciated the thousand-dollar check that accompanied the award. For like the characters in his play, he and his family, while not literally starving, weren't exactly thriving either. No writer could be more prolific than Sam Shepard was; only thirty-two years old, he'd already seen thirty plays produced in universities, coffeehouses, and professional theaters all over the country and abroad. Few playwrights his age had ever been so acclaimed; nine of his works had won Obie awards, and in the spring of 1976 he won the Brandeis University Creative Arts Award citation for achievement in midcareer. It's indicative of the sad plight of the American playwright, however, that he could barely make a living. In 1974 and 1975 his annual income from his plays totaled less than six thousand dollars. He'd gotten a mere five hundred dollars upfront for *Curse of the Starving Class,* and he was offered only another five hundred by Urizen Books, who published the play, until he talked them up to fifteen hundred.

From these measly sums, plus whatever grants and award money came his way, Shepard was trying to put food on the table and keep his horse ranch running. O-Lan worked some as an actress; besides *Action* and *Angel City*, she appeared in Len Jenkin's *The Death and Life of Jesse James* at the Magic and Harold Pinter's *The Birthday Party* at the Eureka Theater. But these weren't paying jobs—San Francisco actors in local theater productions were lucky to get carfare. Shepard had medical bills to pay—his son Jesse had had a serious operation—and he had his father to take care of. Yet at the same time that Sam Sr. was writing to say he couldn't afford a doctor for his infected elbow, Shepard was confessing to his agent that *Curse of the Starving Class* was such a long play that he couldn't even afford to make a photocopy of it.

All these pressures made it easy, if not mandatory, for Shepard to accept an odd offer that came his way that summer—to go to Canada for thirteen weeks and act in Terrence Malick's movie *Days of Heaven*. Malick was having trouble casting the part of a middle-aged Texas farmer who becomes part of a romantic triangle involving a couple of young migrant workers; he wanted someone like Warren Oates or Ben Johnson, but for lack of available old geezers, he decided to make the farmer the same age as the other characters. The idea of casting Sam Shepard came from Rudy Wurlitzer, who had met Shepard through Bob Dylan and the Rolling Thunder Revue. Malick knew that Shepard was a writer but had never even seen a picture of him. He flew up to Shepard's ranch in California, responded immediately to his authentic Southern quality, and offered him the role on the spot.

It was quite bewildering. Except for a few, half-joking performances in his own plays, Shepard hadn't really acted since he was nineteen years old playing in *Winnie the Pooh* with the Bishop's Repertory Company. But he admired Malick as a director on the basis of his first film, *Badlands*, a commercially marginal but very artistic portrait of a Charlie Starkweather-like killer and his teen-aged girlfriend, played by Martin Sheen and Sissy Spacek. He read the script and liked the character of a rich though frail American farmer who falls in love with a poor girl passing through. And what the heck, it was a thousand dollars a week—barely union scale, but the same that his co-stars Brooke Adams and Richard Gere got.

Actually, Shepard was cast before they were; John Travolta and Genevieve Bujold were originally supposed to play the other characters, and when they dropped out, Shepard drove down to Los Angeles to help read with various actresses auditioning for the part finally played by Brooke Adams. Then he spent most of the fall on location in Canada. The experience got off to a bad start;

driving to Alberta from San Francisco across Montana, he had some trouble with his papers at the border, and somebody from the film crew had to go down and fetch him. Then the cost of his car rental was more than had been allotted, and he had to hassle about being reimbursed with the producers, whom he accused of trying to stiff him. Once he bought himself a new pickup truck in Canada, Shepard settled down and was happy, though he didn't stay a minute longer than he had to. On his last scheduled shooting day, he packed his truck early in the morning and left without saying good-bye, before anyone could tell him he was needed for a few pick-up shots.

The last bits of filming took place in Hollywood the following spring, around Easter. While Shepard was gone doing that, his son Jesse entered an Easter egg-coloring contest, determined to win, and Johnny Dark told him if he was anything like his father, he would win—and get a film contract out of it too.

When he finished his chores on *Days of Heaven*, Shepard went to work on a very ambitious project. On a fifteen-thousand-dollar grant from the Rockefeller Foundation, he spent six weeks in a workshop with eight actors and eight musicians developing an improvisational jazz opera called *Inacoma*. Shepard's first attempt at building an Open Theater-style ensemble to create theater pieces using the techniques of Joseph Chaikin, the workshop focused on what it's like to be a victim of coma, an idea that had long interested Shepard. The case of Karen Ann Quinlan, a brain-dead woman whose parents went to court for permission to turn off her life-support system, was all over the news, and perhaps his son Jesse's recent operation brought it close to home. *Inacoma* opened in March for six weeks of performances at the Fort Mason Cultural Center, a former army installation near the Golden Gate Bridge, where the Magic Theater had relocated from Berkeley, and the results were decidedly mixed. Even as a work-in-progress, it seemed to wobble somewhere between documentary and satire, but as an experiment it was an opportunity for Shepard to try his hand at engaging actors in creative collaboration, though not one he would repeat again soon. The next time he did it was under more manageable circumstances—with one actor, Joe Chaikin.

Collaborating with Shepard was something that had been on Chaikin's mind for a few years. The playwright had sent him *Man-fly* to consider directing, but it didn't suit Chaikin; he had in mind a storytelling piece, not a play but "thought music," and he had a semi-mystical hunch he would end up doing it with Shepard. They finally got together for three weeks in May 1978 to make a piece. "It began from almost nothing but the desire to work together," said Shepard.

"Sam suggested we write together, and I perform in, a tale about somebody who might be reborn and reborn and reborn and reborn," Chaikin recalled. "Sam likes egg foo yung, so we'd go to this Chinese restaurant, or we'd go to the park or to the zoo, or we'd stay in my hotel room. We would sit there and make something up. I'd sometimes make up a line, he'd follow it; he'd make up a line, I'd follow it."

In many ways they were an odd team. Shepard was a Western farmboy, Chaikin an Eastern Jew. The playwright was aggressively heterosexual, the actor quietly gay. Although they weren't far apart in age, Shepard was much more the young punk, Chaikin the wise old man, practically a guru of the theater. Although he admired *The Tooth of Crime* and had considered directing it, that play's violent rock 'n' roll sensibility couldn't be further from Chaikin's; the work he directed was usually much more contemplative, and he felt most at home performing Beckett. Both sought to express the same thing in theater, though—the inner life of man—and the extremes of their personalities actually made their collaboration a perfect balance.

What emerged from it was *Tongues*, a series of different voices speaking through the actor, sparked by the idea of structuring the work as a fantasy of the former lives of a dying man:

Today the wind roared through the center of town.
    Tonight I hear its voice.

Today the river lay wide open to the sun.
    Tonight I hear it speaking.

Today the moon remained in the sky.
    Tonight I feel it moving.

Today the people talked without speaking.
    Tonight I can hear what they're saying.

Today the tree bloomed without a word.
    Tonight I'm learning its language.

They originally thought that Chaikin would perform alone, but they also wanted music, and during the final week Shepard decided he would perform the music himself on percussion (bongos, cymbals, maracas, African drum, tambourine, bells, chains, pipes, kitchenware). They performed it for three weeks at the Magic, and the response was so gratifying that Shepard and Chaikin decided to make another piece. After writing letters back and forth all winter, they spent three weeks together composing *Savage/Love*; this time a horn player and percussionist supplied the crucial element of musical counterpoint.

One of Shepard's tenderest writings ever, *Savage/Love* is a series of vignettes exploring romance from every angle—what Chaikin calls "common poems of real and imagined moments in the spell of love." Chaikin performed the piece together with *Tongues* at the Magic, later at the Public Theater in New York, and on tour throughout Europe. Both pieces were recorded for posterity in superb videotapes by experimental filmmaker Shirley Clarke.

Shepard gained much from his collaboration with Chaikin, including (no doubt) a true understanding of the difficulties inherent in collective creation. He recognized that, at least for the time being, he felt more comfortable contributing to a collaborative situation not as an auteur-like director but purely as a writer. He welcomed those situations; when choreographer Daniel Nagrin wrote tentatively commissioning a libretto for a dance, he was shocked when Shepard responded immediately with a text called *Jacaranda*. "A man wakes up in his lover's rather extravagant bed. She's not there. She's gone off. He'd like not to be tied down to anybody, but it's quite possible he's tied to her and doesn't want to be," said Nagrin, summarizing the text of *Jacaranda*. "The title is the name of a very beautiful tree, and Shepard thinks of it as her name."

Although he never succeeded in creating a permanent acting ensemble at the Magic Theater, he became very involved with writers' workshops, leading seminars at the Bay Area Playwrights Festival and its southern California counterpart, the Padua Hills Writers Conference run by his old friend from Theater Genesis, Murray Mednick. The fledgling playwrights were thrilled at the opportunity to learn secrets of the trade from such a renegade hotshot; the Bay Area workshop was quickly nicknamed "Camp

Shepard." It wasn't just a one-way thrill: the workshop also gave Shepard an opportunity to pass along to others the valuable lessons he'd picked up from Chaikin and other major thinkers as well as to pinpoint how he did his best writing.

"The more you penetrate into the smallest thing, the more it sends off sparks to the biggest," he would tell them, lighting up an Old Gold. Most people do it backwards and go for the grand thesis first, but Shepard stressed that writers have to start with what they know, and the best place to start is the body, a repository of experiences rather than ideas. He gave them an exercise to do: go sit somewhere, feel what's happening in your body, then write a detailed description of all the movements and sensations going on at that moment. "You have to get in there and discover what the experience is," he said. "Imagination only takes you so far, as far as your experience goes. It isn't a question of having to write about ourselves, but of contacting in ourselves the elements—forces and tendencies—that are characters. The voices of a lot of external-world characters are inside you.... For instance, if you're writing about a nun on a train, that's imaginary. Then you've got to draw upon all your train experiences—what it sounds like, how it feels and smells. But if you remain in the imaginary—'What would happen if'—you're not going to go very far with it."

Shepard described his own working habits, how he saw each writing spell as having its own life. "What I'm interested in now is getting a little taste of a voice, in terms of attitude, and letting it start to speak. Then listening closely and trying to follow where it wants to go, as far as it wants to take you. Then giving it a rest and coming back and letting it take you further." He said he always stopped while a piece of writing was still building, because that way when he went back to it there would still be some momentum going. And he admitted that he always had problems with endings.

"I never know when to end a play. I'd just as soon not end anything. But you have to stop at some point, just to let people out of the theater. I don't like endings and I have a hard time with them," he said. "I think it's a cheap trick to resolve things. It's totally a complete lie to make resolutions. I've always felt that, particularly in theater when everything's tied up at the end with a neat little ribbon and you've delivered this package. You walk out of the theater feeling that everything's resolved and you know what the play's about. So what? It's almost as though why go through all that if you're just going to tie it all up at the end? It seems like a lie to me—the resolutions, the denouement and all the rest of it. And it's been handed down as if that is the way to write plays. If you're only interested in taking a couple of characters, however many, and having them clash for a while, and then resolve their problems, then why not go to group therapy or something?"

So what was the point, Shepard was asked—to keep the audience hanging? "No, no. I'm not intentionally trying to leave people up in the air. But I also don't want to give people the impression that it's over," he said with a grin, and everybody laughed.

Shepard tried to be just-folks with the other playwrights, showing up on a bicycle when his truck was in the shop and wearing blue jeans, T-shirt, and cowboy boots like everybody else. Oh, hell, maybe a beat-up leather jacket and reflecting sunglasses, just to complete the image. Shepard was not unaware of the adulation he inspired. On the first day of one workshop he asked the participants to write down exactly what they were thinking at the time. When one woman got up to read hers and it said, "I want to fuck Sam Shepard," he seemed to take it in stride behind his mirrored shades.

After one of these workshop sessions, Shepard admitted that they were his way of paying some dues. "If there was one thing I wanted to accomplish it was to try to inspire the writers to trust their own material, to feed the connection between their experience and their writing. And I got the sense that people in the workshop came around to the idea that their experience was valuable, not something to throw out the window or to avoid in preference to literature. The fact is, writers' own experience is the best thing they've got going and too often they betray that for something else."

Shepard knew from experience the traps writers laid for themselves, and even with all his accomplishments he was not immune to them. After *Curse of the Starving Class* he went through one of the longest dry spells of his career. Not that he quit writing. He filled his drawers with unfinished manuscripts. He wrote poems, prose pieces, and scraps of dialogue with titles like "Machismo Mum" and "The Man Who Invented His Self." He fiddled with screenplays, film treatments, and notes on possible movies like

Baseball Card—The Flipper Hustler Movie or *Hero Movie* based on the Marvel Comics character the Mighty Thor. He started any number of plays: *Freeway Life* about a character named Robin Ross who wants to move in with his friends Case, Frankie, and Ruby because he sees them as true artists; *Madagascar*, about two guys named Mack and Kinney in a hotel room; and *Links*, a play about golf.

Except for *Inacoma*, the only work completed during this period was *Seduced*, a very perfunctory four-character play about a Howard Hughes-like reclusive kazillionaire. Hughes is just the sort of warped American hero who would seem ripe for the Shepard treatment, but the playwright simply used him as a grandiose projection of the artist-as-visionary characters in *Angel City* and *Suicide in B-flat*—self-indulgence compounded with infantilism. The only interesting thing about it is the surprising lack of irony in Shepard's perspective on Hughes, signaling perhaps his own desperation and sense of being isolated in San Francisco from the lifeblood of his profession. Although it provided the occasion for a sensational performance by Rip Torn at the American Place Theater (after premiering in Providence at the Trinity Square Repertory Company), almost everyone agreed that it was one of Shepard's least interesting works.

The playwright himself felt stymied, unsatisfied. He complained in his journal that he felt like writing but had nothing to say, and then he berated himself for complaining. He brooded around the house, causing O-Lan to protest that she had to read his writing just to know what he was thinking. He read a lot of Jack London, William Faulkner, James Joyce, *The Story of Secretariat*, and especially Flann O'Brien (*At Swim-Two-Birds*, *The Third Policeman*). He went through an Irish phase; in fact, ever since he returned from England he'd been referring to himself as a mick, and he and Johnny Dark went through a spell of compulsively talking in phony brogues. He spent a lot of time staring at himself in the mirror, noticing how his right eye was more open than his left and speculating that the good eye came from his mother, the bad eye from his father. During the summer of 1977, one of his lowest points, Shepard made up a sort of Dewar's profile of himself for amusement, giving his age (33), height (6'1"), weight (160), etc., and listing as his ambition—salvation.

That salvation—or at least a step toward it—came by turning back to the family. To whatever extent *Curse of the Starving Class* was autobiographical (evidence suggests it was considerable), *Buried Child* picks up where the earlier play left off. If *Curse* was a fictional account of events leading up to his leaving home as a teenager, *Buried Child* picks up the family saga about six years later when Vince (an older version of Wesley, or young Sam) stops to visit his grandparents in Illinois on the way to see his father in New Mexico. The two plays are clearly companion pieces, almost conventional three-act dramas exploring the underbelly of the family. *Curse* seems like the warm-up in that it takes place on two distinct planes, one poetic (its long speeches, its symbols strewn like birdseed), the other narrative (its get-the-money plot). *Buried Child* is paradoxically both more conventional and more original: its explosive actions and visual images are more overtly tied to a melodramatic plot.

Set in a ramshackle two-story family house, the play opens during a rainstorm with invalid Dodge parked in front of the TV set sneaking sips of whiskey while carrying on a banal conversation with his wife Halie, upstairs and offstage. His oldest son Tilden comes in muddy from the backyard with his arms full of freshly picked corn and proceeds to clean it, tossing the husks on the floor and the ears in a bucket. Announcing that she's having lunch with Father Dewis to discuss a commemorative plaque for her dead basketball-hero son Ansel, Halie comes down the stairs dressed in black and accuses Tilden of stealing the corn, since nothing has grown in the backyard since 1935. It seems Tilden has had some trouble with the law back in New Mexico, because Halie warns that he'll be run out of Illinois if he doesn't return the corn. She leaves Tilden in charge of watching over Dodge, whose cryptic remark "My flesh and blood's buried in the back yard!" hangs in the air. When Dodge nods off, Tilden steals away with his whiskey, and his brother Bradley, who lost a leg in a chain saw accident, hobbles in to cut Dodge's hair while he sleeps.

Vince shows up from New York with his giggly girlfriend Shelly, but his grandfather doesn't recognize him. And his father Tilden comes in from the backyard, this time with his arms full of carrots, and says, "I had a son once but we buried him." Vince's attempts to jog their memories fail. He agrees to go to the liquor store to get Dodge two dollars' worth of sour mash, and Shelly offers to clean the carrots. Tilden tells her that there had been a little baby in the house but Dodge drowned it and buried it. Bradley arrives with his squeaking wooden leg, scares off Tilden, and makes Shelly let him stick his fingers in her mouth.

The next morning the rain has stopped, and while Bradley sleeps (his false leg propped against the sofa), Shelly has a friendly conversation with Dodge. Halie returns dressed in bright yellow with Father Dewis, both of them slightly tipsy. When Halie insults Shelly, Dodge retaliates by telling the whole story of how, after the boys were grown and she'd stopped sleeping with Dodge, Halie became pregnant, how Tilden loved and looked after the child, and how he killed it because "it made everything we'd accomplished look like nothin'." Just as Halie cries, "What's happened to the men in this family!" Vince comes home, suddenly recognized by everyone in the family—perhaps because he's drunk as a skunk and starts smashing empty liquor bottles against the side of the porch—and Dodge even bequeaths the house to him. Vince cuts a hole in the screen window to let Shelly out, while he crawls back in, explaining that he was going to run away the night before but something stopped him.

> I could see myself in the windshield. My face. My eyes. I studied my face. Studied everything about it. As though I was looking at another man. As though I could see his whole race behind him. . . . And then his face changed. His face became his father's face. Same bones. Same eyes. Same nose. Same breath. And his father's face changed to his Grandfather's face. And it went on like that. Changing. Clear on back to faces I'd never seen before but still recognized. Still recognized the bones underneath. The eyes. The breath. The mouth. I followed my family clear into Iowa. Every last one. Straight into the Corn Belt and further. Straight back as far as they'd take me. Then it all dissolved. Everything dissolved.

Shelly leaves by herself, Vince throws Bradley's leg offstage and he crawls after it, and Father Dewis slinks away. Vince is left sitting on one end of the sofa opposite Dodge, who has died, and as Halie's voice proclaims from upstairs that the backyard is full of corn, carrots, and other vegetables, Tilden enters carrying the muddy corpse of a small child. "It's a miracle, Dodge. I've never seen a crop like this in my whole life," says Halie's disembodied voice as Tilden makes his way up the stairs. "Maybe it's the sun. Maybe that's it. Maybe it's the sun."

Buried Child is the theatrical equivalent of an optical illusion: it messes with your mind. Thematically you could sum it up very simply as an eloquent depiction of the inescapability of the family bond, a favorite subject for Shepard and indeed many American playwrights, and in that respect it ranks right up there with *The Glass Menagerie* and *Long Day's Journey Into Night*. But what's extraordinary about *Buried Child* is that, like Shepard's best plays and decidedly unlike most conventional family dramas, it acts on the audience the same way the tensions of the play act on the characters. It becomes the things it is about—emotional violence and the mystery of the family bond.

Shepard masterfully draws the audience into what seems, despite its creepy overtones, a comfortable and recognizable family story. He drops hints of secrets, creates disturbing stage pictures, and eventually makes palpable to the audience the emotions of the play. Just when he's got everybody's nerves on edge, Vince comes in and starts smashing those bottles—the single most effective onstage action in Shepard's work. There's no more violent action that can actually be performed onstage without faking than smashing bottles against a wall. In *Buried Child* the actual wall is offstage, with a groundcloth spread to catch the flying glass, but you see Vince throwing bottle after bottle; it goes on for several minutes, and no matter how big the theater is, an audience cannot fail to feel the assault on their senses.

Likewise, after dropping numerous pointed yet confusing clues, Shepard never solves the riddle of the buried child. Who was the father? Tilden? Ansel? Someone else? Why did Dodge kill it? And why does nobody recognize Vince when he arrives? A true mystery, Shepard suggests—such as how we were chosen to be born into a particular family, or how we turn out the way we do— remains a mystery. The only solution the play offers is an "impossible" one: that Vince and the buried child are the same person, each one a fantasy of what the other might have become under different circumstances. This duality, this sense of split self, would certainly be felt by someone who grew up as Steve Rogers and turned himself into Sam Shepard. But the family secret, the unsolvable mystery, is universal. As Tolstoy pointed out, happy families are all alike, but each unhappy family is unhappy in its own way. In *Buried Child* every member of the family has a different version of what went wrong, and they don't necessarily add up.

Buried Child is another watershed play for Shepard. It's full of echoes from previous works, all the way back to the woman's one-sided conversation in *The Rock Garden*. The familiar yet stylized domestic activity recalls *Action*, the overlapping realities *Suicide in B-flat*, the flying veggies *Curse of the Starving Class*. Set-piece monologues aren't as prominent as before—the dialogue is much more "naturalistic" and conversational—though Dodge's instructions for disposing of his estate resemble the ritual that ends *The Holy Ghostly*. (The presumably autobiographical description of Pop's family in *The Holy Ghostly* also fits the household of *Buried Child*, including the uncle with the wooden leg.) Critics have found resemblances to Pinter's *The Homecoming*, and a very persuasive parallel can be drawn between *Buried Child* and Ibsen's *Ghosts* with its intimations of incest, inherited poisons, even its closing line, spoken by the syphilis-blinded Oswald: "The sun . . . the sun." (Shepard's terse response to this theory? He "never read Ibsen.") But *Buried Child* stands as a unique achievement. Even though Shepard claims to be embarrassed by a "lot of toe-scrunchers in there"—probably referring to such blatantly melodramatic lines as "I know you've got a secret. You've all got a secret"—it is the control he exerts over the language and action of the play that gives its unorthodox effects such theatrical power.

Shepard decided *Buried Child* was too tricky to direct himself, so he turned it over to Robert Woodruff (commonly known as Woody), who staged the play at the Magic Theater with different actors from the ones Shepard had been using. They were both very pleased with the results, and the show got good reviews when it opened in June 1978. But a six-week run in a 99-seat theater didn't rescue Shepard from his financial straits. When his lease on the Flying Y ranch ran out, he wanted to buy the property but he didn't have the cash, so it was snatched away by developers, and the Shepard-Dark household moved once more—to a modest family house in Mill Valley.

After writing *Buried Child*, Shepard was back in the doldrums again, doodling in his diary, venting his impatience, trying this and that. Meanwhile, he was reading Peter Handke, poems by Richard Hugo, Thomas Wolfe's *A Western Journal*, and Thomas Pynchon's *The Crying of Lot 49*. At the Bay Area Playwrights Festival that summer he collaborated with Maria Irene Fornes on a four-page sketch called *Red Woman*, about a man named Dan talking to a statue of St. Teresa, and in the fall he started a play called *Rage of Unknown Origin*, toying with the idea of using the pseudonym Eamon Reese, but he had abandoned the play by Christmas.

Curse of the Starving Class had finally opened in New York earlier in the year, and although the play was admired, Woodruff's production was not, so the show ran only its scheduled five-week run at the Public Theater. Shepard was so financially strapped that he made a deal with Joseph Papp to get a one-thousand-dollar-a-year advance in return for the right to produce any new plays he wrote in the next five years. He had already promised *Buried Child*, however, to Theater for the New City, a small off-off-Broadway theater run by Crystal Field and George Bartenieff, whom Shepard knew from his New York days and who were able to give him a small commission for the play. The advantage was that Field and Bartenieff were happy to have Woodruff direct the play (with New York actors), but the disadvantage was that they could only guarantee a three-week run in a tiny theater.

The only bright spot on the financial horizon was that in September, as the New York production of *Buried Child* went into rehearsal, *Days of Heaven*—two years in the making—was finally released to critical acclaim, and Shepard in particular received very strong notices for his performance. Even his literary agent, Lois Berman, after having a conversation with a movie executive about what a fine leading man he would make, wondered if Shepard could be lured from playwriting into becoming a movie star. Little did she know! His dazzling debut immediately catapulted him to Hollywood's list of most-wanted men, and within a month he was fielding offers. By now he had an agent for acting jobs as well as one for plays and one for screenplays. Daniel Petrie's *Resurrection* wasn't necessarily the biggest or splashiest movie offered to him after *Days of Heaven*, but it starred Ellen Burstyn, and he wanted to work with her. "I think she's a genius," he said. So in January he was off to Texas for a thirteen-week shoot. It was lonesome between takes, and he missed O-Lan. She wrote him chatty letters about household matters, saying—only half-jokingly—that if things got too bad, she and her mother could go back to taking in ironing.

Meanwhile, *Buried Child* had opened in New York to unanimously favorable reviews and transferred immediately to off-Broadway—the first time a Shepard play had been mounted commercially in New York since 1970, when *The Unseen Hand* and *Forensic and the Navigators* played for a mere thirty-one performances. In fact, *Buried Child* was probably the single best production of a Shepard play that had yet been seen in New York, thanks to Robert Woodruff's direction and an excellent cast. The show did good business at the Theater de Lys in Greenwich Village throughout the winter, though after four months attendance dropped off, and the play closed on April 15.

Around the same time, Shepard finished up work on *Resurrection* and headed home in his truck, stopping along the way to visit his father in Santa Fe for the first time. His father gave him the whole tour, pointing out his collection of cigarette butts and jazz records, including an Al Jolson 78 he was sure was worth a thousand dollars. Over the sink was a picture from a magazine of a Spanish senorita covered in whipped cream. "She's supposed to be naked under there, but I'll bet she's wearing something," Sam Sr. cracked. The walls were practically papered with pictures of a waterfall, a dog with a fish in its mouth, saguaro cactus, B-52 bombers in formation, and so forth. "He spent all the food money I'd gave him on Bourbon. Filled the ice box with bottles. Had his hair cut short like a World War II fighter pilot. . . . Showed me how the shrapnel scars still showed on the nape of his neck," Shepard noted. "My Dad lives alone on the desert. He says he doesn't fit with people."

On April 16, 1979, the day after his play closed in New York and while Shepard was driving home from the set of *Resurrection*, a telegram arrived at his house in Mill Valley from the president of Columbia University:

YOU WERE AWARDED PULITZER DRAMA PRIZE TODAY FOR BURIED CHILD. CONGRATULATIONS.

Chapter Seven:

WAR IN HEAVEN

RAUL: I've always respected your vision sir.
HENRY: My vision? That's right. My vision. I still see. Even in the dark, I still see. Do you want to know what I see, Raul? It's the same thing I saw in Texas when I was a boy. The thing I've always seen. I saw myself. Alone. Standing in open country. Flat, barren. Wasted. As far as the eyes could take in. Enormous country. Primitive. Screaming with hostility toward men. Toward us. Toward me. As though men didn't belong there. As though men were a joke in the face of it. I heard rattlesnakes laughing. Coyotes. Cactus stabbing the blue air. Miles of heat and wind and red rock where nothing grew but the sand. And far off, invisible little men were huddled against it in cities. In tiny towns. In organizations. Protected. I saw the whole world of men as pathetic. Sad, demented little morons moving in circles. Always in the same circles. Always away from the truth. Getting smaller and smaller until they finally disappeared.
RAUL: I think your plane is ready sir. Is there any business you want to finish before we leave?

—Seduced, Sam Shepard

After he won the Pulitzer Prize in 1979 and became, unexpectedly, a movie star, it seemed like Sam Shepard had it made. Professionally and financially, he more or less did. But peace of mind is not so easily guaranteed. There was a demon in the air, and whether he fought it or made friends with it, the next few years would turn out to be the most emotionally turbulent period of his life so far.

The Pulitzer Prize changed everything. The prize itself didn't mean all that much to Shepard—he had plenty of awards to show for his work—but it suddenly brought this independent and proudly renegade playwright into the mainstream of American theater. He had never been produced on Broadway, his plays had never crossed the country in touring productions, he had never played ball with the Shuberts and the Nederlanders (the theater owners and producing organizations who dominate commercial theater in America), he rarely mingled with writers or critics or theater people outside his own working circle, and he never expected his plays to make much money for him or anybody else. Even the off-Broadway production of *Buried Child*, the play that won him the Pulitzer, had to close the day before the prize was announced.

Still, the prize had a great deal of significance for its official recognition of Shepard's status in the theater. He had produced an enormous body of work, and to a younger generation he was already a culture hero, inspiring the kind of admiration and emulation more common to poets or rockers or movie stars than to playwrights—partly because he retained both the character and image of an outlaw. Although every Pulitzer Prize-winning drama in the previous ten years had begun in a not-for-profit regional theater (except Edward Albee's 1975 *Seascape*), *Buried Child* was the first to get the award without ever playing Broadway.

Until the Pulitzer he was much better known in the regional theaters than to people who got their culture from the Arts and Leisure section of the Sunday *New York Times,* and while Neil Simon's mechanical comedies epitomized contemporary Broadway drama, overseas it was Sam Shepard who succeeded Tennessee Williams as the quintessential American playwright. *The Tooth of Crime* was translated into Inuit and performed for Eskimos on Baffin Island, and in Antwerp a Belgian company mounted a production of *Curse of the Starving Class* that exploded its kitchen-sink realism into grotesque theatrical spectacle. After the Pulitzer, American theatergoers who'd never heard of Sam Shepard had to sit up and pay attention. Some television producers became interested in doing *Buried Child* on TV, tentatively enlisting such actors as Henry Fonda and Robert de Niro, though nothing came of the project. Shepard was invited to the White House by President Carter to attend a Kennedy Center honors ceremony, however, and he soon ranked second to Shakespeare as the most-produced playwright in America.

The New York production of *Buried Child,* which had opened off-off-Broadway at Theater for the New City and had then moved to the off-Broadway Theater de Lys, reopened at the Circle Repertory Theater just down the street shortly after it won the Pulitzer and played through the end of September for a total run of almost a year—the longest any Shepard play had run in New York. The prize also brought Shepard a lot of publicity. *Esquire* magazine sent a writer out to San Francisco to profile Shepard, and when the article came out Shepard heard from numerous friends and relatives he hadn't seen in a long time; one congratulated him and suggested he would soon have his own box on *Hollywood Squares.* His Aunt Nancy sent him a long letter, with prayer cards attached, saluting his courage in exposing the sins of many Americans, specifically those of his father, grandfather, and grandmother. Sam Sr. himself wrote to say how proud he was of his son, despite their battles in the past, and to remind Shepard that his literary genius was inherited from his father, because he had been the sports editor of his high school newspaper.

Not surprisingly, the Pulitzer also triggered something of a backlash against Shepard, both among long-time champions and Broadway snobs who viewed him as so much unwashed laundry. Critic and professor Ruby Cohn dropped him a note breezily assuring him that *Curse of the Starving Class* and *Buried Child* couldn't be very good if they were so well-liked. And Otis L. Guernsey, Jr., in his introduction to the 1978–1979 volume of *Best Plays*, turned up his nose at *Buried Child*, calling it "a dismal, unstructured exploitation of both our malaise and our patience, describing the economic and spiritual decay of an American family in terms of faddist character poses flapping like wash on a line, in a fashionably masochistic and unbearably tedious work. What we need in our 1980s scripts is more attention to craft," Guernsey wrote, "not more emotion or flagellative insight, of which we have more than plenty."

Shepard was no stranger to this kind of criticism. Although he always got intelligent if not unqualified critical support from *The Village Voice* (which had awarded him a by now almost obligatory Obie for *Buried Child*), the truth is that for many years he also had to endure asinine and dismissive reviews from critics on major daily newspapers who frequently praised well-tailored trivialities over Shepard's jagged poetry. The Pulitzer stamp of approval meant he could tell his hostile critics where to go.

If he really cared, which he didn't. "I've been in a few rodeos, and the first team roping that I won gave me more of a feeling of accomplishment and pride of achievement than I ever got winning the Pulitzer Prize," he said. For him, life went on as usual.

After shooting *Resurrection,* he went home and started preparing to collaborate on *Savage/Love* with Joe Chaikin, who'd sent him a number of books to read—stories by Franz Kafka, a James Dickey poem called "Sheep Child," a volume by Simone de Beauvoir—and suggested other texts by Bruno Bettelheim, Nietzsche, Kierkegaard, and Merleau-Ponty that might be inspiring. Shepard dutifully looked into Chaikin's suggestions, but it sometimes felt like dull homework. Bored with Kafka's parables, he'd pick up the Stark Brothers Fruit Tree catalogue and find that he was much more interested in ordering a semidwarf Golden Delicious than contemplating guilt. He did enjoy reading *Calamity Jane's Letters to Her Daughter,* though, as well as old favorites Beckett, Joyce, Brecht, and Wolfe. In August 1979 he spent some time at his mother's house in Pasadena while she was away on a vacation trip to Alaska, which is when the seeds for *True West* were planted.

In September 1979, back in Mill Valley, misfortune struck the Shepard household. While the others were out riding bikes, O-Lan's mother Scarlett collapsed in the middle of doing exercises; rushed to the hospital, she turned out to have a cerebral hemorrhage, and the doctors said she stood only a twenty-percent chance of surviving surgery. The family located a brain surgeon at another hospital in San Francisco who had performed this particular operation sixty times, losing only one patient. Although only a minuscule blood clot was keeping her from bleeding to death, they decided to take the risk of transferring her to the other hospital. When they met the doctor, "he shook our hands perfunctorily and spoke with a South Texas drawl. The drawl itself filled me with confidence," wrote Shepard in his harrowingly matter-of-fact account of all this in *Motel Chronicles*. Scarlett survived the operation, though she was unconscious for a week, required phenobarbital for a year, and suffered for a long time from aphasia. She had to relearn motor and language skills, and although it was recommended that she move to a therapy center, the family elected to take her home; when she left the hospital, the nurses handed Shepard a bag with Scarlett's long red hair in it.

Her pain, fear, and suffering frightened and saddened the family, especially when she accused them of trying to kill her and repeatedly asked for her long-dead mother. Caring for Scarlett at home took a heavy emotional and psychological toll, but a year after the accident Shepard reported, "She walks on her own now. She feeds herself. She speaks with a strange accent but takes part in our conversations. She still falls silent and sits and stares into space for long periods of time. She refers to her past as the time before she was 'blown away.' "

Winning the Pulitzer meant Shepard was no longer the most-promising-young anything—he was the hottest playwright in America. This made him the recipient of untold numbers of offers and requests, large and small. His agent joked that she could probably sell his chili recipe if he wanted to write it down. Typically, Shepard had little concern for cashing in, but when a country schoolteacher in Big Sandy, Tennessee, wrote asking for material to "auction" for a reading project, he responded right away. He sent off his Little League baseball pin, which unfortunately fell out of the envelope en route, but he still got forty handwritten letters with the kids' photos attached thanking him anyway. Joe Chaikin opened at the Public Theater that winter in *Tongues* and *Savage/Love* to excellent reviews, and come Obie time *The Village Voice* was not content to honor just one more fine play: Shepard received the Sustained Achievement award previously bestowed only upon such off-off-Broadway pioneers as Chaikin, Ellen Stewart, and Al Carmines.

Much as he tried to deny it, all of this unavoidably put pressure on Shepard when it came time to writing the next play, The One After the Prize. He spent more time and worked harder on True West than on any of his earlier plays, rewriting it thirteen times until it was "down to the bone"—a distinctly new experience. "I used to avoid that process I think because I was basically lazy and I wanted to get on to the next thing and I was compulsive. And a lot of things just weren't worth rewriting," he said. "After Buried Child I wanted to simplify, to refine, and distill. That is the general direction I'm moving in."

True West is certainly a distillation. Combining the mythical masculine struggle of earlier work with the mundane circumstances of the recent family dramas, it is his most straightforward play yet. Clean-cut screenwriter Austin is holed up at his mother's house in Southern California while she's on vacation in Alaska. Slaving over a project he's pitching to a Hollywood producer, he is distracted by his older brother Lee, a slovenly drifter and cat burglar who takes after his father, now living "out on the desert," drunk and broke. While the producer meets with Austin, Lee butts in, claiming that he has a good idea for a Western. Something happens over a game of golf—you're not sure whether the producer lost a bet or Lee threatened the guy—and he decides to drop Austin's "simple love story" and do Lee's tale about "two lamebrains chasing each other across Texas."

The two brothers switch roles, but it's ridiculous. Lee can't spell, let alone type, and Austin's idea of crime is stealing all the toasters in the neighborhood. Mom arrives home from Alaska, disappointed with the last Western frontier, just in time to catch Picasso at the local museum (she thinks—but how could she?—it's Picasso himself). She takes one look at her ravaged bungalow and her drunken, brawling boys and decides to check into a motel. Moonlight settles on the two brothers circling each other in silent, deadly combat. It's the classic confrontation of good guy and bad guy. But there's no woman in the picture, no new world to be built, no land to be settled—there's the form of the cowboy showdown without the content. They're out there stalking each other in the desert. They might as well be animals. They might as well be one guy, just good and bad tussling on metaphysical territory, wrestling with the modern-day mystery of identity. The true West is in the mind. No, the true West is in the soul.

The good son/bad son motif runs through Shepard's plays in various guises—from the androgynes of *Cowboy Mouth* to the rock stars of *The Tooth of Crime* to the real blood relations in *Buried Child*—but his characters don't act out the traditional sibling rivalry ("Mother always liked you best"). His contemporary Cains and Abels struggle to integrate contrasting images of masculinity: the idealized Western movie hero and the disappointingly average (or even lousy) all-American dad. The quest for the "true West" has a lot to do with what it means to be a real man in today's world. Austin faces this challenge as a suburban husband-father and aspiring screenwriter—a tamed Wild Westerner. Lee is a wilder creature, a degenerate cowboy with a bulldog instead of a bronco. Though he seems more in touch with some spirit of the mythical West, he's hardly heroic; with the specter of his desert-rat daddy hanging over him, the outcome of Lee's maverick antics is all too predictable.

There's a lot about *True West* that is explicitly autobiographical. Like Austin, Shepard himself has put in time as a would-be screenwriter, but he's also been known to share in Lee's sticky fingers: in his book *Motel Chronicles,* he describes an attempt to steal a practically worthless painting from a room in the Chateau Marmont in Hollywood. And all the stuff in the play about "the old man" clearly relates to Shepard's father. When *True West* was first published in a paperback anthology called *Seven Plays,* the dedication read "for my father, Sam."

"I never intended the play to be a documentary of my personal life," the playwright admonishes. "It's always a mixture. But you can't get away from certain personal elements. I don't want to get away from certain personal elements that you use as hooks in a certain way. The further I get away from those personal things the more in the dark I am. *True West* is riddled with personal sketches like the tooth story for example." In one of the play's few long speeches, Austin tells Lee about visiting their father and taking him out to a Chinese restaurant; the old man took out his ill-fitting false teeth and put them in a doggie bag with some leftover chop suey, and afterwards while the two of them were touring the local saloons, the doggie bag got left behind and thrown away, teeth and all. "Now that's a true story. True to life," says Austin, and apparently it was, although it was Shepard's sister Roxanne who took the old man out for the Chinese meal that cost him his teeth.

The basic truth of *True West* transcends its autobiographical impulse. The notion that each man has to face the other side of himself, the person he might have been if he had (or hadn't) followed in his father's footsteps, is a chief obsession for Bruce Springsteen or, for that matter, any kid from a working-class family who outachieved his father simply by going to college. By internalizing this conflict—by suggesting that on some level Lee and Austin are the same person—Shepard steers clear of the facile Freudianism and soap-opera sentimentality that floods most American drama. "I wanted to write a play about double nature," Shepard said, "one that wouldn't be symbolic or metaphorical or any of that stuff. I just wanted to give a taste of what it feels like to be two-sided. It's a real thing, double nature. I think we're split in a much more devastating way than psychology can ever reveal. It's not so cute. Not some little thing we can get over. It's something we've got to live with."

True West's production history is a saga almost as fascinating as the play itself. The Magic Theater, as usual, hosted the first production, directed by Robert Woodruff in July 1980. Shepard was around for all the rehearsals, smoking Old Golds and taking notes, though he ducked out once to attend the closed-circuit simulcast of the Roberto Duran–Sugar Ray Leonard fight; boxing had temporarily replaced hunting and horse racing as his favorite macho sport. On the opening night of *True West*, drama critics from all over the country outnumbered the paying customers in the audience, but Shepard still showed up in aviator glasses and cowboy boots, blue jeans, orange T-shirt, and silver-and-turquoise belt buckle. "This is the first one of my plays I've been able to sit through night after night and not have my stomach ball up in knots of embarrassment," he said.

At the Magic, the comic performances by leading actors Peter Coyote and Jim Haynie, both veterans of the San Francisco Mime Troupe's street theater, thoroughly entertained hometown audiences, who treated the play as the latest of several original scripts by a popular local playwright. It wasn't until it got to New York that *True West* got bogged down in Great Expectations. By the time it opened at Joseph Papp's Public Theater the following fall, it had become a media event, breathlessly anticipated as the latest work by the hottest young playwright in America. Robert Woodruff again directed the play, not with the original cast (which Shepard lobbied for) but with moderately well-known movie stars Tommy Lee Jones as Austin and Peter Boyle as Lee. After three weeks of previews, Woody resigned as director because, he said, "I didn't feel it was going to work," and Papp took over the direction.

Shepard, on location in Texas filming *Raggedy Man,* issued an outraged statement: "I would like it to be known that the 'production' of my play *True West* at the Public Theater is in no way a representation of my intentions or of Robert Woodruff's." In an interview with *The New York Times* he accused Papp of coercing Woody into hiring movie stars and said that the producer would never see another of his scripts. "He just has no respect for the relationship that exists between Woodruff and me, no idea of how we work together," Shepard fumed. "His judgments are out to lunch." When the play finally opened after several delays, a cloud of gloom hung over it. The performances were listless, and the reviews were correspondingly negative. After a mere eight weeks the play more or less limped offstage and out of sight.

Afterwards, the general perception lingered that Joe Papp destroyed *True West,* and perhaps it's true that he should have closed the show if Woodruff felt it didn't work. But it seems more fair to say that it was Shepard himself who sabotaged the production by telling *The New York Times* that Papp hired movie stars over his objection. No wonder the actors were so demoralized; it must be tough when the author goes around saying publicly you've ruined his play, especially since Shepard had not even seen the actors' work. For the playwright, his sudden status as a "hot" playwright quickly turned cold. Critics called the play "two acts of tedious wrangling, recrimination, and vicious infighting" and "conceivably the least satisfactory Shepard play I have yet come across," which didn't exactly make regional theaters rush to book the play into their next subscription season.

In the middle of all this mess, *Resurrection* was released, and Shepard got very good reviews for his performance, his second in a major film. Although he was broke, Shepard's father got someone to take him to see *Resurrection,* which he liked very much. He wrote Sam a letter saying that in *Days of Heaven* he just seemed like Steve, his father's son, but in *Resurrection* he proved that he was a real actor.

Sam Shepard in front of the Caffe Cino, the legendary birthplace of off-off-Broadway theater, in New York's Greenwich Village. His play *Icarus's Mother* premiered there in 1965. (New York Times)

Sam and O-Lan Shepard: newlyweds in 1969. (copyright Henry Grossman)

McCarty, Sam Shepard, Richard Tyler, and Steve Weber. (copyright 1970 Henri Dauman)

Sam Shepard and Patti Smith in rehearsal for *Cowboy Mouth*, 1971. (copyright Gerard Malanga)

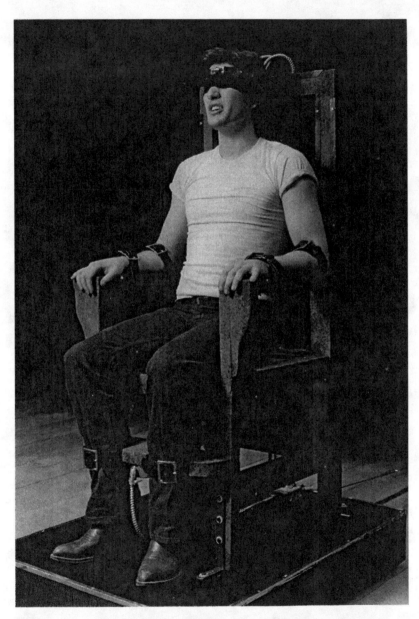

Richard Gere in the 1975 premiere of *Killer's Head* at the American Place Theatre in New York. (photo by Martha Homes)

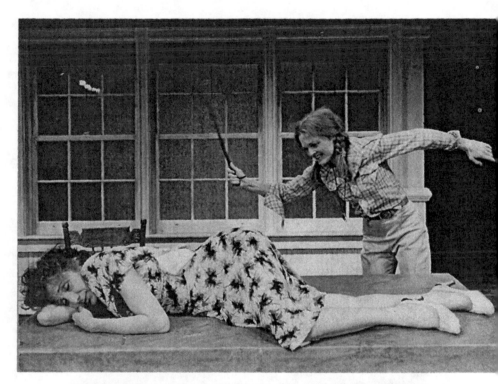

Olympia Dukakis and Pamela Reed in the 1978 premiere of *Curse of the Starving Class* at the Public Theater in New York. (photo by Frederic Ohringer)

John Malkovich and Gary Sinise in the 1982 Steppenwolf Theater revival of *True West*. Directed by Sinise, the show was first produced in Chicago and transferred to a long off-Broadway run in New York. (photo courtesy of Photofest)

Shepard won an Oscar nomination for his 1983 performance as Chuck Yeager in
The Right Stuff.

Sam Shepard and Jessica Lange in the 1984 movie *Country*. (photo courtesy of Photofest)

The 1993 European premiere of *States of Shock* at Staddttheater Konstanz, directed by Harmut Wickert (l. to r.): Hartmut Lange, Rainer Piwek, Ursula Minelic, Markus Graf, and Martina Struppek. As pictured here, the production incorporated Edward Kienholz's sculpture *The Portable War Memorial* and Bruce Naumann's neon sculpture *EAT/DEATH*. (copyright Guido Kasper)

Buried Child, which won the Pulitzer Prize for drama in 1979, was revived by Steppenwolf Theater in 1995 and transferred to Broadway in 1996, when it was nominated for the Tony Award for best play of the year. Pictured here in the revival (l. to r.): Jim Mohr, James Gammon, Lois Smith, and Leo Burmester. (copyright T. Charles Erickson)

The movie elevated Shepard's status from novice film actor to sex symbol. Even his wife O-Lan said later, "Sam was so hot in *Resurrection* that I wrote him a filthy fan letter." And *Playgirl* magazine named Sam Shepard one of the ten sexiest men in America that year (some of the others were Senator Gary Hart, Willie Nelson, David Steinberg, Tom Brokaw, Billy Dee Williams, and Bob Seger).

The Magic Theater revived its production of *True West* the following summer and moved it to a larger commercial theater in San Francisco, but it was an enterprising young theater company in Chicago that redeemed the play's reputation in New York. Steppenwolf Theater, a thirteen-member acting ensemble, mounted a rip-roaring comic production which promptly moved to off-Broadway, where critics proclaimed it "the true *True West.*" Directed by Gary Sinise, who also played Austin as a bespectacled wimp (unlike Peter Coyote—the Magic Theater's Austin—and Tommy Lee Jones, who were hunky Shepard lookalikes), the Steppenwolf production downplayed the play's mythical aspects and exploited its comic anarchy by turning the relationship between Austin and Lee into a sort of Blues Brothers slapstick routine. The star of the show was a young actor never before seen in New York named John Malkovich, who out-Belushied Belushi as Lee: picking his nose with the fervor of an archaeologist uncovering Mayan treasures, exploding into terrifying violence when his brother tries to push money on him, using a butter knife to help load paper into a typewriter. Sinise said he directed Malkovich "to find the dumbest side of himself, the place where his brain just stops." But his finest moments revealed the soulful side of scuzzy Lee, the patch of poetry that Shepard sews into the collar of his filthy white T-shirt, as in this exchange about a suburban house he's thinking of burgling:

Austin: What kind of a place was it?

Lee: Like a paradise. Kinda' place that sorta' kills ya' inside. Warm yellow lights. Mexican tile all around. Copper pots hangin' over the stove. Ya' know like they got in the magazines. Blonde people movin' in and outa' the rooms, talkin' to each other. Kinda' place you wish you sorta' grew up in, ya know.

"People kept saying *True West* is so commercial, but I think it's a more personal play than most of his," Malkovich said in an interview with *The Village Voice.* "Shepard, like Lee, defies all the things we're told we have to do to be successful. He spent years in a loft picking his nose and writing really punk stuff with Patti Smith, and then he wins a Pulitzer. He's like Austin when he shrugs off his writing to go make all these movies, but then he'll turn around and, like, trash Papp in *The New York Times*—that's such a Lee-like thing to do. Lee is the side of Shepard that's always being strangled but never quite killed."

True West settled down for a long off-Broadway run at the Cherry Lane Theater. And partly because of Malkovich's exciting New York debut, the show actually became something of a chic event, attracting such celebrities as Lauren Bacall, Morgan Fairchild, David Rabe, Jill Clayburgh, Stiller and Meara, Susan Sarandon, Kurt Vonnegut, Jamie Lee Curtis, John Denver, and Jacqueline Onassis accompanied by her son John Kennedy, Jr. As the show went on, the Steppenwolf actors left and were replaced by such up-and coming movie and TV stars as James Belushi, Tim Matheson, Daniel Stern, Randy and Dennis Quaid, and Erik Estrada. It was also produced at the National Theater in London under the direction of filmmaker John Schlesinger. But when the production was videotaped for the PBS series *American Playhouse*—the first major play of Shepard's to be done in any other medium—the cast featured Sinise and Malkovich. The videotape, first shown nationally in January 1984, is even better than the live version of the Steppenwolf production and a first-class documentation of Shepard's play.

After the initial brouhaha, Shepard had little to do with the various productions of *True West,* but he did say, "Right now I don't want to open anything in New York. I'd rather open everything here with no strings attached"—here being San Francisco. He canceled the five-year first-refusal arrangement he had with Joe Papp after *True West.* "I paid Papp back what I owed him and said sayonara," Shepard explained. "I'm not saying I'd never do another show in New York. . . . But there's no reason we couldn't do something here and take it to New York. We've got actors out here who are every bit as good as New York actors."

Ironically, the next Shepard play to open in New York was by O-Lan, a musical called *After Stardrive* co-written with Kathleen Cramer. *After Stardrive* was originally produced in 1979 by the

Overtone Theater, a music-theater company that O-Lan founded with the twenty thousand dollars she received on being fired from the cast of the Goldie Hawn movie *Private Benjamin* when a different director took over. In its first season, Overtone presented a jazz concert cum percussion demonstration called *Drum War,* which Sam Shepard conceived, directed, and played in with five other drummers. And the Overtone company featured, among others, Shepard's sister Roxanne Rogers, an actress who had appeared in several plays at the Magic Theater. *After Stardrive* was nominated for a Bay Area Theater Critics award, and in 1980 O-Lan Shepard and Kathleen Cramer won the award for their original score to *Katy Cruel,* another Overtone production. *After Stardrive,* a funky-cosmic tale about a woman whose mystical experiences renew her appreciation of life's small wonders, played at La Mama in May 1981.

O-Lan traveled to New York for rehearsals and the opening. Unlike her husband, she had nothing against New York and was happy to see old friends from Theater Genesis like Walter Hadler and Barbara Eda-Young, who were in her play. But she went right back to San Francisco to begin work on a new Overtone piece called *Superstitions* based on the prose pieces and journal entries that would eventually become *Motel Chronicles,* with music by Catherine Stone. When *Superstitions* opened at the Intersection Theater, its author was given as Walker Hayes who was supposedly born in Del Rio, attended the University of Oklahoma, and was currently residing with his mother on a cattle ranch in Texas. But everybody in town suspected what O-Lan didn't try to hide for long, that "Walker Hayes" was really a pseudonym for Sam Shepard. "Sam didn't want the hoopla," she said.

Together at the theater, the Shepards were a fascinating pair, Sam more than a foot taller than his tiny wife, though they both smoked constantly and had the same crooked front teeth. "In his worn leather jacket and jeans, he looked like one of the mythological cowboys he writes about. She was dressed all in black. With her long straight hair and saucer brown eyes, she was the epitome of a beatnik as painted by Keane," wrote Ruthe Stein, a *San Francisco Chronicle* reporter who met them backstage. "O-Lan was as bubbly as her husband was reserved. She warmly greeted friends in her dressing room, while Shepard, who has the reputation of being reclusive, sat quietly on a bench in the lobby, oblivious to the people staring at him."

At the time, Shepard was completely preoccupied with putting together *Motel Chronicles* (published in November 1982 and dedicated to his mother) and told his agent he hadn't thought about writing a play for months. He told John Lion he was on a "redhaired people from Texas" kick, studying up on Texas history, but nothing came of that. A lot of his energy went into movies.

He went off to Seattle to film *Frances* in the fall, and in January 1982, in Los Angeles, he had a dinner date with Jessica Lange that made headlines. Approached by three celebrity-hound photographers outside the Ports Restaurant in West Hollywood, Shepard blew his top: he screamed obscenities and slung his leather jacket at the paparazzi, whose blurry snaps of a wild-eyed guy with a contorted face and a blond woman with her hands over her mouth made the wire services the next day. The incident supplied gossip columnists with the first evidence of an offscreen romance between Shepard and Lange; the next evidence was probably the film itself, in which Shepard was extremely convincing as the devil-may-care intimate playmate of an ambitious, independent movie actress. Driving back home to San Francisco after finishing *Frances,* he conceived a screenplay that he wanted to direct himself called *Synthetic Tears* about a guy who tries to rehabilitate his long-lost father and reunite him with his family. He took meetings on this movie and that movie, met Chuck Yeager to prepare for shooting *The Right Stuff*, and huddled with Wim Wenders to discard one movie idea after another until they hit on *Paris, Texas*.

Not a lot of writing got done. The truth was, he was slowing down, taking it easy, spending time with his son Jesse, a happy blond kid who was now eleven years old. When people asked him what he wanted to be when he grew up, Jesse often said, "A football player and a poet," but he was showing signs of catching the theater bug from his parents: he acted in a play with two other kids at the 1984 Padua Hill Playwrights Festival. For Shepard, hanging out with his son meant teaching him to rope cattle or taking him on camping trips—"macho cowboy stuff," as O-Lan called it.

Shepard was also working on his relationship with his own father. In April 1982 Sam and O-Lan took a trip to New Mexico with Scarlett and Johnny to visit Sam Sr.—a visit that probably formed the basis of a father-son encounter described in *Motel Chronicles*. "The old man was sitting hunched over in a Maple rocker with stained pillows strapped to the seat and back. He was just sitting there in a barren cement room. His beard was long and red. His hair stood up at the back like a rooster. He wore an old black quilted jacket that had faded yellow spots from the sun," Shepard recalled. "He hadn't been visited in quite a while. On the floor beside him was a bottle of Dickel's Sour Mash in a brown bag, a white plastic plate overflowing with cigarette butts, and a small cardboard box with newspaper sticking out the top of it."

The father picked up the cardboard box and started unwrapping strange little presents and handing them to his son: a black and white plastic horse with a rubber saddle, a silver belt buckle saying "State of Texas," a green ceramic frog with some initials carved on the bottom, a black rock from the desert. "The son kept collecting all the objects in his lap and wished he'd brought something for the old man," Shepard wrote in his memoir. "He took off his straw Resistol cowboy hat, reached over and placed it on his father's head. It fit perfect."

While *The Right Stuff* was being filmed, a new play started forming in Shepard's mind. Drawn from his new life in films, his reestablished contact with his father, and his budding romance with Jessica Lange, the play was already being listed in the Magic Theater's subscription brochure as an upcoming attraction before it was even finished. It had a title, and a provocative one—*Fool for Love*—but its birth was slow and painful; by comparison *True West* was a snap. "I wrote about 16 versions of it, and every time I came back to the first five pages. I'd write like 70, 80 pages and then bring it all the way back to the first five pages and start again—throw out 60, 70 pages. So I've got literally at least a dozen different versions of the play, but the first five pages are the same in every one," said Shepard. "They weren't just drafts. Every time I think *this is the play.* I'm not writing a draft—I wrote twelve *plays.*"

Fool for Love takes place in a motel room on the edge of the Mojave Desert, where two estranged lovers meet like a couple of storm clouds. Eddie's been off having an affair with a glamor queen, and May's divided her time between cursing him and weeping for his return. Until now, that is—she's getting ready to go out with another man. She isn't happy to see Eddie, but she doesn't want him to go, either. They scream, they kiss, they cry, they attack each other, they bang on the walls, they slam the doors, they show off for each other: he practices roping the corners of the bedstead, and she changes clothes from a drab skirt to a black slip and sexy red dress right in front of him. Eddie's girl-friend, whom May calls "the Countess," drives by outside and shoots out the windshield of his truck; later she returns to blow up his rig and let his horses go. May's date, a regular fellow named Martin, walks in on them fighting and stays to hear the story of their forbidden love. Together since high school, Eddie and May discovered too late that both their mothers loved, lived with, and had a child by the same man—who sits onstage in his rocking chair drinking whiskey, though he exists only in the minds of May and Eddie.

When Shepard finally showed up at the Magic Theater with the play, it still wasn't done. "I suppose I saw about the eleventh draft of *Fool.*" said John Lion. "Anyway, the draft I finally saw had Ed-die, May, and Martin in it but not the 'princess.' This was odd to me, because we had auditioned about a hundred actresses for the part of the 'princess,' sight unseen. This draft, draft eleven, also didn't have 'the old man' in it, but the story was essentially there. I was convinced it would play like gangbusters, but it somehow seemed 'square.' (I don't mean the attitude, I mean the shape.) It was pretty linear, unusual for Sam, and I remarked on it. 'Maybe it needs a three-quarter circle surrounding three points of the square,' I said. Three weeks later, we had the completed script, with 'the old man.' "

As writers sometimes do, Shepard later came to feel that he may have gone too far in rewriting *Fool for Love*. "Basically when you get down to it, I worked it *too much*. I tried to hone it so carefully that I think I overcrafted it," he told the *New Yorker*'s Stephen Schiff. "I knew there was the thing going on between these two forces, but it seemed to want to go in so many different directions. I tried a lot of different streets with it. The one I ended up with, which is the sister-brother thing, now seems kind of like a cop-out. At the time it didn't seem easy or facile, but now I feel like I turned a trick on it where it didn't need a trick. It needed something else. I did like including the old man, the narrator. But when it suddenly goes off into this sister-brother, it goes haywire. I don't mind admitting that, because I see it as a misfire. I don't even know what I'd do now if I was going to re-write it, but I think the brother-sister thing is an attempt to bring a wholeness to it that didn't work."

It doesn't take much guessing to figure out that "the old man" is Sam Sr., especially when the script describes the character as having "a scraggly red beard" and wearing "a sun-bleached dark quilted jacket." Shepard readily admits that there are autobiographical references in *Fool for Love*. "One little talk, about Barbara Mandrell, is almost a verbatim conversation with my dad the last time I saw him. And there's a story about a cow field that he told my sister and she told me." What he doesn't acknowledge is how much the story of *Fool for Love*—a movie stuntman who's run off with a rich cover girl has it out in a motel room with his childhood sweetheart—sounds like the final blowout in his thirteen-year marriage to O-Lan. And who else could the Countess be but Jessica Lange?

May: You missed my neck?

Eddie: I missed all of you but your neck kept coming up for some reason. I kept crying about your neck.

May: Crying?

Eddie: Yeah. Weeping. Like a little baby....

May: Was this before or after your little fling with the Countess?

Eddie: There wasn't any fling with any Countess!

May: You're a liar.

Eddie: I took her out to dinner once, okay?

May: Ha!

Eddie: Twice.

May: You were bumping her on a regular basis! Don't gimme that shit.

Eddie: You can believe whatever you want.

May: I'll believe the truth! It's less confusing.

It's true that almost as soon as he finished directing the first production of *Fool for Love* at the Magic, Shepard left his family home to move in with Lange, who had bought some land near Santa Fe. And his anthology *Fool for Love and Other Plays* is dedicated to Jessica. But it would be a mistake to narrowly interpret the play as autobiography. *Fool for Love* is basically a continuation of *True West* by other means, an investigation of "double nature" pitting not man against himself but man against woman, or the male part against the female part of the same person. "I was determined to write some kind of confrontation between a man and a woman, as opposed to just men," Shepard told Bernard Weiner of the *San Francisco Chronicle*. "I wanted to try to take this leap into a female character, which I had never really done. I felt obliged to, somehow. But it's hard for a man to say he can speak from the point of view of a woman. But you make the attempt."

The play might well be called *True Love*: it wants to know where love comes from and where it goes when it's gone. Eddie and May each received by inheritance two incompatible attitudes toward love—their mothers were each in their own ways devoted to one man, while their father was torn between two. Is the man destined to be the one who always runs away? Will the woman always be left behind? Or will they torture each other forever, bouncing back and forth between those two attitudes, only occasionally connecting?

At first *Fool for Love* seems like a simple, straightforward, incredibly passionate love story, the theatrical equivalent of a corny but heartfelt country-and-western ballad. Shepard's first instruction in the script is "This play is to be performed relentlessly without a break," and he opens and closes the play with Merle Haggard songs, first "Wake Up" and then "I'm the One Who Loves You." The sheer physical force of the play inspired one critic to call it "a motel-room *Phèdre.*" And directing the play himself, Shepard emphasized both the musicality of *Fool for Love* and its relentlessness by miking the walls of the set so every slam of the door was emphasized. What can be more resounding than the sound of your lover walking out the door? It doesn't happen just once, either, like at the end of *A Doll's House,* but over and over again until it becomes torturous music, a repeating pattern of physical rejection.

For such a simple play, *Fool for Love* has a lot in it. When the play opened at the Magic Theater in February 1983, the leading roles featured Ed Harris, who had acted in productions of *Cowboy Mouth* and *True West* in Los Angeles and had co-starred with Shepard in *The Right Stuff;* and Kathy Whitton Baker, who'd appeared at the Magic Theater in *Seduced* and *Curse of the Starving Class.* The entire production moved to New York intact and opened in June at the Circle Repertory Theater, a respected off-

Broadway theater not much larger than the Magic. Ed Harris was indisputably the star of the show—his blazing good looks and charging-bull performance had the impact of a nuclear reaction going off right there in the room.

Harris had to leave the production after only three weeks in New York to make a movie (Robert Benton's *Places in the Heart*), and he was replaced by Will Patton, a young actor who had worked extensively with Joe Chaikin. Although he looked remarkably similar to Harris—blond, balding, soft-spoken, muscular, sexy—Patton radically changed how the play came across to the audience. Harris so dominated the stage as Eddie that *Fool for Love* seemed to be saying that sex roles are fixed, the woman is always the helpless victim, and the man is always the one who comes and goes as he pleases. When Patton took over the role, he made it less macho and more androgynous, and Kathy Baker became more an equal partner in the battle of the sexes, suggesting that their roles were more fluid, that they both had mixed blood, one minute emotionally dependent, the next minute ready to hit the road. Without changing a word of the script, they gave the play a different, somehow more hopeful interpretation.

Fool for Love became an instant smash hit—like Steppenwolf's *True West*, which was still running—and eventually moved to a larger theater. As usual, there was a certain amount of turnover in the cast, partly because of the long run and partly because the play is so physically arduous. On opening night Ed Harris scraped his knuckle, and the steady trickle of blood throughout the performance only made it more riveting. During his stint in the play, Patton suffered many injuries and his hands swelled to twice their original size. Ellen Barkin, the popular young actress from *Diner* and *Tender Mercies*, was signed to replace Kathy Baker, but during rehearsals she broke her arm and had to drop out. At the end of the season Ed Harris and Kathy Baker both received Obie awards for their performances in *Fool for Love*, as did Will Patton—the first time in Obie history that a replacement won an acting award. Shepard received his ninth Obie, breaking his own record for number of awards over the years, but what made him especially proud was that he won it not only for writing but also for directing *Fool for Love*.

In terms of conventional drama, *True West* and *Fool for Love* are by far Shepard's best-written plays. They are masterfully crafted, at once suspenseful, funny, and moving. They each pay homage to his fetish for real-time stage actions—a dozen toasters sending up smoke signals in act two of *True West,* Eddie's roping the bedstead and the amplified door-slamming in *Fool*—and they're not entirely without flights into monologue. But they display much more control and discipline than previous Shepard plays, which was an advantage in two respects: it silenced critics who complained that Shepard purposely left plays unfinished or in first-draft form, and more important, it expanded his audience to include regular theatergoers—the kind who may go to movies and musicals but would be scared off by an "avant-garde" play.

While appreciating *True West* and *Fool for Love* as good plays, however, many long-time Shepard fans felt that his most recent plays lacked daring. *True West* did smack of sit-coms, and *Fool for Love* was a kind of soap opera, even though both of them were much better than anything you'd actually see on television. But that's just it—here was a writer at the peak of his powers turning out plays that, however thoughtful and well-written, didn't project much further than his own personal life. The movies that he chose to act in, whether *Days of Heaven* or *The Right Stuff* or *Country,* allowed him to invest some of his imagination in projects of a larger scale that made some comment on society. What if Shepard used the full extent of his writing talent to probe for deeper gold, or to take in more of the world at large?

It's possible that he chose not to because he wanted to keep his plays small enough to be done at intimate theaters like the Magic. Once you start having lavish sets and too many characters, you have to think in terms of Broadway, which doesn't interest Shepard. "I don't know who to address on Broadway," he said once. "I always felt I was writing for people who would understand me. I never had any aspiration to talk to people I don't know. It's a question of strangers versus friends. I'm not interested in speaking to a big mass audience. I don't see the point."

It might also be that he felt he didn't have the chops to write plays any more ambitious than these. He liked this passage from Flann O'Brien's *The Third Policeman* enough to quote it in the program when the Magic revived *Suicide in B-flat:* "The night seemed to have reached its middle point of intensity and the darkness was now much darker than before. My brain was brimming with half-formed ideas of the most far-reaching character but I repressed them firmly and determined to confine myself wholly to finding the bicycle and going home." And he hinted that he might have exhausted his theatrical imagination, which didn't necessarily disturb him. "I can't seem to quit. I'd like to be free of it once and for all," he said once. "I hope I write something that's, you know, a grand finale, and I won't have to go on, or else I'll be able to change to something else, like a novel."

But Shepard had barely turned forty when he said that. He'd never been a writer to coast on his credentials or to let his imagination go unchallenged for long. It's not surprising, then, that after *Fool for Love* he decided to collaborate once more with his friend and mentor Joseph Chaikin.

Their first discussions took the form of notes and letters exchanged by mail. The gestation period of the play that would be called *The War in Heaven*—1982 and 1983—coincided with the time of Shepard's meeting Jessica Lange and leaving his wife for her. In February of 1983 he wrote to Chaikin, "These days I keep getting hit in the chest by a sadness I can't even name. It seems at times like it's much broader than a personal loss over 'someone.' Anything can trigger it off—but especially Vivaldi. I never really listened to his stuff before, but it carries some kind of humbling testimony—to God, I guess. The music seems to celebrate a victory where man is the loser. I know I indulge myself in these feelings and I'm always alone when they're expressed. They seem to be a dialogue between me and myself, but I'm not sure what their purpose is. I guess I dread this aloneness more than anything, but it always returns no matter who I'm with or how much I'm in love."

By August of that year, Shepard was writing to Chaikin from a new address. He had permanently moved out on O-Lan, and Jessica Lange had ended her six-year-long relationship with ballet superstar Mikhail Baryshnikov. Together they resettled with Lange's baby daughter, Shura, on a ranch they bought outside of Santa Fe. The area suited both of them perfectly. For one thing, there was plenty of space for the horses (Jessica rides, too). And it was close enough to dreaded Hollywood that they could go back and forth on movie business if need be, yet off the beaten path so they could maintain a semblance of anonymity. Nowadays, either one of them was sufficient to draw a crowd of celebrity seekers, and the sight of the two of them together was liable to disturb the peace. Santa Fe was either pokey enough or sufficiently sophisticated not to gawk if Jessica and Sam chose to perform a steamy screen kiss in the middle of lunch at the Staab House or if Sam observed the local custom of forgoing the indoor facilities to relieve himself against the wall of his favorite bar, the Pink Adobe.

Besides, being in Santa Fe meant that Shepard could keep an eye on his father, who was drinking heavily and becoming quite senile. When he went to see a local production of *True West,* the first play by his son he'd ever seen, Sam Sr. was drunk and talked back to the play—not unlike Bob Dylan at *Geography of a Horse Dreamer* in New York. "He could recognize little bits and pieces of the family, so he would get up and talk," said Shepard. "I wasn't there, but I heard that after the play was over somebody found out he was my old man, and the entire audience applauded him. It made his day."

Still, it wasn't easy to forget about the family life he'd left behind in San Francisco, any easier than it was for O-Lan and the others to detach themselves from him. Even as O-Lan's divorce papers were making their way through the courts, she was appearing in New York at La Mama with the Overtone Theater's double bill of *Superstitions* and Shepard's bicentennial opus *The Sad Lament of Pecos Bill on the Eve of Killing His Wife.*

Writing from Santa Fe, Shepard confessed to Chaikin that he was "exhausted" and "still in a strange transition," as if he'd been "swept up in a hurricane and landed in a strange land." He'd been doing some writing for film, "but I have a dread of movie executives," he said. "The thing is, with film you can get into so many states. Theater has such limitations—language and the body of the actor. . . . I just can't write another play right now." He proposed trying the kind of free-form workshop situation that produced *Tongues* and *Savage/Love,* perhaps at a university. Chaikin called up Robert Brustein at Harvard's American Repertory Theater, who quickly agreed to sponsor the project.

The workshop began in the middle of January 1984, as soon as Shepard could travel to Boston after *Country* finished its location shooting in Iowa. The American Repertory Theater provided them with a working space, a musician, and a lighting designer, and they went to work. For a while there was a possibility that Jessica Lange would participate in the workshop, too, but Shepard and Chaikin ultimately decided to bring in Michelle George, an actress who had worked with Peter Brook's company and had directed several of Shepard's plays in Canada. Some theater students who volunteered to do research were asked to locate a copy of Thomas Mann's essay on Schopenhauer, to make photocopies of all references to angels in the Bible, and to find out about an angel who had supposedly been put in jail in Utah.

"This thing that me and Sam are doing, there's no setup for this kind of impromptu work," said Chaikin about the ART workshop. "Sam and I have a long and deep friendship. He's reeling from his different identities. We talked a lot about directions in the theater. How he feels stuck yet excited is something we talked about all along. We started in one direction, abandoned it, started in a second direction and left that, started a third time, and we're staying on it. The way we work is I improvise once we come up with a character. The working title is *War in Heaven,* but that can always change. He said, 'The last thing I wanna do is write a play now.' He said, 'I've come all this way to work with you, not to write a play.' "

While Shepard and Chaikin spent seven or eight hours a day in a windowless room working, the actors and administration of the ART walked around in something of a tizzy at the star in their midst. "I'm agog," Brustein admitted. "All the women in the company are out of their minds. He has some special charisma." One day a young fan brought a present for Shepard in a cardboard tube and gave it to Jan Geidt, the publicity director for the theater. She picked up the tube, and a bottle of tequila fell out and shattered on the floor. Mortified, she went downstairs and explained the situation to Shepard, whose only response was, "Well, you've got a worm on your floor somewhere." Just then Geidt's assistant came running in with a paper towel saying, "Jan, look what I found!" Shepard said, "There it is," and popped the worm into his mouth.

While he was at Harvard, Shepard was very gracious with the students, speaking at seminars to young actors, directors, and playwrights. He looked in on a rehearsal of *Big River,* a musical based on *Huckleberry Finn* that the ART was producing, and he and Lange attended a performance of Brecht's *Mother Courage,* starring Linda Hunt, at the Boston Shakespeare Company. He and Chaikin were supposed to do a public presentation of their work-in-progress, but they decided that they had to work on the piece a lot more before showing it to anyone, even in an open-rehearsal situation. And since Chaikin had an immediate commitment to direct a play in Israel, they disbanded the workshop after two weeks.

To make matters worse, Shepard had started attracting so much publicity that it was impossible for him to work. A local gossip columnist printed an item saying that he and Jessica Lange had been spotted frequently at a particular coffee shop on Beacon Hill, and when newspapers announced that he would lecture at Harvard about his and Chaikin's workshop process, photographers showed up on the lawn at the place where he was staying. Shepard got so pissed off that he canceled the talk and refused to go out of the house. As soon as he could, he left town and drove back to Santa Fe. He and Chaikin agreed that they would resume their workshop later in the year, and if a play came out of it Brustein would produce it the following season at the ART.

It was not to be. On May 7, Chaikin underwent emergency heart surgery, and although he had survived two heart attacks before, this time heart failure was accompanied by a stroke that left him seriously ill and incapable of speaking, making it extremely doubtful that he would ever be able to perform again. Chaikin's illness was one of three severe emotional blows that Shepard received in the spring of 1984. In March came the death of Lord Pentland, the English-born leader of the Gurdjieff movement in America. And Shepard had barely returned from Pentland's funeral in suburban New York when his own father got hit by a car in Santa Fe and died at the age of sixty-seven.

His father's death was devastating to Shepard. After fighting with the old man all through adolescence and keeping his distance throughout much of his adult life, he was just beginning to make peace with his father, to care for him as a person, to recognize in his father many aspects of himself. Especially now that he had an adolescent son of his own, especially now that he had left his son's mother to go live on the edge of the desert with another woman, Shepard found himself *becoming* his father in ways he'd never dreamed of, and he felt a new compassion for this wizened, helpless old man he'd judged so harshly for so long. And now he was gone.

"I think there are basically two roads: You either die like a dog or you die like a man. And if you die like a dog, you just go back to dust. All that stuff in the Bible is absolutely true. Dust to dust," Shepard mused. "I had my dad cremated, you know? There wasn't much left of him to begin with. They give you this box with the ashes in it. The box is like it's got a spotlight on it or something, because that's *him,* and yet it's just this little leather box."

Sam's father received a veteran's funeral at the National Cemetery in Santa Fe. Shepard attended with his two sisters, his Uncle Buzz, and his uncle's wife. He was surprised at how many people showed up for the service — drinking buddies, neighbors from the housing complex, his father's Mexican caretaker Esteban. "Me and my younger sister took turns reading some Lorca poems (my dad's favorite poet)," he later recalled, "and I even attempted a passage from the Bible but choked on the words 'All is vanity,' because I suddenly saw my own in reading this as though I understood its true meaning. I couldn't speak at all for a while. Nothing came out. My whole face quivered, and I could sense the embarrassment from the gathering. I felt no embarrassment myself, only a terrible knotted grief that couldn't find expression. I stood there, waiting for it to pass, but it didn't. It held me there for what seemed like a very long time, until finally it dissolved enough to allow me to finish. I read the rest of the passage without emotion and with no connection to any of the words. I was just grateful to get through it."

Shepard never felt more torn in his whole life—cut off from his past, uprooted from his wife and child, euphorically pitching himself into an uncertain but absorbing future with his new love. The frenzy of emotions was almost overpowering. Christmas of 1983 had been particularly hard. It was the first time he'd been separated from his family for Christmas since his son Jesse was born. He spent the holidays in Iowa with Jessica Lange and her three-year-old daughter Shura, who missed her own daddy something fierce too. Trying to console a kicking and screaming little girl who regarded him as a well-intentioned stranger, Shepard thought about the various places he'd set down roots. He owned an overgrown farm on the Bay of Fundy in Nova Scotia. He had a ranch for raising horses in California just north of San Francisco. He lived in New Mexico with a tin-roofed barn out back full of alfalfa. Yet here he was, thousands of miles from any of those places, buffeted by forces of nature and the human heart that he just didn't understand.

Suddenly, it all felt strangely familiar.

It felt like it had always been this way.

He was the successful son of a man who died with no money and broken dreams, and his father's example lived on in his blood, the hidden side, the dark side, the path not taken. He remained emotionally tied to his wife through their son and the history of their fifteen-year marriage, even as he carried on a highly publicized affair with another film celebrity. He was a poor boy from a California avocado farm who never finished college, and now he was one of the most famous writers and familiar faces of his generation. All the questions he had ever pursued in his work came flying back at him with the full strength of their mystery.

Who am I? Who is the real me—the inside me or the outside me, the person I know or the person I show to the world?

Chapter Eight:

SPLIT SCREEN

I look at the screen and I am the screen. I'm not me. I don't know who I am. I look at the movie and I am the movie. I am the star. I am the star in the movie. For days I am the star and I'm not me. I'm me being the star.

—Miss Scoons in *Angel City*

When Sam Shepard met Peter Brook in London in 1973, the renowned stage director asked the playwright, "What is character?" Shepard really had to stop and think. When he was younger, he would probably have shrugged and said, "A person and what he's doing that day." That was the distinction of Shepard's early plays. His characters weren't realistically drawn, psychologically calibrated individuals introduced by occupation, appearance, and attitude in half-page descriptions like the people in plays by Shaw or O'Neill. They were fluid images, overlapping personas moving through the world, changing faces and identities according to whim, survival instinct, or chemical inspiration. Kids in the sixties, in other words, liberated from the past enough to live out their dreams in public. "When I started writing, I wasn't interested in character at all. In fact, I thought it was useless, old-fashioned, stuck in a certain way," he says. "But I had broken away from the idea of character without understanding it."

Shepard's ideas about character started changing while he was in England, for three reasons. One was his contact with Brook, who like Shepard was a student of Gurdjieff, or as they say, "in the work." (Brook directed the 1979 film *Meetings With Remarkable Men* based on Gurdjieff's philosophical memoir.) "Character has become much more important to me. I learned that from Peter Brook," says Shepard. "I don't know him that well, and I've had only a few brief meetings with him, but he's had a real influence on me over the years. He's presented things to me that I still think about *now*, that were presented to me back in the early seventies."

The playwright also turned thirty in 1973 while living in England, and he was getting old enough to realize that underneath the variety of images he had been playing out in his life and work—cowboy, rock star, musician, playwright, father, lover—was something constant, steady, possibly old as the hills, something that defines identity, character. If only he could figure out what it was. That dichotomy between the self that changes and the self that stays the same, the self that you make up and the self that your family/society/culture makes up for you, runs through Shepard's work. And always, the struggle to integrate the two.

Finally, when he started acting in films, it gave him a new perspective on character from the inside. He found himself doing the kind of exercises he'd ridiculed Method actors for, like making up personal histories of the characters he played. It was scary, and that's what he liked. "When you put yourself in the position of being an actor, you not only learn about your vulnerabilities, but also about the ways in which you're not vulnerable," he says. "For me, it has to do with opening up, and there are certain dangerous areas that are very closed."

To some extent Sam Shepard has always been a movie star, at least in his head. "I remember trying to imitate Burt Lancaster's smile after I saw him and Gary Cooper in *Vera Cruz*," he wrote in *Motel Chronicles,* the journal he kept when he started spending a lot of time in rented rooms while making movies. "For days I practiced in the back yard. Weaving through the tomato plants. Sneering. Grinning that grin. Sliding my upper lip up over my teeth. After a few days of practice I tried it out on the girls at school. They didn't seem to notice. I broadened my interpretation until I started getting strange reactions from the other kids. They would look straight at my teeth and a fear would creep into their eyes. I'd forgotten how bad my teeth were. How one of the front ones was dead and brown and overlapped the broken one right next to it. I'd actually come to believe I was in possession of a full head of perfect pearly Burt Lancaster-type of teeth. I didn't want to scare anyone so I stopped grinning after that. I only did it in private. Pretty soon even that faded. I returned to my empty face."

When Shepard did become a film star (bad teeth and all), the ironic thing was that it came after literally years of serious effort to break into the movies—but as a writer. Like everybody else in his generation he grew up on John Wayne and John Huston, James Dean and James Bond, the ideal entertainment and the great escape. " 'What dya' say we take in a movie?' What a great sound that has," says Tympani in one of *Angel City*'s most hilarious speeches. "What dya' say we just lose ourselves forever in the miracle of film? We nestle down, just the two of us, with a big box of buttered popcorn, a big cup of Seven-Up, a big box of Milk Duds, a giant box of Black Crows, and we just chew ourselves straight into oblivion?" And throughout his writing there are flickering references to movies as a model art form. Various plays are subtitled "a staged film" or "a movie for the stage," and he always said that *The Tooth of Crime* was "built like *High Noon*, like a machine Western."

Shepard had his eye on the real thing, too. He first tried his hand at screenwriting as long ago as 1965, when he worked on a film called *Me and My Brother* by Robert Frank, a documentary filmmaker famous for *Pull My Daisy*, a portrait of Jack Kerouac and friends, and *Cocksucker Blues*, his movie about the Rolling Stones. *Me and My Brother* was about Julius Orlovsky, the clinically schizophrenic brother of Peter Orlovsky, poet and companion of Allen Ginsberg; the film featured footage of Julius as well as of Joe Chaikin playing the role of Julius, and Shepard apparently contributed dialogue for the nondocumentary scenes. When the film opened in 1969, the credits said "written and directed by Robert Frank," but Shepard always claimed it among his early movie credits, along with *Zabriskie Point*.

After *Zabriskie Point* his feelings about working in film were mixed. Well, not even mixed. "I hate it," he said at the time, "because it's never just that. It has to do with studios, with pleasing certain people, cutting things down, and rewriting. It's not a writer's medium, it's a director's medium—the writer is just superfluous." Still, Shepard got plenty of mileage out of being handpicked to write Antonioni's first American film. "As soon as you start writing a movie you get these scripts showing up in the mail. Can you do this one? Can you do that one? Twenty thousand for this one and thirty thousand for that one. It's like an open auction—suddenly you're in the screenwriters' market."

He did spend some time working with Tony Richardson, then very hot for directing *Tom Jones*, on his adaptation of the Jacobean play *The Changeling* called *The Bodyguard*, but they were never able to sell the finished screenplay. The same thing happened with *Maxagasm*, the movie he wrote for the Rolling Stones. (The film world is so small—instead of *The Bodyguard* or *Maxagasm*, Tony Richardson and Mick Jagger went off to Australia together and made *Ned Kelly*.) There was also *Ringaleevio*, a dense, *Operation Sidewinder*-ish screenplay he wrote with Murray Mednick and dedicated to Crazy Horse, Mangas Coloradas, Jedediah

Smith, The Holy Yehudi, Kathleen and O-Lan (the writers' spouses), and Immanuel Velikofsky.

Once he resettled in California, Shepard spent a lot of serious time and work trying to crack the movie industry. His lack of success no doubt contributed to his periodic depression, and he vented his frustration, of course, in *Angel City*. He really thought that the Rolling Thunder experience with Bob Dylan would turn into a real movie. He started writing a screenplay about Koko the talking gorilla for German director Barbet Schroeder, but that didn't get very far. He wrote a treatment for a film called *Kindred Ties* about a couple who hires an Indian girl to have their baby, and he completed a screenplay called *Seventh Son* about warring gangsters in the child-pornography trade.

The screenplay that he got most involved with and that went the farthest was *Fractured,* which he conceived soon after moving to Marin County, finished while he was directing *Action* at the Magic Theater, and sent around to many of the same people who read *Manfly,* his adaptation of the Faust legend. *Fractured* was a comic/romantic extrapolation of Shepard's own life as a suburban rancher who makes his money from show business. In the script the hero's name is Massey (Shepard's family and dear friends called him Sammy), and his wife is Lou-Anne (just like O-Lan, whose nickname is Lo). The story opens with an Appaloosa mare rampaging through the living room of a modern suburban California home—wonderful frightening image—and the wife fleeing with her kid in a pickup to visit her sister in San Francisco. Lou-Anne complains that the mailbox is always full of magazines like the *Western Horseman* and the *Quarter Horse Journal* and that her husband spends all his time at rodeos when he should be at auditions. It turns out that Massey is a model for commercials—he's literally a Marlboro Man—but would rather be racing horses, and probably the reason the screenplay never made it to film was that it ended with a horse race that had little to do with the rest of the story.

The idea of modeling, having a face that could make money, must have been in Shepard's head. He wasn't unaware of his striking appearance, because he'd been hearing about it for years. During his days in New York, he acted in a couple of underground films that nobody ever saw: one called *Brand X* by Win Chamberlin and one made by his roommate Bill Hart called *Blood,* which was heavily influenced by John Cassavetes's *Faces* and consisted mostly of Shepard, Joyce Aaron, and Charles Mingus, Jr., sitting around talking and doing crazy things. The footage of *Blood* still exists, but it's never been put together. Hart says that Shepard was just as movie-star beautiful back then as he is now—enough so that he was offered the part in *Two-Lane Blacktop* that James Taylor ended up playing. Shepard turned it down because his wife was pregnant.

When *Days of Heaven* came along, it wasn't just a paying acting gig or an opportunity to exercise his vanity. Everything about the script must have rung Shepard's bells, from the fragment of Hamlin Garland's 1899 journal, *Boy Life on the Prairie,* which director Terrence Malick copied on the first page, to the showdown on the Texas wheatfield where his character ends up with a screwdriver in his chest. And the film was being shot on location in Alberta, Canada, mostly outdoors and far from Hollywood. It was irresistible. Shepard drove up from San Francisco in the middle of August 1976 and checked into the Holiday Inn in Lethbridge to begin the thirteen-week shoot.

Set a few years prior to World War I, at a time when industrialization had not yet overtaken agriculture as the American way of life, *Days of Heaven* concerns a hotheaded laborer named Bill who has to flee Chicago with his girlfriend Abby and his sister Linda when he fights and possibly kills the foreman of a steel mill. Along with a trainful of migrant workers, they end up harvesting wheat in Texas for a wealthy young farmer—"the richest man in the Panhandle"—who has his eye on Abby. Bill, who passes himself off as her brother, overhears a doctor telling the farmer that he has only a year to live and urges Abby to marry him, foreseeing a quick inheritance but not the genuine love that she conceives for the farmer. Looming behind the romantic triangle may be a morality play about the destruction of the land by men and machines, but the two levels don't connect in any obvious way (the farmer is not the villain, and Bill is not the hero).

The director's intent in casting Shepard as the farmer clearly had something to do with establishing that ambiguity. He wanted a wealthy gentleman who was also down-to-earth, a simple man with complicated feelings, a still-waters-run-deep kind of guy, and that's what he got. "The tension in Shepard's paradoxical self— the mind of a Kafka trapped in the body of a Jimmy Stewart— probably explains the triumphant success of his screen persona in *Days of Heaven,*" one critic wrote. "Everything the movie is busily declining to say out loud about the pioneer spirit as a vehicle for its own corruption, about the cult of the rugged individualist as a recourse for the frightened and sensitive, about a close relation with Nature as a tactic for suppressing one's human conscious- ness—is summed up in the lingering closeups of Shepard's face, handsome and expressionless."

The idea of acting under the scrutiny of a camera intimidated Shepard at first. He read some books and talked to a bunch of actors in advance to find out what it was like, he confided to a friend. But he discovered about movie acting the same thing he learned his first time out as a director—you just have to plunge in and do it. Jacob Brackman, who was Malick's second-unit di- rector on *Days of Heaven,* recalls that Shepard had trouble with some of the big emotional scenes he had to play. "When Terry would ask him to do something over and over, making it bigger, you'd see him off by himself just in a state, in a state of high anxi- ety, trying to work himself up for it—probably trying to remember something the other actors had told him about sense memory and so forth," says Brackman. "Terry wasn't very good at teaching him the tricks of acting, so sometimes he resorted to giving him im- ages. Like in the scene where he's supposed to go after Richard Gere in a jealous rage, he had trouble playing the emotion, so Terry had him squint his eyes and think of himself as a Western gunslinger."

As a Western-style hero, Shepard had some definite natural ad- vantages. He could ride a horse, shoot pheasant, and look right at home testing a stalk of wheat by crumpling it in his palm and tast- ing it. He had a sharp-nosed, aristocratic profile, yet from the front his face was round and soft, almost goofy; close-up he looked weathered, canny, possibly insane. "He has a very American face," says Nestor Almendros, the cinematographer on *Days of Heaven.* "Even the fact that his teeth weren't so good added to the credibil- ity of the role. Those people out in the country at that time prob- ably often had crooked or missing teeth. A lot of times it seems silly to me to see people in period movies with perfect teeth."

The lack of readily available orthodontia may, in fact, explain the tight-lipped nature of many Western heroes, not to mention Shepard's character in *Days of Heaven.* He's so laconic he seems like a silent-movie character, and his few lines are incredibly di- rect. "How long would yuh reckon I have?" he asks the doctor, and after "Where are yuh from?" practically the next thing he says to Abby is "I think I love you." But Shepard delivered them with the offhanded conviction of a country-and-western singer. Malick was terrifically impressed with Shepard's performance. "Everything in him is sterling," he told the crew.

Shepard made fun of his becoming an actor, though he wasn't the only novice in the cast. Brooke Adams as Abby had done a lot of television, but this was her first major film role, and Linda Manz as the tough-talking little girl had never acted before at all. The only one who'd been around movies much was Richard Gere, a last-minute replacement for John Travolta; Gere was also one of the few who knew Shepard was a playwright without being told, since he had performed the world premiere of *Killer's Head* and acted in an off-off-Broadway production of *Back Bog Beast Bait*. Gere and Shepard were friendly, but the situation became a little intense when the relationships among the actors, cooped up together in the isolation of Canadian countryside, began to reflect the storyline of the film. Gere and Brooke Adams, who knew each other slightly from before, started having an affair, and then two-thirds of the way through the shooting they broke up, and Brooke started having an affair with Sam. O-Lan came up to visit and went back home after a week, apparently unruffled by the romance with Brooke Adams. "It certainly wasn't the first time Sam had strayed," says Jacob Brackman. "They'd been married a long time and seemed to have some kind of understanding worked out." The emotional turbulence behind the scenes may explain, however, Shepard's hasty departure when his scenes were done.

Shepard enjoyed making the movie, and he enjoyed working with Malick, whom he referred to as an Okie Rhodes scholar. He was very quiet and shy around the set; when the location shifted to Waterton, he hung out some at the Kootemic Lodge, the only action in town, checking out the blond waitresses. Later, his favorite story about shooting *Days of Heaven* had to do with one of those technical tricks that the audience for a movie never even sees. During the scene when the wheat fields are burned to roust the invasion of locusts, crew members dropped the locusts (not real insects, but peanut shells and sycamore seeds) from helicopters first and then reversed the film so it looked like the locusts were flying out of the fire. That meant that during the few nights the scene was being filmed, all the actors and machinery had to do everything backwards, too—a bizarre sight.

Actually, not much of that scene remained in the final film, which underwent tremendous changes during the editing process. The voice-over narration originally done by Adams wound up being spoken by Manz in a blunt, street-angel rasp reminiscent of Patti Smith. And several scenes with Gere and Adams were either trimmed or cut; Gere, who was so exciting as Diane Keaton's S&M lover in *Looking for Mr. Goodbar,* seemed more pretty boy than ruffian, an idealized Ken-doll version of Shepard's natural man. At the Cannes Film Festival in 1979 Malick won the award for best direction, and Nestor Almendros received an Academy Award the following year for his stunning cinematography. But it was Shepard who walked off with the best reviews. "Though the irregularly handsome, slightly snaggletoothed Shepard has almost no lines," wrote Pauline Kael in *The New Yorker,* "he makes a strong impression; he seems authentically an American of an earlier era."

The first time Shepard appears onscreen in *Days of Heaven,* he's decked out in white shirt, tie, and suspenders and standing at a distance in front of his country castle, which rises up alone on the prairie like Reata Ranch in *Giant.* The first time you see him in *Resurrection,* his next movie appearance, he's a rowdy drunk in greasy jeans and a John Deere cap yelling and kicking in the flatbed of a truck with a nasty knife wound that would probably have killed him if Ellen Burstyn hadn't come along and stopped the bleeding with a laying on of hands. After nearly dying in a car crash that killed her husband, Edna Mae McCauley (Burstyn) finds herself blessed with the power of healing—a nosebleed here, a knife wound there—and pretty soon she has tentfuls of people seeking her help. After she saves handsome Calvin Carpenter (Shepard, of course), they become lovers, but Cal's preacher father starts denouncing her publicly for her refusal to attribute her gifts to an act of God. Watching her perform what are clearly miracles, Cal like many of her followers decides she is the living Christ, but the more she refuses to accept that role, the more he suspects she is a tool of Satan. Supposedly a rebel (he rides his motorcycle in a black T-shirt) but still subject to his fundamentalist upbringing, he finally goes berserk and tries to assassinate her.

Shepard is wonderful in *Resurrection,* playing the mean punk side of the same James Dean-like persona that was so romantically doomed in *Days of Heaven.* It's also uncanny how well these performances complement his plays. "On the one hand he is the aloof strangely serene farmer, as American as the soil he works, who hides a foreboding secret," one critic noted; "and on the other hand he is the James Dean rebel who can't escape his spiritual heritage and who therefore turns it toward an aesthetic act of designed cataclysm."

The movie took place in Kansas but was mostly shot in a little town in Texas called Shiner between San Antonio and Houston. Shepard stayed at the Holiday Inn in San Marcos and rode to the set every day with a couple of other actors. He particularly enjoyed studying the driver, "a Wrangler first and a Teamster second," who wore a black cowboy hat with three used toothpicks jammed into the hat band, "one of those braided horsehair kind of hat bands like the convicts make." Shepard spent his spare time listening to Stevie Wonder's *Songs in the Key of Life* and pining for O-Lan.

He took the part primarily because he wanted to work with Ellen Burstyn. "I think she's a genius," he said. "And I'm real interested in acting now. I don't really have my chops as an actor. I think it's easier for a nonactor to work in movies than onstage. Film has to do with the surface of things; onstage, nonactors don't fool you for a second." Burstyn was very impressed with his "nonacting," particularly his unstudied masculine grace. "Sam?" she said. "Sam is Gary Cooper."

The chemistry between Burstyn and Shepard on camera was unmistakable. O-Lan Shepard wasn't the only one who felt like writing her husband "a filthy fan letter" after *Resurrection.* That's more or less what he got from movie critics too. "His rangy sexuality— quiet but threatening—gives their affair a fresh, unpredictable texture," David Ansen wrote in *Newsweek* "There's nothing actorish about him, and his strong natural presence gives weight to a character whose motivations are only sketchily supplied. Shepard, who also happens to be one of our best and most challenging playwrights, invests his role with the same sense of lurking psychic violence that permeates his plays. If he wants it, he stands on the brink of an extraordinary new career in the movies."

Shepard wasn't sure if he wanted it. Robert Redford wanted him to be in *Brubaker,* he could have played Eugene O'Neill in Warren Beatty's *Reds,* and he was offered a leading role in *Urban Cowboy.* "They handed me some *Esquire* article about Gilley's and said, 'We're making a movie out of this.' They were talking about me doing a part, and I didn't see it. Who wants to ride a mechanical bull? I've ridden real ones and they're not fun. I just didn't see how it could make a very exciting film."

He turned them all down to make *Raggedy Man* with Sissy Spacek and Eric Roberts, another film shot in Texas. It was a very down-home production. The director was Jack Fisk, Spacek's husband, who had been the art director on *Days of Heaven,* and the screenwriter/co-producer was William Wittliff, whose previous credits included *Coal Miner's Daughter* (which featured Spacek's Oscar-winning performance as Loretta Lynn), *Honeysuckle Rose,* and *The Black Stallion.* In *Raggedy Man,* Spacek plays a divorcee with two little boys who works as a small-town telephone operator during World War II, and Roberts is a sailor on leave who for a few days relieves her loneliness. Shepard plays the title character, a creepy scarface who wears a long raincoat, drags a lawnmower around all day, and spies on Spacek's house. She complains to the town policeman, who assures her he's harmless ("You mean Bailey, face all boogered up?" goes the cop's succinct description), and only after he dies saving her and her kids from two psychotically horny townies does she discover that the Raggedy Man is her ex-husband, apparently so deformed by war wounds that she doesn't recognize him.

The situation of coming home and not being recognized seems to strike some emotional chord in Shepard (it turns up again and again in his plays, most notably *Buried Child*), but on the whole *Raggedy Man* seems like an unlikely project for him. Even though it's the title role, Bailey doesn't seem like a very interesting character to play. He doesn't really make sense, and he has no lines. "It's a real challenge," Shepard said at the time. "I want to do a kind of Japanese character with this guy. Like the Kurosawa films where characters are like apparitions. They don't speak but they have this whole physical thing."

The Raggedy Man has only a handful of scenes, and in some of them he appears only as a featureless figure in the distance or a silhouette on a windowshade. A stand-in could easily have been used, but Shepard was there for all his shots. (The only close-up of his "boogered up" face was an insert filmed much later when he was back in San Francisco.) He was also in several scenes either planned or actually filmed that didn't end up in the final movie, including some sequences from when he was still married to Spacek. He had prepared elaborately for his performance. "We talked early on about the reality he wanted to create around the Raggedy Man," says cinematographer Ralf Bode, "and he showed me this stuff that the character might have collected. One thing was a cigar box full of these beautifully preserved, dried-out bugs. I asked him where he got them, and he said he picked them off the radiator of his car driving down through Texas from California."

When the filming began in October 1980, the entire company lived near the location in Maxwell at a small Holiday Inn–type place whose regular customers were farm-equipment salesmen and the like. But before long most of the cast and crew moved to more comfortable digs at a Best Western in Austin. Spacek and Roberts rented condominiums, but Shepard decided to stay in Maxwell. He bought a couple of horses, and when he wasn't racing or riding them, he used the nine-week shoot as a quiet time to get some writing done. Among other things he was working on the screenplay of *Fitzcarraldo* for Werner Herzog, who visited the set of *Raggedy Man* to consult with him; at that point the stars of *Fitzcarraldo* were Mick Jagger and Jason Robards, Jr., but they dropped out (as did Shepard) during that movie's legendary mid-production crises, and Herzog rewrote the script for Klaus Kinski.

Frances, Shepard's next film, offered him another small and not terribly persuasive role. He played Harry York, a journalist invented as an all-purpose companion and confidant to the embattled Frances Farmer. The movie crudely dramatizes Farmer's rise to Hollywood fame, the actress's struggle to be accepted as an artist rather than a bimbo, her fights with police, lovers, movie executives, and especially her mother, who has her committed to a mental institution, where she undergoes a lobotomy. Jessica Lange delivers a big, raw, unforgettable performance as Frances Farmer, and it won her an Oscar nomination. Shepard at least looks great playing a city slicker with a handsome moustache. "There were three reasons I wanted Sam for *Frances,*" the Australian-born director Graeme Clifford explains. "One, I wanted an enigma, which Sam is. Two, I wanted a sexuality that wasn't *acted,* which Sam has. And three, I thought he and Jessica would get along well together."

Obviously, Shepard and Lange got along very well together, on camera and off, though they didn't become a couple right away. Before that happened, they each had a major motion picture to complete—*Tootsie* and *The Right Stuff*, which won them both Academy Award nominations. Besides, when *Frances* was shooting on location in Seattle during the fall of 1981, Shepard was happily married. Lange was going through a very painful divorce from her long-estranged husband, Spanish photographer Paco Grande, who had gone blind and was suing her for support. Meanwhile, she was steadily partnered with Mikhail Baryshnikov, the Russian dancer who had defected to the United States and swiftly become the biggest superstar in the world of ballet. Still, as Lange said later, "Movie sets are the most seductive places in the world—there's nothing like them for creating an ambience of romance and passion. I had a feeling Sam and I were going to fall in love."

She vividly remembers the first time they met. "It was one of those horrible meetings in the director's office. He was talking to a couple of different actors for Sam's role," Lange said. "I'd seen Sam in *Resurrection* and there was something about him that struck such a familiar chord. I immediately felt I knew something about him, that wildness, that typically American wildness, a no-restraints outlaw quality. The director introduced us and then he just up and left. We're both terribly shy and we're sitting there. I had Shura in her stroller and Sam looked like he was ready to run out. We're both very judgmental, so we were judging each other.

"Then," Lange added, "we went away on location." At first it was clearly a shipboard romance, not to be confused with bonding for life. "Sam was so mysterious in those days. He was always disappearing. He had this whole thing going on with music and nightlife. I never had any idea what this man was up to." As they spent more time together, though, their liaison began to attract public attention. A TV producer who spied them having dinner in Hollywood commented, "I've never seen anything like it in a restaurant. They were literally *attached* to each other over the top of the table. They kept twisting around, holding hands, then a hand would go up the arm, into Jessica's mouth. I don't think a lot of eating was going on because her mouth was constantly full of his hand. They were just gorgeous and madly, wildly, passionately involved with each other." And of course, there was that embarrassing incident in Los Angeles, when Shepard scuffled with photographers trying to take pictures of him and Lange leaving a restaurant together.

As far as Shepard was concerned, though, this affair could be chalked up to life on movie time, which had its own rules, as he suggested when he wrote in *Motel Chronicles* about encountering a movie extra at the hotel in Seattle, stoned on the last day of shooting and wanting to ball someone on the crew. The way she glamorized the movies and devalued her hometown made Shepard feel ashamed of being an actor and "provoking such stupid illusions." He took her to his room, but when he didn't make a pass at her, she tried to jump out the window. "Look," he told her, "it's just a dumb movie." She said, "It's not as dumb as life."

It was around the same time that he wrote in his journal: "I've about seen all the nose jobs, capped teeth, and silly-cone tits I can handle. I'm heading back to my natural woman." In *Motel Chronicles* this journal entry appears next to a hilarious picture of O-Lan lying on the washing machine with her feet propped up on the ironing board wearing jeans and cowboy boots, cigarette in her hand, looking sultry.

After *Frances,* Shepard went home for his next movie—in more ways than one. For one thing, *The Right Stuff* was filmed almost entirely in Northern California, except for the scenes shot on location at Edwards Air Force Base not far from Los Angeles. Among the picture's huge cast were twenty-two actors who had appeared at the Magic Theater, including John Lion himself, O-Lan Shepard, who plays a girlish test-pilot groupie, and the two actors who would originate the leading roles in *Fool for Love,* Ed Harris and Kathy Baker. It was the closest Shepard had come to finding in the movies the kind of regional repertory situation he sought in the theater. Besides, the director was an old friend of his named Phil Kaufman, whose conception of how to film Tom Wolfe's book about the first astronauts hinged on casting the playwright as Chuck Yeager, the first man to break the sound barrier.

When screenwriter William Goldman originally adapted Wolfe's book for the movies, it was during the Iranian hostage crisis, and he left Yeager out completely, focusing on the seven astronauts as a sort of All-American "Wild Bunch" who probably would have stomped into Iran and rescued the hostages themselves. But that version of *The Right Stuff* would have omitted the crucial ironies Kaufman wanted in the script—the anti-heroic fear experienced by none but the brave (Shepard told friends that if he had been one of the hostages in Iran, he would have been the first to fake sick to get sent home), and the juxtaposition of Yeager's unsung heroism with the astronauts' media-made brand.

"Though its chief subject is the astronauts, Yeager is the apple of Kaufman's heroic eye. He has built the no-nonsense test pilot of the late forties, the man who broke the sound barrier as if getting an aloof girl into bed, into a bridging figure for American tradition: the Cowboy in the X-1," says film critic David Thomson, who accompanied Kaufman throughout the making of *The Right Stuff*. "Just as the 'right stuff' is advertising humbug, so real heroes live out of the light, unsung and unsold, yet succumbing from their distance and their neglect to the fraud of celebrity. Like *True West*, *The Right Stuff* is an ironic title, as sour as your taste buds care to take it. They are both studies in how the American media smother a noble strangeness in hype."

The most entertaining section of the movie starts with the strength and endurance tests the astronauts undergo and follows them through their lionization in the press, their gang-like challenge to the prissy German scientists who would rather treat them like lab animals, and the first four solo flights made by American astronauts. But their story is framed by the pre-NASA adventures of Air Force test pilots both in the sky and at their desert hangout, a dim Wild West bar called Pancho's. These scenes could almost belong to another movie (in fact, Kaufman at one point thought of making them two separate pictures), and they are presided over—you could almost say haunted by—the legend of Yeager. Not the present-day Chuck Yeager, the retired brigadier-general who cleans up on endorsement ads and got himself a handsome fee as technical adviser on the film. As played by Sam Shepard, Kaufman's Yeager "is almost a silent movie hero, lured out of his taciturn watchfulness by an occasional 'Sure thing, honey' to his wife, and the ritual, 'Ridley, you got any Beemans?' to his best supporting mechanic before he goes against danger," as David Thomson observes.

"I think Kaufman picked Shepard for the way he represents the movie star as real man and existentialist, a dramatist whose plays have not been sold to Hollywood and who was for years wary of Broadway production. A rebel with a cause," says Thomson. "Kaufman had cast Shepard a little in the way one puts a poster on one's wall for 'His intense dedication to the manly life, rejecting New York, the taste for cowboys and rodeos—and all with the look of a man in a leather jacket on a horse meeting a jet plane in the desert.' That is an arresting image, and Shepard is all that Kaufman wanted in *The Right Stuff*."

The image of the character was something that Shepard and Kaufman thought about a lot. For instance, during shooting, they went to see *Giant* again to get a hit of James Dean juice. "I always felt, even before I was on *The Right Stuff*, that I wanted to make a film with Sam," says Kaufman. "He has a quality that is so rare now—you don't see it in the streets much, let alone in the movies—a kind of bygone quality of the forties when guys could wear leather jackets and be laconic and still say a lot without verbally saying anything. Most of the great actors of our time tend to be the urban types who are verbal and have a high energy that transmits what they're trying to say, whether it's Hoffman or Pacino or De Niro. Sam is more laid-back, like Gary Cooper."

"They told me for this movie my model should be Gary Cooper. I don't know how to take that," Shepard muses. "I could never connect with Gary Cooper. When I think of a rugged individualist, I right away think of Stan Laurel. Out of all the silent comics, he sort of sticks out in my mind as the truest and also the funniest."

The image of the silent loner wasn't the only thing about *The Right Stuff* that suited Shepard. He shared its attitude toward the media. While the astronauts sign lucrative contracts selling their life stories as part of *Life* magazine's exclusive coverage of the first space shots, Yeager snorts, "Coverage? You mean those little root weevils go around poppin' off cameras in yer eyes?" Shepard was the only actor in *The Right Stuff* who had it written into his contract that he wouldn't have to do publicity for the film. Even when *Newsweek* wanted to run a cover story on him and the producers desperately wanted the exposure, Shepard's answer remained the same. Hold the root weevils, please. And the way the test pilots in the movie, pioneers of outer space, talk about the race to break the sound barrier—trying to "push back the outside of the envelope" and wrestling with "the demon that lived in the air"—uncannily resembles Shepard's attitude that his task in writing for the theater is as a pioneer of inner space.

"I don't know if you feel this or not," Shepard told Amy Lippman, a Harvard undergraduate who wrote him a letter on a whim and was (perversely) granted an interview for the school's literary magazine, "but I feel like there are territories within us that are totally unknown. Huge, mysterious and dangerous territories. We think we know ourselves, when we really know only this little bitty part. We have this social person that we present to each other. We have all these galaxies inside of us. And if we don't enter those in art of one kind or another, whether it's playwriting, or painting, or music, or whatever, then I don't understand the point in doing anything. It's the reason I write. I try to go into parts of myself that are unknown." Writing is not, he stressed, a cathartic act for him: "Catharsis is getting rid of something. I'm not looking to get rid of it; I'm looking to find it. I'm not doing this in order to vent demons. I want to shake hands with them."

When all the fondling of images and synchronizing of attitudes was done, acting in *The Right Stuff* was a job, and Shepard took it seriously, which meant, among other things, getting to know the real Chuck Yeager. "The first day I rolled in for shooting out in the Mojave, at this little motel in Lancaster, California, I came around behind the motel and there's this gravel driveway there. Chuck was just getting out of his truck, and I drove up and got out and said, 'I'm going to change the oil in my truck.' I'd met him in San Francisco. But the first day arriving on the set we changed the oil. It was a great relationship. He was like an uncle to me." They hung out together at the Tosca, a smoky North Beach bar in San Francisco that became for the crew of *The Right Stuff* what Pancho's was for the characters. Shepard's greatest act of bravery was going up with Yeager for his first plane ride since the trip he took to Mexico with Joyce Aaron in 1965 that made him swear off flying. "If I'm gonna die, I might as well die with the world's greatest pilot," he said.

"You know, I asked Chuck one time what he thought set him apart from all those other pilots," Shepard recalls. "He was this ace fighter pilot. He shot down I don't know how many planes. He was regarded as *the* hottest pilot. He said that he had all the same abilities and everything as everybody else and the same training and all that, but he said the one thing that set him apart was his eyes. He said he had great eyes from hunting in West Virginia, hunting deer and bear. And then he got up into the sky."

What impressed Phil Kaufman about Sam Shepard was not his eyesight but his ear for language. "Sam is not an actor in the sense that the astronauts were played by actors," the director says. "Sam is much quieter and, being primarily a writer, responds to different kinds of images. He really has an incredible ear. The lines have to have, for him, a certain rightness before he can say them—a ring of poetry of some kind. Lots of actors can take any word and transform it into something, but Sam waits for the word to feel right. It's a very different experience working with him than it is working with typical actors."

The other actors appreciated Shepard on a more gut level. "When we were on the set, Shepard and I mostly talked about drinking, women, and cars," says Dennis Quaid, who went on to perform in the off-Broadway production of *True West* after co-starring in *The Right Stuff*. "When I read his plays later, I found out that's what they're all about: drinking, women, and cars."

When *The Right Stuff* came out, it wasn't the big hit that it was expected and deserved to be, but the critics unanimously admired it. And as before, when it came to ranking the players, Shepard came out ahead of the pack. There were no real stars in the picture, no single dominating performance, but a genuine ensemble of fine players who were outstanding in supporting roles—not just Ed Harris as the gung-ho John Glenn or Dennis Quaid as the adorable cut-up Gordo Cooper but also the fine cameos by Kim Stanley as Pancho, Donald Moffat as LBJ, Jane Dornacker as the enigmatic, mustachioed Nurse Murch, and Mary Jo Deschanel as the stuttering Mrs. Glenn.

Still, what stuck in almost everybody's mind was the indelible image of a scrappy guy in a leather jacket on horseback riding out into the desert for a showdown with a sinister-looking needle of orange steel. "The right stuff" was not about hairless men in tinfoil diapers floating around the earth in amniotic capsules but about a space-age warrior doing hand-to-hand battle with the sky, his armor a mechanical chassis more frail than his own. The image of Shepard as Yeager walking out of the ocean alive, his face "all boogered up" but his heroic stature untarnished, is almost campy in its unadulterated machismo. "Sir! Over there . . . is that *a man?*" gasps someone in the control tower. His superior studies the horizon and grunts, "Damned right it is!" When February 1984 rolled around, Shepard was the only actor from *The Right Stuff* nominated for an Oscar.

What sets Shepard apart from other actors? Why does his presence take so readily to the camera yet retain a stubborn mystery? What is the source of his undeniable sex appeal? It starts with his beauty, which is not Olympian but human, even animal at times. He's tall with a thick shock of rich, dark hair that sweeps back from a wide forehead in a widow's peak. His squinty eyes glint out from under thick brows, propped up by the kind of American Indian cheekbones that tug the sides of his face up to form, with his cleft chin, a foxy triangle. His nose is hawk-like and severe in profile, and his thick lips pout. He moves with a masculine grace and talks in a kind of self-mocking country twang that serves equally well for sarcasm, humility, and guileless desire.

As with many male sex symbols, Shepard's is a dangerous beauty, too. There's something in his physical attitude, the set of his jaw, his beady, sneering eyes that sometimes comes across as hostile, withholding, coiled like a snake. When he smiles or jokes, his face is like an infectious laugh—you want to give it everything; when it turns cold and white, his eyes shrinking and hardening like meat left in the fire too long, you just want to get out of its way. "His head hangs, the lips hook on to one another and eyes swivel toward you, like a bad horse sensing a coming rider. It is paranoia searching for its grievance," a film critic once wrote. "It is a frightening face, ready to stare a camera down and put a crack in its violet blooming."

Compare Shepard's look with that of Ed Harris. Harris has the face of an actor; he can play with or against his bashful blond looks at will. But Shepard has the face of a mystery—it holds back as much as it gives. They both have blue eyes, but Harris's are baby blue, Shepard's the color of midnight. Harris has wide eyes you could swim in; they say, "Come on in, the water's fine." Shepard's eyes are more wall than window, they shrink in accusation and self-protection, they make their own rules, they say, "You can't have me"—which makes everybody want him.

It was Jessica Lange who got him, of course. To hear her tell it, though, their relationship was never a foregone conclusion. "When we started it, it was never with the intention that we were going to run off, live together, have a family, do all these . . . *regular* . . . things. He was married and I had a little year-old baby. It was just this unbelievably passionate love affair," Lange told *Vanity Fair* magazine. "But then we just couldn't give it up. When we were together we were so wild—drinking, getting into fights, walking down the freeway trying to get away—I mean, just really wild stuff. I didn't want to keep going in that direction. So we quit talking. Then through the works of some good friends, we got back in touch and that was it. He left his wife. I was in Iowa doing pre-production for *Country*, so he met me there, and we drove to New Mexico, and that's where we settled."

Lange commissioned the screenplay for *Country* from William Wittliff (author of *Raggedy Man*), coproduced the movie with Wittliff, and hired Shepard as her co-star. They make a fascinating couple in many ways, both onscreen and in the mind of the public. They are both raw beauties and renegade artists, ambitious and talented and determined to do it their own way.

Like Tuesday Weld, the female idol of Shepard's teen dreams, Jessica Lange has always had the looks but never the temperament of a Hollywood blond starlet. While her performances in *Tootsie* and *The Postman Always Rings Twice* conveyed her wit and sexuality, the very choice to play Frances Farmer—not to mention how well she did it—revealed the hellcat behind her blond beauty and provocative slow takes. The classic moments in *Frances* aren't so much the screaming fights with her mother or being dragged away by the cops as quietly intense scenes like the one where she leans over the desk of the studio psychiatrist and, in the kind of tiny voice a little girl might use to say "Thank you, Daddy," informs him, "I can solve my problems without recourse to a *veterinarian.*"

Her background is surprisingly similar to Shepard's. Born in a tiny Minnesota town, she moved around a lot as a kid because her father was a salesman. Small-town life drove her nuts, so after a year of college she ran off with photographer Paco Grande, whom she'd just married, and landed in New York to study acting. She also had a stint abroad (two years studying mime in Paris) and did some modeling with the Wilhelmina agency in New York. She hated modeling—she felt more honest working as a waitress at the Lion's Head, a writers' pub in Greenwich Village—but that's how Dino De Laurentiis saw her and launched her movie career. The remake of *King Kong*, Bob Fosse's *All That Jazz*, and *How to Beat the High Cost of Living* were hardly masterpieces, and they required her to do little more than moisten her lips and toss her pretty blond head. But they gave her a public identity as something other than Mikhail Baryshnikov's live-in girlfriend, and they paved the way for co-starring with Jack Nicholson in *Postman* and getting the role of a lifetime in *Frances*.

Lange's affair with Mikhail Baryshnikov was hardly parallel to Shepard's fling with Patti Smith. She had a very serious relationship with the ballet superstar and a lovely daughter named Alexandra (nicknamed Shura), as well. But Lange, like Shepard, had little patience with big-time show-biz and spent as much time as possible away from it—either on her 120 acres in Holyoke, Minnesota, near her parents' house, or at the homestead she bought in Wisconsin, or on some land she owned in Taos, New Mexico. Two Midwesterners from farm families, they were perfectly suited for a movie like *Country*.

The movie, which Lange conceived as a contemporary *Grapes of Wrath*, focuses on the plight of the small farmer in America today, squeezed on one side by low prices and grain embargoes, on the other side by banks happy with the efficient profits of agribusiness and increasingly quick to foreclose on small farms for nonpayment of loans. When Gil Ivy lets the humiliating prospect of losing his farm damage his pride, it remains to his wife Jewell to rally other farmers in an attempt to stop the government from taking land that's been in her family for three generations—failing that, to keep her own brood together at least.

The film went into production with a spirit of old-home-week. Jessica Lange's Oscar for *Tootsie*, Shepard's nomination for *The Right Stuff*, and the classic strength of Wittliff's script were sufficient to land the major-studio backing of Walt Disney Productions' Touchstone Films. Lange cast her acting teacher Sandra Seacat in a small role, and Shepard suggested Jim Haynie, who played Lee in the original production of *True West*, for another. But once the cast and crew arrived on location in Waterloo, Iowa, troubles began almost immediately. Wittliff was originally signed to make his debut as a director on *Country*, but after two weeks it was clear that he wasn't going to work out—a hard decision to make, since he was also the co-producer.

"Jessica just didn't like what she was seeing in the dailies, and that was flat *it,* you know?" says Shepard. "She should be a director. She's got a great eye." Luckily, they were able to bring in Richard Pearce, who had directed a small but very well-received movie about turn-of-the-century American farmers called *Heartland,* and shooting began all over. Pearce knew he was walking a tightrope because Lange was the producer, and with Wittliff out of the picture he would have to rely on Shepard to help with last-minute rewrites on the script. But sensing the potential mutiny brewing among a film crew disgruntled by delays, the director made it a condition of participating that he be able to deal with Lange and Shepard individually, rather than as a team.

"Just to rehearse with each of them separately and work with them separately was a critical issue," says Pearce. "She's a very disciplined actress, very smart, very prepared, and she's the producer of the film, and can't goof off. Then her co-star, and the man she lives with, and the man she fights with and screws and whatever else, is arriving late, trying to devise strategies to relax everybody, to loosen the process up. It's a classic, but it worked, because they're alive when they're together, and they're alive on the screen when they're together."

Shepard didn't mind the delays so much. He'd brought his rifle along to do some hunting, the tape deck in his trailer was stocked with the latest albums by Dylan (*Infidels*) and the Stones (*Undercover*), and besides he had worries of his own: it was while he was on the set of *Country* that O-Lan decided to serve him with divorce papers. (The Shepards' divorce became final in July 1984.)

By now it was late October, and winter came early to the Iowa flatlands. The filming proceeded through freezing sleet; outdoor scenes had to be shot in five-minute stretches, with actors running to the barn between takes to thaw out in front of high-powered heaters. It got so cold that they finally had to quit and shoot a lot of the indoor scenes on a replica of the real farmhouse back at Disney's Burbank studios—which is where they also filmed the tornado that picks up a huge gleaner-combine like a baby's rattle and overturns a truck full of grain.

Country is the first contemporary film Shepard has appeared in (Gil's son Carlisle listens to his Walkman while milking the cows), but it covers familiar territory—failing farm, bad daddy, dreamy son. In fact, the movie could almost be a counterpart of *Curse of the Starving Class,* a portrait of a down-but-not-out family that will before long tear itself apart from the inside. In a scene that Shepard might have written himself, Gil comes home from a drinking spree and starts talking to Carlisle about "the sparrows" while he's doing his chores. "The hell with you, you're drunk," says the boy, launching a fistfight in the sheep pen.

Ironically, while *Country* was shooting in Iowa, an original screenplay by Shepard with another father-son relationship at its core started filming in Texas. German director Wim Wenders had been wanting to work with Shepard for years; he offered him the title role, for instance, in his movie *Hammett.* Finally, when Shepard published his *Motel Chronicles,* Wenders read it and felt that pieces from the book could be put together as the basis for a movie. "I like Sam's work enormously—he's really my favorite contemporary American writer," says Wenders, who has made several pictures in the United States, including *The American Friend* starring Dennis Hopper. "We found we had certain common territory, but instead of adapting his work we decided to start this story from scratch."

So the two of them worked together on the story, and the screenplay that resulted was *Paris, Texas*. A deadbeat named Travis (played by Harry Dean Stanton, one of the great desert-rat actors and perfect for a Shepard "hero") returns home after four years of aimless wandering, but his wife Jane (Nastassia Kinski) has disappeared, leaving their son with his brother. To win back the love of his son, Travis sets out to find Jane, who's working in a sex club in Houston. Mother and son reunite, but Travis takes off again in his pickup truck.

Paris, Texas, unlike *Country,* was a very low-budget ($3 million) picture produced without major-studio backing. Although the script was complete before Shepard left for his acting gig, Wenders started changing it almost as soon as shooting began. He brought in screenwriter Kit Carson to help with daily rewriting (Carson's son Hunter was playing the boy in the movie). Toward the end Shepard started phoning in from Iowa with new scenes, including the crucial last scenes of the movie, Travis's angry reaction to his wife's disappearance and his ultimate confession of being responsible for the breakup of their marriage. These scenes were basically monologues, and Harry Dean Stanton had a very hard time doing them at first. "I'd suggested and tried to restructure the material into dialogues," says Kit Carson. "Wim considered, then rejected this. Harry had talked to Shepard by phone about his problems; but Shepard simply insisted: 'It's all there. Just don't act it. Don't act it.'

"Wim's covering the scenes from several angles. As the crew works almost silently setting up, Harry sits on the set in a chair, meticulously reading his monologue word-for-word out loud," Carson remembered. "I'm standing off-set listening to Harry. Over and over, stopping halfway, starting again. Four, five, six times; talking through the story of Travis's and Jane's last night together. Suddenly, I start to hear something under the flow of speech—a heart-breaking inevitable pulse-like rhythm. A tragic sound. It shakes me up, sends actual shivers, stands the hairs up on the back of my neck. Shepard was right: *don't act this*. He'd put all the terrible, necessary power of the scenes into just the bare, unhidden sequence of the words."

The film opened at the Cannes Film Festival in May 1984; it became the hit of the festival and took the Golden Palm award for best film. And in the fall Sam Shepard nailed down the two most prestigious slots in the New York Film Festival—*Country* had its world premiere on the opening night of the festival, and the gala closing night presentation was *Paris, Texas*. The esteem accorded *Paris, Texas* was particularly gratifying to Shepard. It meant that after almost twenty years he was finally accepted in the movie business doing what he wanted to do.

"I'm a writer. The more I act, the more resistance I have to it," he says. "If you accept to work in a movie, you accept to be entrapped for a certain part of time, but you know you're getting out. I'm also earning enough to keep my horses, buying some time to write, and learning how to act—something that really interests me."

Shepard's attitude toward acting was ambivalent at best. On one hand, he didn't think of acting as a career—"It's just something I do"—and didn't think he'd be doing it for very much longer. On the other hand, he had to admit that it's hard to resist the temptation when project after project is laid at his feet, with handsome amounts of money attached.

After *Country* he did turn down a fair amount of work. After signing the deal to star in Richard Brooks's new movie *Fever,* a story about another of his obsessions, gambling, he changed his mind and dropped out because he "just didn't want to go to work in Las Vegas for three months." Even Jessica Lange couldn't persuade him to take the male lead in her next movie, *Sweet Dreams*. Lange won an Oscar nomination for her wonderful performance as Patsy Cline, the country music star who died in a plane crash at the age of 31. Lange didn't attempt to sing but simply lip-synched to Cline's classic recordings. And Ed Harris took the role of Cline's husband, to whom she turns in the middle of a knockdown drag-out fight and snarls, "You got me confused with someone who gives a shit!"

At the end of 1984, a year full of satisfactions, Shepard was content not to be wasting his time on one more movie set. He had bigger fish to fry.

Chapter Nine:

FIRE IN THE SNOW

SAM: I've heard this theory that women are rhythmically different from men. By nature . . . That the female rhythm is a side-to-side, horizontal movement and the male rhythm is vertical—up and down . . . Do you feel those two different kinds of rhythms in you?

BOB: Yeah, sure. We all do. There's that slinky, side-to-side thing and the jerky, up-and-down one. But they're a part of each other. One can't do without the other. Like God and the Devil.

Shepard interviewing Bob Dylan (*True Dylan*)

John Malkovich had never met Shepard throughout the long run of *True West*. Then one day in the fall of 1984 he was standing outside the Circle Repertory Theater in Greenwich Village's Sheridan Square, where he was directing the Steppenwolf Theater Company in Lanford Wilson's *Balm in Gilead*. Out of the blue, Shepard walked by on his way to visit Joe Chaikin, who was still recovering from his stroke and very ill. "He just walked up to me and said, 'Hi, how are ya?'" Malkovich said later. "He told me about this new play he was writing. And he asked me would I be interested in coming down and reading a few scenes with some people." The reading took place at the Minetta Lane, another Off-Broadway theater in the Village, and the "some people" included Harry Dean Stanton, Diane Venora, and Geraldine Page. Shepard was shooting for a dream cast that included Malkovich, Page, Amanda Plummer, Jessica Tandy, Jason Robards, Ed Harris, and Amy Madigan—"a cast of unknowns," as Malkovich drily put it.

Malkovich went back and forth with Shepard about doing the play. The actor had never been in the first production of a new play, and he wanted that experience. Besides, he admired Shepard tremendously. "I'd feel really weird if I didn't do it, frankly," Malkovich said. "I gave him some dates when I could do it, and he said, 'Well, that's right in the middle of polo season'—but real serious. God forbid I get involved in that." Ultimately, he decided the role was too similar to Lee in *True West* and to Wesley in *Curse of the Starving Class*, which he'd also played at Steppenwolf in Chicago.

Word started circulating in the New York theater scene that Shepard was conducting these all-star readings of a big new three-act play that was still unfinished. Malkovich summarized the script he'd read: "This guy I play, his wife's an actress, and he gets kinda mad that she wears too many oils on her body and goes to rehearsal wearing stockings and high heels and stuff. And he warns her once not to do it. But then she does it, and so he beats her to death. Like, you know . . . Sam's answer to Noel Coward, I guess."

The new play was called *A Lie of the Mind*. When it premiered in the fall of 1985, it appeared to encapsulate the previous four of Shepard's major plays, which themselves were an imaginative reflection of his own life story. *Curse of the Starving Class* takes place on an avocado ranch in Southern California and portrays a family— alcoholic father, coping mother, brooding teenage son, tomboy daughter—tearing itself apart from the inside, not unlike the real family of Shepard's adolescence. Similar drunken-daddy and sensitive-son characters appear in *Buried Child*. Visiting his grandparents in rural Illinois, young Vince unexpectedly encounters his derelict father and uncovers some family secrets. *True West* pits a clean-cut, aspiring Hollywood screenwriter against his brother, a good-for-nothing drifter said to resemble his father. And *Fool for Love* features the last blowout between a movie stuntman and his childhood sweetheart, who's also his half-sister.

Though it's never explicitly stated, the central characters in these plays could be said to represent Shepard at various stages of his life—withdrawn teenager, estranged son, struggling writer, straying lover. In each case, Shepard subsumed the autobiographical elements to a deeper philosophical investigation. The family plays explored heredity as destiny, while *True West* and *Fool for Love* examined what Shepard has called "double nature," the ongoing clash of good and bad, male and female in a single individual.

A Lie of the Mind picks up almost exactly where *Fool for Love* left off. On the phone with his brother Frankie, Jake confesses that he's just had a brutal argument with his wife, Beth, and he's beaten her to death. It turns out that Beth isn't dead, though she's suffered severe brain damage. Still, Jake experiences the catastrophe as a kind of death and returns to his family to mourn. While enduring the doting concern of his mother and tomboy sister, he contemplates the demons he inherited from his father, recently run over by a truck during a drinking spree. Meanwhile, Frankie follows Beth to her family's house to determine the exact nature of her injuries and winds up winning her heart.

The end of the play becomes thick with freighted visual images. Jake's mother and sister burn down their house in southern California and take off for Ireland. Wearing only his boxer shorts and the

American flag from his father's funeral, Jake crawls all the way to Beth's house, which is somewhere in the cold North (Montana?), to apologize to her before he disappears into the dark. While Beth and Frankie gaze at each other googly-eyed, her ditsy mother Meg and hard-bitten father Baylor fold up the flag in proper military style, and then Baylor gives her a peck on the cheek—"the first time in twenty years," Meg exclaims. Standing on the porch touching the cheek where her husband kissed her, she looks across the stage at the flames Jake's mother set and utters the play's last line: "Looks like a fire in the snow. How could that be?"

Anyone well-versed in Shepard's work could recognize in *A Lie in the Mind* relationships from other plays (the brothers in *True West*, the lovers in *Fool for Love*—all of whom have counterparts in the film *Paris, Texas*). The play also contains echoes of the playwright's personal history: the breakup of his fourteen-year marriage when he left his wife, O-Lan, for Jessica Lange; his father's death in an auto accident; Chaikin's debilitating stroke. Shepard could be and was accused of merely recycling familiar obsessions and autobiographical fragments to the point of self-parody. But *A Lie of the Mind* tells a different story than Shepard's family history. It's a meditation on loss and the tricks it plays on the human psyche, making a grieving survivor feel responsible for a loved one's death or turning emotional crimes into physical ones.

Clearly, *A Lie of the Mind* makes use of "certain personal elements," as Shepard admitted *True West* had. By the time they get to the stage, though, these scraps of personal experience have undergone a transformation. Both biography and art involve the process of constructing narrative from life's vast database, converting prosaic details into poetry through selection, shaping, speculation. As a character in John Guare's play *Six Degrees of Separation* says, "The imagination—that's God's gift to make the act of self-examination bearable." *A Lie of the Mind* provides a textbook example of how Shepard alchemically recasts material that comes from his own life.

Here's the playwright in a magazine interview, describing his last glimpse of his father: "I had my dad cremated, you know? There wasn't much left of him to begin with. They gave you this box with the ashes in it. The box is like it's got a spotlight on it or something, because that's him, and yet it's just this little leather box.

"Two objects are the centerpieces of the service, the box and a little folded-up flag. I kept staring at the box the whole time I was reading. I was reading these Lorca poems he liked. Then the service was over and everybody got up—we had it outdoors under a tent—and everybody started to walk away. I turned back and saw that the box and the flag were still sitting on the table. Nobody was there, and I wondered if I was supposed to take the box or . . . I walked over and I picked up the box and I was . . . it was so heavy. You wouldn't think that the ashes of a man would be that heavy.

"I saw these two little Mexican guys sitting in a green truck with shovels in the back. They were waiting for everybody to clear out so they could come get the box and put it in the hole. So I put the box back on the table and left. I waited by the car and watched until they went over and picked him up. It was a funny kind of moment."

Here's the same scene as it appears in the stage directions at the end of Act 1 of *A Lie of the Mind*. Jake is onstage alone in his mother's house; he's wearing boxer shorts and his father's leather flight jacket. "All the rest of the lights black out except for a tight spotlight on his father's box of ashes. Jake crosses back to the box, picks it up, opens it and stares into it for a second. He blows lightly into the box sending a soft puff of ashes up into the beam of the spotlight. Spotlight fades slowly to black."

The production of *A Lie of the Mind* was a big event for Shepard. For one thing, it was the first play he chose to premiere in New York in fourteen years, since he left Patti Smith stranded at the stage door of *Cowboy Mouth*. The intervening plays had opened first either in London, at regional theaters, or at the Magic Theatre. Now that Shepard no longer lived in the Bay Area, he'd lost his home base. Considering that it was a big play and that he wanted to cast it with heavy-duty actors, he decided to go for a splashy commercial New York production rather than open the play in the financially protected environment of a subscription-based regional theater. To steer him through the treacherous waters of commercial theater, he chose classy Broadway veteran Lewis Allen and his partner Stephen Graham (the son of *Washington Post* publisher Katharine Graham), smart producers with good taste who'd recently produced a successful Broadway revival of Eugene O'Neill's dark epic *The Iceman Cometh* starring Jason Robards. The general manager for the show was Albert Poland, who had produced Shepard's first commercial Off-Broadway production. Shepard is nothing if not loyal to his friends. As with *Fool for Love*, Shepard decided to direct the new play himself.

The cast he assembled was extraordinary. When John Malkovich turned down the leading role of Jake, he snared Harvey Keitel, who had appeared in Shepard's early play *Up to Thursday* Off-Off-Broadway years before he made his name in Martin Scorsese films like *Mean Streets* and *Taxi Driver*. Amanda Plummer, whose fierceness and originality make her every bit the female counterpart to John Malkovich, accepted the role of brain-damaged Beth. Ann Wedgeworth played Beth's mother; she met Shepard on the set of *Sweet Dreams*, where she had played mother to Jessica Lange's Patsy Cline. James Gammon, who'd taken a small part in the New York premiere of *Curse of the Starving Class*, played Beth's father Baylor, the first of a long string of roles he'd perform under Shepard's direction. Jake's mother Lorraine was played by the great Geraldine Page, in one of her last stage performances before she died. Judith Ivey, who was Jake's sister in the early readings, fell out along the way, to be replaced by Rebecca de Mornay, who left after six weeks of rehearsal and was replaced by Karen Young. Will Patton and Aidan Quinn, two exciting young actors who had each succeeded Ed Harris in *Fool for Love*, played the antagonistic brothers of Beth and Jake. (Patton would subsequently take the leading role of Jake in the London production.) It was a powerhouse ensemble, each of whom gave an excellent performance. When it came right down to it, though, Plummer surpassed them all. A mysterious, emotionally free, idiosyncratic actress, she managed to convey the several aspects of Beth—crippled, powerfully sensual, otherworldly, and heartbreaking—all at once.

"I like actors who are incredibly courageous and enthusiastic," Shepard said. "I don't like sulking actors. I don't like actors who I have to pamper or who I have to go through a big song and dance with to come at a very simple thing. I like actors who are pretty much their own person and don't need a lot of care. It's a waste of time. I'd sooner start with somebody who already is his own person, and not only that, has a combination of enthusiasm and courage. And intelligence. I don't want to work with dumb actors. Because I've found the essence of comedy, great comedians, is intelligence. Maybe sometimes they come off very stupid, but they're the smartest actors. Like Buster Keaton. I think John

Malkovich is a good example: extremely intelligent, fearless, and enthusiastic. Just does not give a shit about how this fits into somebody else's idea of what it should be, just goes for ideas that are completely off the wall. They may be wrong but he'll go for them."

As a director, Shepard was unusually casual about telling the actors where to go and what to do, which the actors found both freeing and frustrating. "This is a very competitive bunch of actors, to put it mildly," said Geraldine Page. "Sometimes I'd get weary fighting for my share of space. I'd feel like saying, 'Sam, you've got to block this.'" He was equally casual about such practical matters as hiring understudies, which he didn't do until the play was in previews. One night Ann Wedgeworth was out sick, and Page had to play both mothers. When Harvey Keitel missed a performance to be with his wife who was having a baby, his newly-hired understudy, Bill Raymond, had to go onstage with the script in his hand. As John Malkovich once said of Shepard, "That man is vaguer than I am, which ought to be illegal." On the whole, though, the actors found it stimulating to work with Shepard. "He's quiet—he doesn't talk much," said Amanda Plummer. "Then when he gets excited, his eyes come out. They look out in wonder as if he's never seen this before."

Actors of this stature would usually be found in a Broadway theater. Economics made it more advantageous, however, to produce the play at the Promenade, Off-Broadway's most prestigious theater. The previous year, the Promenade had housed the all-star production of David Rabe's *Hurlyburly*, featuring William Hurt, Harvey Keitel, Christopher Walken, Sigourney Weaver, Judith Ivey, Jerry Stiller, and Cynthia Nixon, which later moved to Broadway. When *A Lie of the Mind* went into rehearsal, the Promenade's current tenant was a revival of *Curse of the Starving Class* starring Kathy Bates. Shepard and Jessica Lange showed up one night to see the play and check out the theater. (Lange, who was very pregnant with her and Shepard's first child, had moved to New York for the time being and enrolled her daughter Shura in a kindergarten on the Upper East Side.) When they picked up their tickets at the box office, producer Patricia Daily rushed over to say Bates was out that night, and she hoped the author would come back to see her in the play. He said okay, went away, and returned the following Sunday night. He sat in the back row, went backstage afterwards, and told the cast they'd done a good job.

A Lie of the Mind rehearsed for two months, more than twice as long as most Off Broadway productions. Of course, the play itself was very long. "It's a big-assed play," Shepard admitted. "That's twenty-one years of work there." The three acts ran for four hours in rehearsal, even before Shepard decided he wanted to have live music in the show. By chance, he spotted an old theater poster for a 1975 Off-Broadway musical called *Diamond Studs* that had featured a bluegrass band called the Red Clay Ramblers. He remembered having heard the band on a college radio station when he was out in Iowa filming *Country*. He had his sister Roxanne, who was working as his assistant director, track them down at home in Chapel Hill, North Carolina. "We got a call—'Come immediately,'" said the band's Tommy Thompson. He and the group's musical director met in New York with Shepard. "He told us he wanted songs to open and close each act, as well as material for scene changes and underscoring," Thompson said.

The band canceled its concert bookings and flew to New York, where they became an integral part of the production of *A Lie of the Mind*. They created a score that combined new originals, some older songs from their repertoire, and traditional folk tunes, performed by a five-piece combo playing guitar, banjo, mandolin, bass, piano, and fiddle. The Red Clay Ramblers' old-timey country music was very much to Shepard's taste and ideally suited to *A Lie of the Mind*, which the playwright once described as "a little love ballad." Well, maybe not so little. The running time had swollen to five hours. Throughout rehearsals, Shepard made tiny cuts here and there, but when the show got onstage for previews he finally started chopping out whole chunks so the audience could get out of the theater before midnight.

When the show opened December 5, 1985, Shepard received some of the best reviews of his career. The crucial daily critics lavished praise. Clive Barnes of the *New York Post* called it "the class event of the season," and Frank Rich waxed poetic in the *New York Times*. "*A Lie of the Mind* may be its author's most romantic play. However bleak and chilly its terrain—some of it unfolds, in more ways than one, in a blizzard—no character, alive or dead, is beyond redemption: There is always hope, as Mr. Shepard's closing metaphor has it, for a miraculous 'fire in the snow,'" Rich wrote. "By turns aching and hilarious—and always as lyrical as its accompanying country music—*A Lie of the Mind* is the unmistakeable expression of a major writer nearing the height of his powers

... When Jake tries to achieve communion with his father by gently blowing a plume of his ashes into the moonlight, it's as if Mr. Shepard had emblazoned a man's timeless destiny like a star shower across a Western sky." These were what's called in the business "money reviews." In three days, the play sold over $100,000 in tickets, breaking box-office records at the Promenade Theater.

Shepard's champions in the weekly papers also flipped over *A Lie of the Mind*. "These families are Shepard's most incisive explorations of the people he grew up among, the dislocated, deracinated working-class Westerners whose odyssey brought them to California," wrote Jack Kroll in *Newsweek*. "These people are battered travesties of the American pioneer energy, but something of that energy survives in their often comically desperate attempts at survival. Shepard is their William Faulkner; like Faulkner, he writes about them with a powerful blend of wild humor and tragic force." Gordon Rogoff seconded the motion in the *Village Voice*: "A fearless national treasure, he has become a playwright willing to be big, epic, demanding and ironic without ever quite knowing how to contain his visions and desires in the recalcitrant limits of theater ... The play is consistently enthralling and explosively funny." *Time* magazine said it was Shepard's best play to date. At the end of the season, *A Lie of the Mind* won the New York Drama Critics Circle Award for Best Play.

Even critics who had mixed feelings about the play respected Shepard's efforts and wrote thoughtfully about the play's shortcomings. "*A Lie of the Mind* is Sam Shepard's most ambitious play to date, the closest he has come to entering the mainstream of American drama," Robert Brustein said in the *New Republic*. "Shepard is moving inexorably toward the heart of American realism, where audiences have the opportunity to identify him as a family member like themselves—son, brother, lover, husband. This has advantages: greater clarity, concentration and recognition. It also has disadvantages, in that Shepard is now displaying what he has in common with the spectator rather than what the spectator unwittingly shares with him. Another disadvantage is that as Shepard's life gets increasingly familiar from interviews, his work seems to get increasingly biographical—and confined."

The *San Francisco Chronicle*'s Bernard Weiner, who'd closely covered Shepard's work at the Magic Theatre, agreed with Brustein. "Though there are moments in *Lie of the Mind* that are as powerful, evocative and touching as anything he's ever written, the play as a whole seems to come from a shaft that has been overmined by the playwright. At times, the script even approaches the outskirts of self-parody, as Shepard once again focuses on the grotesquerie of the American family and its corrosive effect on the possibilities of love."

The parallels between *A Lie of the Mind* and the traces of Shepard's own life tangled up in the plays that preceded it are so glaringly obvious as to be unavoidable. However, in retrospect it's possible to analyze the play from perspectives other than the autobiographical. On the level of technical development, Shepard began in *A Lie of the Mind* to experiment with sustaining parallel narratives within one piece of work—an experiment which would carry over to the screenplays he would subsequently write and direct, *Far North* and *Silent Tongue*. *Lie* also played some subtle tricks with theatrical time and space. Most of the play sticks to scrupulously naturalistic language and behavior—Shepard's production certainly did—so only afterward does the viewer register the incongruities. How did Jake get from southern California to Montana in his boxer shorts? And how could Meg see Lorraine's house burning down from her front porch? A similarly unobtrusive time/space discontinuity would figure heavily in Shepard's later play *Simpatico*.

Another thread that emerges from *A Lie of the Mind* is Shepard's increasing investment in examining the female psyche— or, as Shepard is always careful to assert when people ask him about the way he writes about women, "the female part" of the human psyche. Much of his work consumes itself with masculine mythology and identity. The conflicts almost always boil down to a stand-off between two men, often clearly signifying an inner conflict between the civilized man and the wild man. Beginning with *Fool for Love*, though, the dramatic warfare began to shift toward men and women. Perhaps the demise of his marriage inspired Shepard's new interest in gender conflict and made him examine why men mistreat women. Perhaps he felt guilty about abandoning one woman for another and sought to dramatize his emotional turmoil. It's possible, though, that *Fool for Love* and *A Lie of the Mind* represent as much of an inner conflict as, say, *True West*, and that the abused women he's writing about are part of his own psyche.

In a *Village Voice* interview with Carol Rosen, Shepard said, "the female force in nature . . . became more and more interesting to me because of how that female thing relates to being a man. You know, in yourself, that the female part of one's self as a man is, for the most part, battered and beaten up and kicked to shit just like some women in relationships. That men themselves batter their own female part to their own detriment. And it became interesting from that angle—as a man, what is it like to embrace the female part of yourself that you historically damaged for one reason or another?"

The published text of *A Lie of the Mind* carries a dedication "to the memory of L.P." Who is L.P.? Two events that heavily influenced the writing of *A Lie of the Mind* were his father's death in March, 1984, and Chaikin's stroke in April that same year. Around the same time, Shepard attended the funeral of Henry John Sinclair, better known as Lord Pentland, the British businessman who served as president of the Gurdjieff Foundation in New York for 31 years. Shepard has long been involved with the Gurdjieff work but, like most Gurdjieffians, has never spoken about it publicly. The wall of secrecy that successfully shields the Gurdjieff work from any but the most committed students has presumably contributed to Shepard's steadfastness in refusing to seek publicity and maintaining a personal life that is private. It's hard to say what influence Gurdjieff's esoteric teachings have had on Shepard's work, because they cannot be reduced to doctrine or dogma. One of his disciples, Claudio Naranjo, has noted that Gurdjieff "took it upon himself to show the Western world that mankind is asleep, that there are higher levels of being, and that there are somewhere people who know."

Dedicating *A Lie of the Mind* to the memory of Lord Pentland, however, invites a reading of the play that has little to do with Shepard's biography. What if the play is much more dreamlike than it appears on the surface? What if the various characters represent aspects of the same psyche? What if Beth's recovery from her brutalization at the hands of Jake and her awakening to a loving kinship with Frankie holds a mystical or spiritual meaning for Shepard?

In any case, there is an overwhelming sense of finality to the play. It's as if Shepard intentionally conjures elements from earlier plays to bid them farewell. *A Lie of the Mind* so boldly announced itself as a career summary of sorts that one wondered where

Shepard could possibly go next. It would be six years before he brought another play to the stage.

In the hiatus from the stage that followed *A Lie of the Mind*, Shepard occupied himself with three things: his family, his horses, and acting in movies (not necessarily in that order of importance).

The family was expanding. Shepard and Lange's first child, Hannah June, was born January 13, 1986. Lange gave birth to their second child June 14, 1987; he was named Samuel Walker Shepard and called Walker. "I was pregnant for three years," joked Lange, who gained fifty pounds when she had Hannah. "Sam's one of those men who loves you when you're pregnant— just thinks you look more beautiful than ever before, loves the big belly. It was great, except I get real dark sometimes when I'm pregnant. My mood swings are extreme anyhow, but when I'm pregnant I could be like Medea any moment, I'm so hard to live with. Sam says he went through it twice, he doesn't want to live through it again."

It was during one of those "mood swings" when Lange decided it was time to move. She and Shepard had been living with Lange's daughter Shura, two dogs, and a horse in Santa Fe. They occupied a $450,000 log cabin on five acres with a barn and a state-of-the-art security system designed to deter anyone who might even think about messing with two movie stars and their celebrity babies. Suddenly, living in New Mexico "just didn't feel right" to Lange. "You know you can feel when you're meant to be in some place and then you know your time there is past. And it's time to move on. And I really felt that strongly," Lange said. "We were in New York. Sam was doing his play. I was pregnant and very . . . I don't know, moody and restless and feeling crazy and one day I looked in the *New York Times* and I saw this picture of a farm down in Virginia, and I thought, Well, we're going to look at this place. And that was it."

At the end of April, they packed up the house in Santa Fe and moved to Scottsville, Virginia, about 25 miles south of Charlottesville. "Whoever built the house around 1790 also planted an extraordinary variety of great American trees. We have lindens and beeches and lots of maples. My favorite tree is a beautiful American elm which must be at least two hundred years old," Lange told Linda Bird Franke (daughter of former President Lyndon B. Johnson) in a 1988 conversation published in *Interview* magazine.

"We use [the farm] now mostly as a horse farm, breeding and raising Thoroughbreds. Sam sold his first yearling at the Fasig-Tipton
sales in Kentucky this fall and actually did great. We have just two
brood mares now, but we're starting. Sam plays polo, and we have
ten polo ponies, and three hunter-jumpers, which Sam and I ride."
They lived not far from Sissy Spacek and her husband Jack Fisk,
who directed *Raggedy Man*. But their 110-acre property was sufficiently off the beaten track not to have an address. Shepard
picked up his mail at a hardware store.

That didn't exactly make him incommunicato, however. After his
Oscar nomination for *The Right Stuff*, Shepard discovered that he
could work pretty much continuously in movies if he wanted to. His
acting career came about so unexpectedly, even accidentally, that
he seemed content to treat it as a kind of running joke. In movie
after movie, whether he was a farmer or a doctor or a drifter or a
bad cop, he generally played some version of what Hollywood considers a Sam Shepard character. And for a while, anyway, he didn't
seem to mind. Put him in a pickup truck, surround him with animals, and call him Spud or Doc or Cooch, and he was happy. The
most curious thing about the movies Shepard made in this period is
that he didn't seem to care if they were any good or not, as long as
they allowed him to inhabit some aspect of his favorite masculine
iconography. As often as not, his motivation for appearing in a film
seemed to have more to do with loyalty to friends or colleagues
than anything the movie wanted to say.

Much of what looks like aesthetic indifference on Shepard's
part may come from his effort to conceal his distate at the waste-
fulness and obsequiousness that goes with the territory of moviemaking. "Movie acting is all about narcissism," he told *Newsweek*
in 1985. "Terry Malick called it 'sanctioned vanity.' Everything is
attended to. Would you like some Perrier? Anything we can do?
May we throw ourselves on the ground in front of you? It's this
unbelievable barrage of indulgence."

When Shepard did apply himself to the craftsmanlike aspects
of film acting, he was frequently frustrated because he encoun-
tered standards of quality that weren't as rigorous as those he
held for himself in writing or making theater. "There's no honor
in acting for the movies, because there's no real respect for acting
in the movies. What they do is idolize the actor. They don't have
any idea what the actor's up to. Nobody. Least of all the director,"
he said. "Film directors are visual artists, they're perceiving the

exteriors of things. They don't give a shit about the interior. So the actor has to go off and work that out by himself. A lot of actors worry about that, but I prefer to be left alone because all of my mistakes are my own."

Fool for Love was the first Shepard play to be filmed, and the first time he played one of his own characters in a movie. Directed by Robert Altman, one of the renegade masters of American cinema, it was treated as a big deal. The release date of the film was scheduled to coincide with the New York opening of *A Lie of the Mind*, for that all-important one-two media push. Unfortunately, the movie was a Big Mistake.

Originally, the plan was for Shepard and Jessica Lange to star in the film, along with Randy Quaid (who appeared in *True West* onstage in New York) and Harry Dean Stanton (who played the lead in *Paris, Texas*)—in other words, a true "family affair." But family got in the way: Lange became pregnant and wisely chose not to do the movie. Everything about it is misguided. Robert Altman has made some great movies, some of them based on stage plays (*Streamers; Come Back to the Five and Dime, Jimmy Dean, Jimmy Dean*). He's also made some stinkers, and this is one of them. The director perversely took a play set in a tiny motel room made claustrophobic with erotic tension and spread it out over the desert sky. "Quite simply, a very effective play has been stretched out into a very ineffective movie," wrote film critic Andrew Sarris. "What was ritualized, stylized, or merely mentioned on the stage has been rendered with a brooding 'realism' on the screen." To give just one example of wrongheaded direction, instead of practicing his rope tricks on the bedpost, Altman has Shepard lasso a garbage can and drag it around the parking lot.

Shepard turns out to be all wrong as Eddie. Pale, scrawny, beady-eyed, he acts more like a mangy sidekick than the irresistible leading man. The erotic presence he commands in other films disappears when he has to say more than a few words. This unfortunate performance initiated a critical backlash against Shepard as a potential matinee idol. "The only thing we can be sure of is that the movie will end the news-magazine talk of Sam Shepard as the next Redford or Newman," wrote *New York* magazine's David Denby. "Not only is Sam Shepard not a movie superstar, Sam Shepard isn't really an actor. In *Fool for Love*, he appears thin and rather drawn, and he speaks in a sharp, querulous, unappealing voice; worst of all, ducking his head and looking away, he barely makes contact with his co-star, Kim Basinger."

Basinger, who replaced Jessica Lange, is equally blonde but virtually talent-free. As one critic pointed out, "46 other American actresses could have made some emotional sense out of May, or at least sent her smoldering in mystery." Onstage the figure of the Old Man occupied his own mysterious theatrical space; in the film, Harry Dean Stanton simply tiptoes around the motel, eavesdropping and looking embarrassed. The pacing of the scenes is strangely slow and slack, as if to leave room for the numerous country-and-western songs written for the film by Shepard's sister, Sandy Rogers. The only consolation for Shepard was that he got to drive a pickup and ride a horse. The debacle with *Fool for Love* may have led Shepard to say no when Milos Forman (the Academy Award-winning director of *Amadeus* and *One Flew Over the Cuckoo's Nest*) wanted to make a film of *A Lie of the Mind*.

In Bruce Beresford's 1986 film of Beth Henley's Pulitzer Prize-winning comedy, *Crimes of the Heart*, about a day in the life of three Mississippi sisters, Shepard plays the small part of Doc Porter, a married man who fools around with wayward sister Meg, played by Jessica Lange. It's not an especially good movie. Shepard's character wears glasses and walks with a limp (something about an accident during Hurricane Cordelia). It's apparent that Shepard has really long legs and a small high butt. It's also apparent that Lange is a bit chubby, having recently given birth to Hannah. Shepard and Lange definitely appear to be enjoying themselves in the scene where they take a ride in the country to look at the moon. They dance in a field as the sun comes up while the radio plays Willie Nelson singing "Don't Fence Me In," and they get back to town falling down drunk. Obviously, Shepard wanted to do the movie to work with Lange, but as a bonus he also got to drive a pickup. And perhaps he also enjoyed the dark Southern humor of Beth Henley's play, which manages to get a big laugh with the line "Granddaddy's in a coma."

Shepard didn't care much for Beresford, who didn't trust actors enough to let them rehearse or improvise. An Australian director who made his name with *Breaker Morant* and impressed Hollywood with his American debut, *Tender Mercies*, Beresford wrote the screenplay for an excruciating 1994 cable-TV film of *Curse of the Starving Class*. Director J. Michael McClary made many of the same mistakes as Altman in adapting Shepard to the screen. The action becomes overemphatic and sentimental. Except for Kathy Bates, reprising her performance as the mother in the successful Off-Broadway revival, the roles are badly cast and badly acted. James Woods, who can be brilliant, is all wrong and desperately overacts as the father. Henry Thomas, the child star of *E.T.*, looks far too well-bred as Wesley and ridiculously plays cello in the barn, as if he were the overprotected brother in Chekhov's *Three Sisters*. The only scene that has the flavor of Shepard is when Emma on horseback crashes through the plate-glass window of a honky-tonk firing an automatic rifle—an image Shepard has been trying to capture on film all his life.

In 1987, Shepard spent several weeks at Astoria Studios in Queens working on Woody Allen's film *September*, a somber drama released on the heels of one of Allen's most popular comedies, *Radio Days*. Like several of Allen's films in the '80s, *September* showcased a serious performance by Mia Farrow, his romantic partner; Woody doesn't appear in the picture at all. In a sort of dynastic casting coup, Allen had Farrow's mother, Maureen O'Sullivan, play her neglectful, show-bizzy mother in the film. Others in the cast included Dianne Wiest and Denholm Elliott. Shepard joined the ensemble late as a replacement for Christopher Walken, who left the picture over "creative differences" with Allen. The idea of Sam Shepard, Mr. True West, in a film by Woody Allen, Mr. New York City, is intriguing and incongruous. Perhaps they first crossed paths at Elaine's, an Upper East Side restaurant famous for catering to writers that Shepard frequented during rehearsals for *A Lie of the Mind*.

September portrayed a group of artists and professionals renting a house together in Vermont. In some ways, it pays homage to Chekhov's play *The Seagull*. (Shepard's character corresponded to Chekhov's Trigorin, a successful second-rate writer irresistibly attractive to women and envied by other men.) After photography was completed, Allen decided he was unhappy with the script and wanted to rewrite and reshoot a number of scenes. Maureen O'Sullivan became seriously ill and wasn't able to go through round two of *September*. Elaine Stritch was hired in her place and gave a stunning performance that remains the best reason to see the movie. Apparently, Shepard, like Christopher Walken, didn't exactly see eye-to-eye with Allen. For the final version of the film, he was replaced by Sam Waterston, who had worked with Allen before.

To many actors, working with directors like Robert Altman and Woody Allen would be a dream come true. After *Fool for Love* and *September*, Shepard had no illusions left about that. "They're piss-poor as actors' directors," he told an interviewer for *Esquire*. "They may be great filmmakers, but they have no respect for actors. Individually, each understands zip about acting. Allen knows even less than Altman, which is nothing." Although he was willing to badmouth him in the press, Shepard liked Woody Allen enough as a person to give him some rare Sidney Bechet recordings that had been in his father's collection of vintage jazz.

Baby Boom, released in 1987, is a completely idiotic screwball comedy. Shepard shows up in the last half hour playing a veterinarian named Dr. Cooper, whose clients include a horse, a pig, a dog, and Diane Keaton. He's the first thing Keaton sees after she comes out of a faint. Shepard has very little to do except stand around with his hands in his pockets, listening politely and trying to keep a straight face. Why would he agree to be in such a silly movie? Probably because he knew Diane Keaton, who was also in *Crimes of the Heart*. Maybe he got a kick out of playing a veterinarian, since he'd worked for a vet the summer he got out of high school and briefly entertained the idea of becoming one himself. Who knows, he might have considered the movie fitting, because he and Lange were having their own baby boom; at the time, Lange was pregnant with their second child, Sam Jr.

In Herbert Ross's 1989 film of Robert Harling's stage comedy *Steel Magnolias*, Shepard has a small part as Spud Jones, the husband of a hairdresser named Truvy, played by Dolly Parton. They have a son named Louie who drives a motorcycle and wears an earring. Onstage *Steel Magnolias* featured an all-female cast. The male characters added for the film are completely overwhelmed by the female stars (Parton, Sally Field, Shirley MacLaine, Olympia Dukakis, and starlet-of-the-moment Julia Roberts, whose brother Eric co-starred with Shepard in *Raggedy Man*).

It's amusing to see Sam Shepard in this predominantly female environment. The film capitalizes on the comic, sexy pairing of Parton and Shepard. He first appears when Truvy yells, "Spud, get in here and finish coloring these Easter eggs." His mock-sullen reply: "I live to serve." In another scene, Truvy brandishes a bottle of champagne she's bought to celebrate Spud's return from a seven-day stretch working on an offshore oil rig. "When he gets home, all he wants to do is sleep," she says, "but I plan to keep him up as long as I can." Besides giving him the opportunity to drive a pickup and play Dolly Parton's husband, *Steel Magnolias* probably also appealed to Shepard's taste in Southern humor. In fact, one line from the play suggested an artistic credo Shepard could endorse: "An ounce of pretension is worth a pound of manure."

Richard Ford, the American author who practices what the British like to call "dirty realism," writes stories about the kind of people who show up in Sam Shepard's plays. So it makes sense that Shepard would be cast in *Bright Angel*, Martin Fields' 1990 film based on Ford's *Rock Springs*. The movie is a rather good coming-of-age story about the adventures that allow a teenager named George to escape a prairie town in Montana. Shepard plays his father, Jack, who struggles without much luck to support his household. He and his son do some illegal duck hunting to raise cash, and he teases his son about his sex life. But then he stands by helplessly as his wife, played by Valerie Perrine, walks out on him with her new boyfriend Woody. Shepard does have an angry scene where he threatens to shoot the boyfriend (played by Will Patton, who performed in *Fool for Love* and *A Lie of the Mind* onstage). After his wife leaves, Shepard cries on his son's shoulder. His crying is awkward and embarrassing to watch, which is probably appropriate for the character. Shepard disappears after the first half hour, when George takes to the road in a dusty pickup.

Shepard ended his streak of driving-a-pickup movies with *Defenseless* (1991) in which he plays a gum-chewing gumshoe named Detective Beutel who smokes Lucky Strikes and says things like "I'm a cop, my job is to find out what happened" and "Just look for the truth, that's all." It's hard to understand why Shepard would bother to take a role in a forgettable cop thriller like this. Again, he probably did it out of loyalty to another leading lady. This time it was Barbara Hershey, who made a sexy and soulful partner playing Shepard's horse-riding wife in *The Right Stuff.*

Voyager, Volker Schlondorff's adaptation of the Max Frisch novel *Homo Faber*, was Shepard's first "star vehicle," the first time his performance had to carry the movie. From beginning to end, it's several cuts above all the Hollywood movies he made after *The Right Stuff*. Shepard plays Walter Faber, a globe-trotting engineer who proudly proclaims his strictly scientific view of the world.

"I don't read fiction," he declares, "and I don't dream." But in the course of two months, between April and June of 1957, he encounters a chain of coincidences that shakes him up and causes him to recognize that there is another level of reality beyond the material.

The film was an international production. Directed by a German, written by a Swiss, photographed by a Greek, with a crew of Frenchmen and Italians, it was shot primarily in Mexico. The script, whose working title was *Last Call for Passenger Faber*, was co-written by Schlondorff and Rudy Wurlitzer, an American hipster who has crossed paths with Shepard many times. Shepard identified with the character of Faber—understandably, because the connections between *Voyager* and his own work and life are numerous. The plane crash in the desert somewhere in Mexico is a perfect Shepard nightmare; it was a turbulent flight back to Oaxaca in 1965 that made Shepard swear off travelling by airplane. While stranded in the desert, Shepard's character occupies himself by typing letters on his manual typewriter and filming the wreckage with his portable movie camera. Wherever he goes, the character is surrounded by willing women. He makes out with the stewardess on the plane. Home in New York, his girlfriend Ivy has a romantic dinner waiting for him. He pulls her fully dressed into the shower. More of Shepard's body is on display than usual in this film. He has rather skinny legs and no muscles to speak of in his upper arms. On board an ocean liner to Europe, he meets a beautiful young French girl named Elisabeth, whom he calls Sabeth, and the night before they land he impulsively proposes marriage to her. Their first kiss at the ship's railing by moonlight has all the steamy eroticism missing from Shepard's scenes with Kim Basinger in *Fool for Love*. And when Faber learns, after consummating his relationship with Sabeth in Avignon, that she is the offspring of a romance with his college sweetheart in Zurich, this conjures the unconsciously incestuous relationship at the heart of *Fool for Love*. Sabeth's mother is named Hanna, which is also the name of Shepard's daughter with Jessica Lange.

Voyager is an unusually classy entry among Shepard's film acting credits, and it's not hard to see why he chose to accept the job. It had a good director, good sex scenes, and a good script. Perhaps Shepard took a special interest in Faber's engineering jargon, as when he gives Sabeth a tour of the ship's machinery and explains to her "what a kilowatt is, what hydraulics is, what an ampere is ... problems of torsion, index of friction, fatigue of the steel through vibration, and so on."

Accepting the job was one thing; executing it was another. The logistics of getting Shepard from Los Angeles to Poza Rica, 700 miles south of the Mexico border, became a big issue. The production company never missed an opportunity to remind Shepard, "It would be a lot easier on all of us if you flew." He was more than willing to drive himself. "Just get me a Chevy," he kept telling Schlondorff's busy assistants. One problem was that American rental car agencies refused to let their cars leave the country, for fear that they wouldn't get them back. So one car had to be arranged from Los Angeles to Laredo, and another car from the Texas border town to the location in Mexico. Another obstacle was the production staff's inability to comprehend that a movie star might not want to travel with a limousine and driver. Despite Shepard's insistent requests for a Chevy or even (at last resort) a Ford, the director's team of assistants triumphantly supplied him with a midnight blue stretch limo.

Not only that, they issued him as driver a tall, blond Austrian-born Viking dressed in a full tuxedo. The driver turned out to be an obnoxious road hog with a leadfoot. He insisted on barreling across the desert at 110 miles an hour. Inevitably, they were stopped just outside of El Paso by a line of heavily armed narcotics patrolmen with lunging German shepherds. Both Shepard and the driver were body-searched and forced to stand by the side of the road for an hour and a half while the cops stripped the car of its headliner, door panels, and carpeting, let the air out of the tires, and rummaged through their luggage. One of the officers made fun of the fancy belly-ostrich cowboy boots Shepard was wearing: "Stretch goddamn limos and bumpy bird boots. Somebody must be livin' right." Shepard drove the rest of the way to Laredo, with the driver asleep in the back seat.

The ordeal of crossing the border wasn't over yet. At customs, when asked what was his business in Mexico, Shepard made the mistake of saying he was there to act in a movie. Without a permit? How dare he! (It would have been so much easier if he flew.) The Mexican driver had to take him back across the border to Laredo to get a permit from the Mexican consulate. The desk clerk there treated him like some kind of arrogant imperialist carpetbagger—until he mentioned, under duress, the movies he was in, some of which she'd seen. Immediately her attitude changed.

She started flirting with him and demanded his autograph. "This is the same woman who, moments before, was ready to crucify me as an American devil. The movies hold a strange international hypnosis, as though real life were suddenly suspended into fantasy land." A hasty signature, not quite legible, got him across the border, and a long drive over the mountains finally landed him in Poza Rica.

Once he arrived at the location, then there was the small matter of actually giving a performance. Shepard had been coasting along in small supporting roles. *Voyager* presented the biggest acting challenge since his first film, *Days of Heaven*. He read Frisch's novel, read the screenplay several times, and took plenty of notes. Still, on the first day of shooting, he found himself in his hotel room, panicking because he didn't have a clue how to play the character. He'd read that Laurence Olivier liked to work from the outside in, so he put on the entire costume that had been carefully selected for him, including handmade English shoes, a period watch, and a snakeskin belt. Nothing. He put on his period hat and period glasses. He tried to scrape up memories of the fifties, but the first things that came to mind—"great Chevy fins and Tijuana girls in tight split skirts"—didn't quite fit the situation. Like Crow strategizing for his showdown with Hoss in *The Tooth of Crime*, he experimented with developing a particular walk for his character. "Just a simple walk. Nothing fancy. I start pacing the aisle of the trailer in full costume, with the suit coat slung over my shoulder. I'm hoping a walk will emerge. A particular walk, characteristic of the character. A walk that feels unlike my own walk yet close enough that I won't feel stupid doing it. I feel stupid enough already in this getup, with no clue who I'm supposed to be." Suddenly, there was a knock on the door. "They want to see me in the makeup trailer. I haven't even found my walk yet, and they want me for makeup!"

As he ambled through the crowd of Tohacatec Indians hired as extras and little boys grabbing his sleeve and pleading for handouts, his acting instincts finally kicked in. "This character is European through and through. Western. American, and gringo to the bones. He's in a foreign land, but he carries all his baggage with him; all his curse of heritage. His sense of superiority is involuntary. Intellectual. It's culturally preordained. He looks into the faces of these Indians without the slightest empathy. They are victims of culture, the same as him. Victims of the jungle; he, of the industrial age. They have nothing in common. He feels no contempt; just indifference. He's not as soft as Robert Morley, yet not as hard as Bogart. He's simply alone."

Working with better material made Shepard started taking his own acting more seriously. "I must say, it's become more interesting over the years," he said in a 1992 *Village Voice* interview. "At first I was really disappointed in film acting. Not only by its possibilities, but by mine. I felt very limited. I felt very intimidated, and unable to take many risks. Now I feel like I'm actually beginning to find a way to make an expression of character and to follow something that wasn't possible when I first started out. I don't know how that's happened, but it's evolved over the years of doing, I guess, just from practice." Now, he said, "the difficult part of film acting is not the acting, but the hanging around and the waiting and all the time that's burned up."

Because he played the central role, Shepard was privy to more of the inner workings of the film production than usual on *Voyager*. And because he'd started directing films himself, he took a new interest in that stuff. Plus, since this was one of his rare acting gigs on a film that didn't involve horses, he was trapped without some of his usual ways to pass all those endless hours of waiting that define life on a movie set. He found himself keeping a detailed journal and fashioning self-contained stories about the absurdities of moviemaking on location and the daily culture clashes between the invading movie crew and the curious or indifferent townspeople. Some of them documented his tangles with Volker Schlondorff. "I never met anyone I liked so much off the set that I felt so much hostility with *on* the set," Shepard said later. Other stories dealt with a hard-drinking veteran stuntman on the picture who turned out to have been at one time a stand-in for Emilio Fernandez, the legendary Mexican actor-director who shot and killed a critic who gave him a bad review. (Shepard loved that story and never tired of retelling it.)

He began to conceive these journal entries as a collection of stories called *Slave of the Camera*. He even published three excerpts in *Antaeus*, the literary journal founded by Paul Bowles, in the Spring 1991 issue, which was devoted to one-act plays by virtually every major American playwright. Apparently, Shepard didn't maintain enough interest to complete *Slave of the Camera*. But ten of the stories he wrote during the *Voyager* experience surfaced years later in *Cruising Paradise*, the collection of "tales"

Shepard published in 1996. Oddly, he left out one of the three stories published in *Antaeus*, the most amusing and perhaps most self-revealing one. Datelined "March 18, El Paso," it transcribes a conversation with a stranger in the next toilet stall in a truck stop bathroom who notices Shepard's ostrich-skin cowboy boots. While conducting an extended tirade about faggots, Jews, and niggers, the unseen trucker keeps asking Shepard, "You sure yer not a faggot?" To which Shepard finally replies, "Well, nobody's ever sure, are they?"

After *Voyager*, Shepard's attitude about participating in "sanctioned vanity" shifted. "I'm an actor now; I confess," he wrote in his journal just before setting off to work with Schlondorff. Still, being an actor meant doing it on his own terms. "I don't fly. I've been having some trouble landing jobs lately because of this not wanting to fly business; plus, I refuse to live in L.A. . . . I don't own a fax machine or an answering service or call forwarding or a cellular car phone or a word processor . . . On top of all this, I'm not getting any younger and my face is falling apart. Most of my lower teeth were knocked out by a yearling colt in the spring of '75. Half my upper teeth are badly discolored, and one of them's been dead for as long as I can remember. When you get right down to it, I'm lucky to even have an agent at this point in time." Mike Figgis, the director of *Leaving Las Vegas* and other good small films, offered Shepard a starring role if he would get his teeth fixed. No deal.

However self-conscious Shepard was about his looks and disdainful of the vanity cultivated by Hollywood's dream factory, he was neither ignorant of his glamorous image nor indifferent to its benefits. He simply preferred to be the one controlling his image. He wouldn't show up for just any old photo opportunity. Nonetheless, he has been repeatedly photographed for magazine spreads and book jackets by some of the most glamorous fashion photographers of the day, including Herb Ritts, Annie Liebovitz, Brigitte Lacombe, and Bruce Weber. Weber even put out a limited edition book of pictures he'd taken of Shepard and Jessica Lange over a three-year period in Santa Fe and in Virginia. Shepard's careful cultivation of an unstudied image did not go unnoticed. As one critic, Katherine Dieckmann, shrewdly noted in the *Village Voice*, "Weber's photos of Shepard have accompanied recent cover stories in *Interview* and *Esquire*, where the T-shirt-

and-jean-clad celeb is captured assuming poses that spell American Classic (in that Ralph Lauren way): casually smoking a cigarette, leading a horse, and brooding, always brooding, his jaggedly handsome face never totally yielding to the PR opportunity at hand."

Taking his image control further in hand, Shepard seemed to get a little pickier about the films he chose to act in after *Voyager*. Michael Apted's 1992 *Thunderheart* opens with a brief visual image of Native Americans "calling the directions" at the beginning of a prayer ceremony. That alone would probably be enough to intrigue Shepard, who has long been interested in Native American lore and sacred rituals. Perversely, in the film Shepard plays an enemy of the Native people, a hardass FBI agent investigating a murder on an Indian reservation that he and some other crooked cops apparently set up to silence political opposition to uranium mining on sacred Indian ground. Shepard's character, Frank Coutelle, is nicknamed Cooch. He leads an FBI raid on a sweat lodge ceremony, and in the course of arresting a suspect, Cooch gets bit by a badger. Throughout the film, Shepard looks tired and smokes a lot of cigarettes. One of the anti-Indian yahoos that Cooch collaborates with is played by Fred Ward, who also played one of the astronauts in *The Right Stuff*.

Shepard gives an especially good performance in *Thunderheart*, playing a man whose belief in *realpolitik* leads him to make choices with disastrous moral consequences. In admirably Brechtian fashion, Cooch's bad example teaches the film's main character, a half-breed FBI agent played by Val Kilmer, to respect his own Native heritage. The movie ends with a somewhat ludicrous car chase in the desert that suggests a Native American *Thelma and Louise*. But overall it's a high-quality film, and the fact that it was filmed in the Badlands of South Dakota was surely a plus for Shepard.

In the spring of 1993, Shepard went to New Orleans to play a role in Alan Pakula's film version of John Grisham's bestselling novel *The Pelican Brief*. Julia Roberts stars as Darby Shaw, a woman law student who investigates the murder of two Supreme Court justices. (After she appeared in *Steel Magnolias* with Shepard, Roberts' performance in the mega-hit *Pretty Woman* catapulted her to Hollywood's A-list of bankable actors.) Denzel Washington plays the *Washington Post* reporter who validates her theory about who's responsible for the assassinations. Shepard plays Tulane Law School professor Thomas Callahan. He first appears lecturing about *Bowers v. Hardwick* and challenging his class to explain the Supreme Court's logic in that case, which upheld the State of Georgia's right to arrest two men for having sex in their own bedroom. "The Supreme Court was wrong," Julia Roberts says. That must be the right answer, because the next thing you know she and Shepard are in bed together. Shepard gives a moving and vulnerable performance as a middle-aged professor perpetually falling in love with students and struggling unsuccessfuly to stay sober. He disappears early in the film, his car fire-bombed in front of Julia Roberts' eyes. Pakula's film is a well-made thriller, almost as good as his *All the President's Men*, and it's a feather in Shepard's cap, although he would later dismiss it as "three weeks' work."

A much cornier piece of fluff is *Safe Passage*, a film by successful New York stage director Robert Allen Ackerman starring Susan Sarandon as a woman with seven sons whom she loves too much. Shepard plays her estranged husband, an inventor who has sudden inexplicable spells of blindness. The movie is set during the 1991 Persian Gulf War. One of Sarandon's sons is stationed there with the Marines, and when the TV news announces that a Marine barracks has been bombed, she freaks out and gathers all her men around her for a vigil. Most of the movie consists of cutesy domestic comedy. Shepard gets on Sarandon's nerves by displaying all the habits that caused them to break up. He lets the family cat inside the house, and he dunks his teabag exactly seven times and tosses it over his shoulder into the sink. At regular intervals, he has to "go blind," which means immediately jumping up and crashing into the furniture. It's not one of Shepard's finest screen moments. But the director of photography was Ralf Bode, with whom Shepard had worked on several films. And it was filmed in New Jersey and gave him something to do in the fall of 1993 while his theater producers were trying, ultimately without success, to scare up the backing to mount his play *Simpatico* on Broadway.

A happier experience was *Lily Dale*, the film version of a play by Horton Foote, another Pulitzer Prize-winning playwright with a distinguished career in films. Besides the screenplays for *To Kill a Mockingbird* and *Tender Mercies*, Foote won an Oscar for *The Trip to Bountiful*, as did the film's star, Geraldine Page. Filmed in Dallas, *Lily Dale* was its own kind of family affair, with Shepard as

invited guest. Like *The Trip to Bountiful*, *Lily Dale* was directed by
Peter Masterson, Horton Foote's cousin, and Mary Stuart Masterson, the director's daughter, played the title role. *Lily Dale* is essentially a Grimm's Fairy Tale set in a genteel Houston household
in the horse-and-buggy era. Shepard plays the evil stepfather
whom everyone calls Mr. Davenport—not just Lily Dale, whom he
pampers and spoils, but also his wife Corella (Stockard Channing)
and her nineteen-year-old son Horace (Tim Guinee), whom he
can't bear to have around the house. Horace has been supporting
himself since the age of twelve because that's how Mr. Davenport
learned to "be a man." It's also clear that Mr. Davenport resents
the emotional intimacy Horace has with his mother, whose first
husband was a drunk. It's an upsetting and minutely detailed
drama about a boy who grows up without a father.

Shepard took the job because "it was just good writing. But
that stuff doesn't come around every day," he told the *New
Yorker*'s Stephen Schiff. The dearth of halfway intelligent scripts
make it easier to decide what roles to take, he said, because the
criteria are simple: "Does this thing have any value at all, or is it
just a vacuous corporate doo-dah? It's unbelievable, some of the
scripts. Where does this come from? There's no dialogue, there's
no character, there's no real situation, it's just somebody's notion
about how to put stars together."

Another made-for-TV film shot in Texas allowed Shepard to re-
turn to his favorite mythological territory. *Streets of Laredo*,
Joseph Sargent's two-part mini-series, was based on Larry
McMurtry's novel, a sequel to his Wild West saga *Lonesome Dove*.
James Garner stars as Capt. Call, the role played by Tommy Lee
Jones in the extremely popular TV mini-series of *Lonesome Dove*.
In *Streets*, Capt. Call is the prairie ranger hired by the railroad to
find the young Mexican bandit who keeps hijacking the train,
stealing payrolls, and gunning down the train crews. Shepard plays
his longtime deputy, Pea Eye Parker, who's now married to Sissy
Spacek, who was a two-dollar whore in the town of Lonesome
Dove but has become a schoolteacher and mother of five. Pea Eye
is reluctant to join Call's latest search party because he and his
wife have a baby girl. Inevitably, though, testosterone gets the better of him. He saddles up and away he rides. He acquires a sidekick named Flat Shoes, a Kickapoo Indian renowned for his
ability to track animals. Flat Shoes is obsessed with learning to
follow tracks on paper—that is, writing—and wonders if Pea Eye

can read. Shepard as Pea Eye shyly but proudly admits that he knows a couple of letters—"P" and "Y." And he promises that his schoolteacher wife will teach Flat Shoes to read if he will help nab the Mexican killer.

Like *Lonesome Dove*, *Streets of Laredo* is part classy Western, well-written and well-acted along the lines of Clint Eastwood's *Unforgiven*, and part prime-time soap opera. McMurtry brings in characters who have been mythologized in story and song, such as Judge Roy Bean (played by Ned Beatty) and John Wesley Hardin (played by Randy Quaid). In addition to a heavy concentration of horse-riding and intensely violent gunplay, McMurtry and co-screenwriter Diana Ossama nurture a strong subplot about the treatment and mistreatment of women in the West, routinely assumed to be present only to provide sexual services. To a certain degree, the women's story, which gives Spacek and Sonia Braga (who plays the bandit's mother) nearly as much air-time as the leading male actors, is welcome for filling in some historical blanks. On the other hand, its depiction of gender relations gets revisionist to the point of sentimentality: it ends with James Garner, as a grizzled old one-legged prairie ranger, deciding it would be a good idea to educate a blind orphaned Mexican girl.

For the most part, though, *Streets of Laredo* works as a good, unromanticized Wild West story. In contrast to the saturated color and aesthetic perfection of, say, *Days of Heaven*, Shepard's looks and performance are strictly anti-glamorous. He's bearded and graying, and he describes himself as "gangly." In fact, he looks eerily like the picture of his own daddy that appears in *Motel Chronicles*. The movie was shot in a number of small towns near the Mexican border—Del Rio, Lajitas, Bracketville, Alpine—and enable Shepard to inhabit some patches of Texas history, which has long been one of his favorite subjects. He was also able to get his son Jesse, now a grown critter in his twenties, hired to do stuntwork on the picture, which aired nationally in November of 1995.

After separating from Shepard, Jesse's mother O-Lan charted her own course as an artist. The first thing she did after the divorce was change her name. Not back to Johnson, the name she was born with, but to Jones—a whole new name for the next stage of her own evolving identity. The Overtone Theater, which she'd founded in San Francisco, transformed into a production company called Overtone Industries, although at first they called themselves

O-Lan Jones and the Overtones. That made them sound like a cross between a theater company and a rock band, which they were. O-Lan also co-founded Pulp Playhouse, an improvisational theater that gained a fanatical following in the Bay Area and played for a while in Los Angeles.

By 1990 O-Lan had enough of a career going in movies to convince her to relocate to L.A. with her son. In addition to small parts in *Married to the Mob* and *Beethoven*, she played the mean-looking, organ-playing fundamentalist in Tim Burton's *Edward Scissorhands* and the all-too-friendly waitress who serves Key Lime pie to Woody Harrelson in the first scene of Oliver Stone's *Natural Born Killers*. She also played a regular role on the CBS-TV series *Harts of the West*. And she wasted no time before plunging into the local theater scene, hooking up with old friends from New York and San Francisco as well as forging relationships with the L.A. equivalent of the Magic Theater's feisty fringe, people like playwright John Steppling and director David Schweizer. She reconnected with Murray Mednick, who'd first cast her at Theater Genesis when she was a teenage actress and who was keeping the Padua Hills Playwrights' Conference alive. She acted in a play with Jim Haynie, the San Francisco Mime Troupe actor who'd played Lee in the premiere of *True West*, and she performed in a musical adaptation of *King Lear* directed by Shepard's sister, Roxanne Rogers. *Shelf Life*, a play she co-wrote and performed with Andrea Stein and Jim Turner, got turned into a film by Paul Bartel. And with the money she made from *Edward Scissorhands*, she commissioned a quartet of short mini-operas based on myths called *String of Pearls*. It was produced at the Met Theatre, a company whose celebrated alumni include longtime Shepard actors Ed Harris and James Gammon.

Without abandoning the past she shared with Shepard, O-Lan Jones carved out a reputation for herself as a talented artist—singer, actor, writer, composer, and producer—with high ambitions. "I see him every couple of years," she said about Shepard. "I had a great time with him. I'm having a great time without him."

The feeling was mutual. "I would have been down the river if I hadn't met Jessica," Shepard said. "There was salvation for me. It's just this suddenly being connected with someone in a way you never knew was possible. It's like a revelation, it's like discovering a whole new life that you didn't know was in you. I'm not saying there are no problems, but I've capsized my life so many times in the past with this thing of burning my bridges and entering new territory that I'm beginning to wonder whether in fact I've really been running away from something that it would be better to turn around and join hands with. And in this case for me it has to do with love and the possibility of a real family."

In *A Lie of the Mind*, Shepard imaginatively sketched out the warring impulses in his blood set off by the very idea of family. The wild man Jake bids farewell to civilization and heads off into the wilderness, where he remains at large. His brother Frankie stays put in the civilized domesticity of the far north. And that side of Shepard would lead him to his next destination as a writer.

Chapter Ten:

THE IDENTITY DANCE

SIMMS: How many lives do you think a man can live, Mr. Webb? How many lives within this *one*?
VINNIE: I'm not sure I understand you, sir.
SIMMS: Well, say for instance, you could put the past to death and start over. Right now. You look like you might be a candidate for that.
VINNIE: That's not possible.

Simpatico, Sam Shepard

Early in 1987 Jessica Lange was having another one of her mood swings. "I was pregnant with the third baby, and there's that restless thing of wanting to do something and not let too many years pass just child bearing," she said. "I thought the only thing I could do in a limited amount of time is a play for cable or something. So I asked Sam if he'd want to direct a play so we could work together. He said yeah, but if I'm going to do that, let me write something for you." Shepard started writing, though he didn't like the idea of doing it as television. And after her experience acting in a TV production of Tennessee Williams' *Cat on a Hot Tin Roof*, Lange became disenchanted with the small screen as well. "The medium doesn't work for me," she said. "So he just continued writing it, but now with the idea of shooting it as a film."

Shepard finished the screenplay for *Far North* in California while recuperating from a serious polo injury. "I cracked two vertebrae and couldn't play, so I was forced to write. I sat down and finished this thing—it took me about two weeks, but I'd already had most of it done." The result was something Shepard had been dreaming of for a long time: his first film not only as writer but also as director. He found a smart and supportive producer in Carolyn Pfeiffer of Alive Films, who had produced a number of good, hip movies, including six by writer-director Alan Rudolph (*Choose Me, The Moderns*)

In *Far North*, Lange plays Kate, a woman who returns to her parents' house in Minnesota from New York after her father has an accident with a runaway horse. The extremely slim plot centers on the promise Kate's father extracts from her to avenge him by shooting his horse. "Yer the only one mean enough!" he tells her. Kate's homecoming is also an opportunity to find refuge in a community of women—her sweetly vague mother (played by Ann Wedgeworth), her cranky 100-year-old grandmother (Nina Draxten), her uptight sister Rita (Tess Harper), and Rita's wild child, Jilly (Patricia Arquette). Essentially the film is a comedy that jokes cartoonishly about strong women and ineffectual men, at times pining nostalgically for a time when men ran the world and all women had to do was make them a hearty breakfast. The somewhat stagy realism and talkiness of the screenplay occasionally gets interrupted with brief flashes of horses running, sometimes ridden by women wearing tribal makeup. Visually, *Far North* is a poem about blonde women and wild horses.

In Shepard's iconography, he associates his central male characters geographically with the south and the west, which correlates with his own family background, and his central female characters with the north and the east, which correlates with Jessica Lange's background (she's from Minnesota). Thematically, you could say that Shepard broke *A Lie of the Mind* in half and further develops the women's side of the story in *Far North*. The family constellation of Beth-Meg-Baylor from *A Lie of the Mind* is represented in *Far North* by Lange, Wedgeworth (who played the same ditsy mother onstage in *A Lie of the Mind*), and Charles Durning (who played opposite Lange in the movie *Tootsie* and opposite Shepard in Woody Allen's *September*). Durning plays the kind of blustery, drunken father who appears throughout Shepard's work. (Marlon Brando was the director's first choice for the role; when Shepard offered it, the actor begged off because of ill health.) The film ends, as so many Shepard pieces do, with a man—Durning's Bertrum—heading out into the unknown all by himself. And the Red Clay Ramblers again supplied a country-bluegrass soundtrack. But the recurring refrain "Where are all the men?" suggests that even in this strong female territory, there is a longing for the other half of the equation.

The movie was shot in Duluth, Jessica Lange's hometown. Her father had a walk-on part in the film, and her sister worked on the costumes. The film crew called it "an homage to Jessica's family," and Shepard admits that the gentleness of the film—in contrast to the hell-raising, hard-drinking families who show up in his plays—has everything to do with her. "Having fallen in love with Jessica, I took a tremendous turn in terms of my own vulnerability. My relationship with Jessica allowed this vulnerability to show itself."

Shepard's debut as a filmmaker didn't set any worlds on fire. It opened in November 1988 to mediocre box office receipts, and film critics found his newfound vulnerability less than compelling. "Unlike most of his plays, and even his bumpy but occasionally very beautiful script for Wim Wenders's *Paris, Texas*, there's no sense of underlying rage, or even strong sentiment, save a warm-milk nostalgia for family (even if they're all nuts) and the good ol' days," said Katherine Dieckmann in the *Village Voice*. The kindest review came from the *New Republic*'s Stanley Kauffmann, who had closely followed Shepard's work in the theater: "This time he leaves his usual Western haunts—and haunted they are for him—to burrow into the home country of his companion, Jessica Lange, who plays a leading role. It's northern Minnesota, not a great way from Duluth and Lake Superior. In this landscape, which feels a bit raw even on sunny days, Shepard fixes his subjects: the persistence of country life in a nation tugged everywhere by urban standards; the disappearance of young men from this countryside; the ancient and now-humorous contest between man and animal—in this case a stubborn horse; the struggle to keep a large scale in a small-scale existence; the explosions of sex. Shepard connects all these subjects with interwoven stories about the members of a stubborn family. Stubbornness is their chief common trait." But most critics agreed with Georgia Brown, who wrote in the Manhattan weekly *7 Days*, "*Far North* reminds us that movies are different from plays. Shepard's theatrical dialogue rings false onscreen. He intends to be visual—especially with some showy compositions featuring birches and a full moon—and some of his best gags are in the editing, but essentially *Far North* looks like moonlighting."

Undeterred, Shepard continued to dream in moviescapes, though the next time around he returned to more familiar territory. His second film, *Silent Tongue*, takes place in New Mexico in 1873 within the context of a Wild West medicine show. This is territory dominated by men and horses, violence and trickery, ancestral crimes and earth wisdom. Essentially, in *Silent Tongue* Shepard took the men's side of the story from *A Lie of the Mind* and tracked it backward in time.

The film tells two parallel stories about fathers and sons. The only women who figure in the movie are a pair of half-breed sisters, one who's living and one who's a ghost. They are, however, central figures. They constitute the currency in a complicated emotional/economic exchange between the male characters. Their mother also appears briefly and symbolically—she is the title character, an Indian woman who had her tongue cut out after being raped by a white man. When one sister dies in childbirth, her young white husband goes crazy with grief and refuses to give her body proper burial. His shocked father returns to the man who sold him the girl—Eamon McCree, master of the bogus "Indian Medicine Show"—and tries to buy her sister, to assuage his son's grief. But the second sister is one of the stars of the medicine show, and besides McCree's own son is in love with her. It's not that women are merely something to be bought and sold. In the language of the film, the female is ultimately the only thing that has value to the men.

The film was originally inspired by the 1964 black-and-white Japanese movie *Onibaba*. "I'm only interested in things that go way beyond the ordinary, beyond the mainstream of what people think of as good. I've always loved those old Japanese films about Shinto legends," said Shepard. But *Silent Tongue* overflows with motifs from his other works: Irish cowboys, half-breed Indians, damaged women, Native ritual, old-time country music, clowns and sideshows. The dualities of good/bad, male/female that Shepard has long struggled with blossom into parallel stories that he tracks with Shakespearean symmetry. Even the name Eamon (an Irish variation on Edmund) is one that Shepard has long been attached to. It turns up in the manuscripts of several unfinished plays. There was a time when Shepard even considered writing under the pseudonym "Eamon Reese."

Silent Tongue was the first ever French-financed Western. Belbo Films put up the money, though Alive Films' Carolyn Pfeiffer oversaw the production, as she did *Far North*. His first picture had been a big educational experience for Shepard. Part of what he learned was strictly technical, "angles, coverage, what works as a master shot and what doesn't, and where you look good and where you don't, things like that. And lenses, I learned a helluva lot about what sizes relate to what you actually see onscreen." He also picked up some lessons about writing for the screen that basically meant re-learning what he discovered when he started directing his plays onstage. "I've learned to cut my speeches way down. You can't get away with long stage monologues. Everything is minimalized, tight, short, cut away fast," he said. "'Course *Far North* was entirely different, a domestic film. This is big screen, animals, land, epic scenes, more dramatic." For *Silent Tongue*, he made it a point to lean more in the direction of favorite filmmakers like Luis Buñuel, Akira Kurosawa, and Jacques Tati, whose works so overwhelmingly concentrate on visuals over dialogue that they nearly function as silent films.

Perhaps most humbling, Shepard saw for the first time making *Far North* "how easy it is to neglect actors. When you're directing you've got so many other things to worry about—the lens, the effects, the lighting, acting and the budget, writing, cameras, costumes, the animals, all the other stuff going on. So when the actor steps in, it's like he's a piece of furniture, you know what I mean? All that makes it difficult for the actor to feel like an artist."

That Shepard got a chance to make *Silent Tongue* at all owed a lot to the commercial success of Kevin Costner's *Dances with Wolves*, which swept the Academy Awards in 1990. (Shepard is quick to let it be known, though, that he wrote the script in 1988, well before *Dances with Wolves*.) Originally *Silent Tongue* was going to star two movie legends, Gregory Peck and Albert Finney, as well as Val Kilmer, with whom Shepard had recently acted in *Thunderheart*. In the years-long hunt for financing that's maddeningly common for independent filmmaking—the picture finally went into production in 1992—Shepard lost those actors, but the cast he got was not too shabby, either. Alan Bates played Eamon McCree, the Medicine Show owner, and Shepard cast Dermot Mulroney, who starred in *Bright Angel*, as his half-Indian son. Richard Harris, who'd recently appeared in Clint Eastwood's downbeat Western *Unforgiven* and won an Oscar nomination for *The Field*, played Prescott, and River Phoenix, a talented young actor with traces of James Dean's quiet soulfulness, was his grief-crazed son Talbot.

Sheila Tousey, whom Shepard had met making *Thunderheart*, took the role of the avenging ghost, Awbonnie. For the role of Velada, her half-breed sister, Shepard insisted on hiring a Native American actress who could also ride. Over 200 women auditioned before Jeri Arrendondo, a full-blooded Mescalero-Apache Indian, got the part. The Medicine Show performers included Bill Irwin and David Shiner, two physical comedians acclaimed in the hip performance art field known as "New Vaudeville," as well as Shepard's favorite music group, the Red Clay Ramblers. The two clowns liked the musicians so much that afterwards they all put together a successful Broadway show called *Fool Moon*.

Shooting a Western in New Mexico surrounded by guys and horses, Shepard was totally in his element. On location, Shepard made time to follow the races and place bets at the nearby Ruidoso Tracks. The cast and crew got swept up in the betting fever as well. The set bustled with real cowboys working as wranglers and real Native American stuntmen. "A big cowboy-boot fetish has gripped them all, and a bigger baseball-cap or black-ponytail cult," an observer who visited the set reported. "Shepard himself favors an old cap, and has chosen to look as un-Hollywood and un-leading man as he can."

River Phoenix spent a good deal of time working on his performance as the demented, love-crazed Talbot, who won't leave the dead body of his half-breed wife. He loved working with Shepard. "The first time I met Sam, I felt like we were an uncle and nephew out doing their chores on the farm," he told the unit publicist. "Without a word spoken, I felt warm and secure and there was an instant trust. I knew it would be a pure experience." Phoenix hung around with the Kiowa Indians, wore burnt cork on his face, and rumpled his hair with his fists. Every so often he would throw himself to the ground and writhe in the dirt.

Shepard encouraged Phoenix's intense efforts to get into character. To reinforce the bond Talbot feels to his dead wife, during rehearsals Shepard literally tied Phoenix to Sheila Tousey with a piece of twine. "Grotowski once said a great thing about directing. He said you have to *seduce* the actors; you actually have to invite actors into a world where they feel they've never been before, but which they're willing to try out. That's the kind of thing I'm after," Shepard said. "You make an invitation. There's a demand, too, but the demand has to do with something that's gonna pay off. It's not for nothing; it's not for its own sake. The payoff is that the actor discovers a *life*. And you hope that it's a life that they haven't really found before. Or maybe they've found a little part of it, and you'll help them to find more. More than anything you have to encourage actors to be courageous. Most of them want to be, but there's a tremendous fear. Almost every really good actor I've come across in some part of himself is terrified. And you have to make that terror less prevalent by inviting him to explore something that may be dangerous but in the end is going to pay off." Unfortunately, by the time *Silent Tongue* opened, River Phoenix was dead, another sad drug casualty, at age 23.

The most important character in the film was the land itself. The film was shot near Roswell, New Mexico, on prairies that have changed very little since European settlers first ventured into Kiowa territory. "The prairie is so barren, desolate, austere and empty, and that's what the characters are," said Richard Harris. "Half the work is done for the actor by the location. We just stand in the settings Shepard has picked for us and we don't have to say a word."

Shooting *Silent Tongue* was a very different experience for Shepard from making *Far North*. "One of the things that drove me nuts about *Far North* was interiors," he said. "I don't feel at home shooting interiors in terms of picking and choosing camera angles. I can do it, but I don't feel excited about it." When he wrote *Silent Tongue*, he made sure that all but one of the scenes could be shot outdoors. "When I get outdoors, immediately everything seems to fall into certain patterns and structures. That's one of the reasons I wrote something that was predominately exteriors. If you embrace the landscape, it isn't daunting. I loved the framing possibilities the prairie offered."

Shepard finished editing the film in time to show it at the Sundance Film Festival in Utah and then at the Cannes Film Festival, both in the spring of 1993. Once more, though, the world was not on the edge of its collective seat waiting to see Shepard's poetic preoccupations transferred to the screen. Reviewing the film at Cannes, *Variety* called *Silent Tongue* a "mystic oater" and predicted dim commercial prospects. It took more than a year for the producers to find a company willing to distribute the film. When it was released commercially, it got some reviews comparing it favorably to *Unforgiven* and *Dances with Wolves*. "*Far North* was a facile comedy-drama about a contemporary farm family falling apart. *Silent Tongue* comes from a deeper part of Mr. Shepard's imagination," Caryn James wrote in the *New York Times*. "It deals with mysticism, history, and the kind of profound family tangles that echoes his best plays (*Buried Child, True West, A Lie of the Mind*). But while *Silent Tongue* is powerfully connected to Mr. Shepard's dramas, here he truly becomes a film maker. He composes eloquent pictures within the vast space of the plains, and uses his images to tell a story layered with meaning."

Silent Tongue does look gorgeous. The camera etches the actors against the Western sky with a classic pictorial elegance that recalls *Days of Heaven*. But the drama of the movie is almost entirely conceptual, interior, and static, several layers removed from engaging an audience emotionally. *Variety*'s prediction turned out to be accurate. The movie did no business and was in and out of theaters in ten minutes.

The commercial failure of his first two films put Shepard's future as a filmmaker in jeopardy. "I'm a slow learner and I saw them as experiments, but there's very little room for that in American film-making," he said. "I'd love to direct another film. But I refuse to go through that circle dance they put you through to beg for money, to beg for validity, to keep begging all the way through the process in order to make the thing you want to make. I don't have to beg in the theater, but I do have to beg in movies. And I don't want to be a beggar."

Hollywood still seemed to respect Shepard as a writer. Producers continued to approach him about adapting books for the screen, but that kind of hired-gun work didn't appeal to him. "The struggle to do that is not worth it," he said. "You're just not really able to do your own work. That's what's so great about writing a novel or a play, you don't have to answer to anyone."

Case in point: his 1991 play *States of Shock*. All he had to do was let it be known that he had completed a new play, and Shepard had everything he needed at his disposal: a theater (the American Place, site of past Shepard triumphs), a star (John Malkovich, at last agreeing to be in a Shepard premiere), and a sold-out run. After a six-year hiatus from the theater, it was in some ways the perfect—that is to say, perfectly perverse—follow-up to a long, laboriously worked-out play like *A Lie of the Mind*. *States of Shock* is the kind of play Shepard used to toss off in the late '60s, full of repetitious dialogue, raw images, food fights, and other juvenile comic gestures.

Stubbs, a young man in a wheelchair, keeps pulling up his shirt to show off a ghastly war wound and to complain, "My thing hangs like dead meat!" His companion, a crypto-fascist military man known only as the Colonel, smashes banana splits in half. A waitress struggles to carry cups of coffee across the stage without spilling them. An elderly man dressed in white, waiting with his white wife to be served their clam chowder, masturbates underneath his dinner napkin. Two drummers create an ominous racket behind a scrim.

Clearly written very fast, in an all-night frenzy of pounding at the typewriter fueled these days by coffee and cigarettes rather than a handful of amphetamines, the play was, Shepard acknowledged, his response to the Persian Gulf War. In that conflict, the United States used Iraq's invasion of oil-rich Kuwait as an opportunity to flaunt its military might. Vastly overequipped in personnel and firepower compared to the Iraqi army, U.S. military forces devastated Baghdad and other Iraqi locations with computer-operated "smart bombs" that created a never-tallied number of casualties said to be in excess of 100,000. The American media covered the event with all the jingoistic fervor of a small-town TV station reporting on the home team's comeback victory.

"I was in Kentucky when the war opened," Shepard told Carol Rosen in a Village Voice interview. "I was in a bar that I go to a lot down there because it's a horsemen's bar. Normally that bar is just a din of conversation and people having a great time and talking about horses and this, that, and the other. And I walked in the bar and it was stone silence. The TV was on, and these planes were coming in, and suddenly . . . It just seemed like doomsday to me. I could not believe the systematic kind of insensitivity of it. That there was this punitive attitude—we're going to just knock these people off the face of the earth. And then it's devastating. Not only that, but they've convinced the American public that this was a good deed, that this was in fact a heroic fucking war, and welcome the heroes back. What fucking heroes, man? I mean, they bombed the shit out of these people. They knocked the stew out of them over there with bombing and bombing and bombing. The notion of this being a heroic event is just outrageous. I couldn't believe it.

"I still can't believe it," he said. "I can't believe that, having come out of the '60s and the incredible reaction to Vietnam, that voice has all but disappeared. Vanished. There's no voice anymore. This is supposed to be what America's about? This fucking military? . . . I just got so outraged by the whole hoax of it, and the way everything is choked down and censored in the media . . . I wanted to create a character of such outrageous, repulsive, military, fascist demonism that the audience would recognize it and say, 'Oh this is the essence of this thing.' I thought Malkovich came pretty close to it. Just creating this monster fascist."

Shepard didn't direct SOS but turned it over to his old friend Bill Hart, who had made a bit of a name for himself directing

Robert De Niro in *Cuba and His Teddy Bear* first at the Public Theater and then on Broadway. The playwright made it a point to be around for rehearsals, though, thrilled at last to be working with Malkovich, whose humor and gutsiness he admired.

While he was in New York, Shepard found out that Sam Waterston was doing a reading of work by Primo Levi at Manhattan Theatre Club and invited himself along. An Italian Jewish writer and philosopher, Levi had survived Auschwitz and written books about the Nazi concentration camps; in his old age, Levi rather surprisingly committed suicide. He appears as a somewhat puzzling moral inspiration to the Woody Allen character in one of Allen's best movies, *Crimes and Misdemeanors*, in which Waterston also played a major role. Waterston, of course, acted in Shepard's *Red Cross* and *La Turista* before going on to a major career in TV, films, and Broadway. At the reading, he and Shepard took turns reading from Levi's work, sometimes playing parts in a dialogue. One of the stories Shepard read was a delightful fable about an Italian village girl who suddenly sprouts wings and begins to fly—a story that may have turned up in the research about angels he and Chaikin did during their aborted workshop production of *The War in Heaven* at Harvard.

States of Shock opened in May 1993, but it didn't get the warm welcome the playwright might have desired. "Sam Shepard has been away from the New York theater for only six years—since the epic *Lie of the Mind*—but *States of Shock*, his new play at the American Place, could lead you to believe he has been hibernating since his East Village emergence in the Vietnam era," Frank Rich wrote in the *New York Times*. "With manifest sincerity and some courage, Mr. Shepard wishes to examine the casualties, corporal and spiritual alike, of even a fast, victorious, morally right-minded war, and he also wishes to question the values of a society that leaps so readily into the fray." However, Rich said, the long one-act play "does not really go anywhere intellectually or theatrically once it has established its basic thematic attack." The actors got high praise, though. "Wielding props that include a retractable military-briefing pointer, a ferocious saber and a particularly runny banana split, Mr. Malkovich disrupts a coffee shop with more malicious glee than anyone since Jack Nicholson in *Five Easy Pieces*."

Shepard himself later said about *States of Shock*, "I think there was an intrinsic misunderstanding about it, which was probably my fault. I think the audience, and obviously everybody else, had a hard time realizing that this was indeed about a father and son relationship." This intriguing comment suggests a biographical element to the play beyond the topical Gulf War context. As a child Shepard frequently heard his father crow about the bombing missions he conducted over Europe during World War II. In *States of Shock*, Shepard separates himself from his father to make a somewhat obvious point: that the glorification of war conditions young guys to consider such supposed shows of strength as the primary measure of manhood.

The most admirable thing about *States of Shock* is that Shepard chose to do it at all: to confound critical expectations, to ignore his reputation, to work fast and messy as if he were a young punk doing midnight shows at La Mama. In the Shepard canon, it seemed to be a distinctly minor item, though not everybody held the same opinion. The British premiere, which took place in June 1993, was coproduced by the National Theatre's Studio and the Salisbury Playhouse. Though it didn't pull in many ticket-buyers, it got mostly favorable reviews—one critic called it "a weird blend of groan, curse and threat, an angry, alienated babble directed at some prime American vices." And in the first German production at Stadttheater Konstanz that same year, the young director-dramaturg team of Hartmut Wickert and Alfred Nordmann undertook a fascinating reconsideration of the play.

Wickert and Nordmann were intrigued by Shepard's account in the *Village Voice* of the play's genesis as a response to the Persian Gulf War. They decided, however, that this interpretation was too narrow to interest a European audience. Examining the play carefully, they considered several other approaches they thought might give the play resonance for German theatergoers. "America is everywhere," for example. "Most European productions of Shepard's plays are implicitly premised on this postulate," Wickert and Nordmann explained in an essay they wrote about *States of Shock*, "certainly all those which in outward appearance differ very little from American stagings and which straightforwardly reproduce the American setting and idiom. Whether it is explicitly elaborated or not, the postulate expresses the recognition that . . . simply by eating hamburgers and watching Hollywood movies we are Americans already." Other statements around which a production could be built, they suggested, were "*States of Shock* invokes all wars at all times" and, most intriguing, "If violence is the means of proving to ourselves that we are healthy, that we are someone, that we can act again, then we should *beware of the healthy*."

Ultimately, Wickert and Nordmann gave themselves the challenge of incorporating these various interpretations not by expressing them directly but by rigorously exploring Shepard's concrete-theater aesthetics. That is, by creating a world for the play that doesn't refer to anything beyond the time and space shared by the actors and audience in the course of the performance. This is precisely the aesthetic at work in *Action*, one of Shepard's best plays, and indeed in all the work of Samuel Beckett, an early influence. Taking inspiration from Jack Gelber's 1976 essay on Shepard called "The Playwright as Shaman," Wickert and Nordmann conceived *States of Shock*—ostensibly an absurdist one-act about a retired military man and a wheelchair-bound Vietnam vet terrorizing an elderly couple and an inept waitress in a roadside diner—as a shamanic session in which urgently needed healing energy arrives not as the gentle, beneficent "white light" of New Age visualizations but in the raging, disruptive form of a "monster-fascist."

Wickert and Nordmann's brilliant conception reflected a profound inquiry into shamanism. Acknowledging that the concept of shamanism is often appropriated from indigenous cultures and liberally applied to describe LSD trips or rock stars' charisma, they made it clear that they understood shamanism (based on a 1988 study by German anthropologist Alfred Stolz) as "traffic with supernatural powers for the purposes of 'preserving societal norms and values and of treating their violation on an emotional level.'" The Colonel "thus becomes a shaman who takes upon himself all that is vilified by society, violence and unruliness or disorder . . . and he uses all this evil matter to cast the fragmented elements of society into a closed form and to reconstitute society as a real community."

The guys from Konstanz gave a presentation about their production of *States of Shock* at an international symposium on Shepard's work held in Brussels in May 1993. The conference, titled "Between the Margin and the Center," was organized by Johan Callens, the energetic young president of the Belgian Luxembourg American Studies Association. The guest of honor was Joseph Chaikin, who on opening night held the conference spellbound with a performance of *The War in Heaven* delivered simply from his chair in a small hotel conference room. But the revelation of the conference was the paper given by Wickert and Nordmann, who also showed on videotape the first scene from *States of Shock* in Konstanz. In addition to its bold interpretation of the text, their production was extraordinary to look at. The director had gotten permission to incorporate into the set replicas of sculptures by two prominent contemporary American artists—Edward Kienholz's *The Portable War Memorial* and Bruce Naumann's take-off on roadside diner signage, a neon sign that alternately flashes "EAT" and "DEATH." The show also included lots of music in addition to two live drummers and stylized lighting that suggested a production of *The Tooth of Crime* staged by avant-garde master Robert Wilson.

The Brussels symposium revealed a lot about Shepard's international reputation. European theater makers viewed Shepard's plays as opportunities for extravagant theatrical experimentation, his recent plays no less than his wilder early plays. Clearly, the American critics and scholars, who dominated the conference, did not. The string of family plays from *Curse of the Starving Class* to *A Lie of the Mind* had moved Shepard inexorably in the direction of traditional American naturalistic theater that the critical consensus seemed to view as drab, dramaturgically dated, used up, and basically boring. As hot as Shepard's critical reputation had been in the '60s and '70s, it was now stone cold. One commentator at the conference dropped an extremely authoritative reference to "Shepard's cultural moment, 1979–86," which prompted another to wonder aloud, "Are we dancing around the grave?"

When he wasn't acting in movies or in rehearsals for a play, Shepard spent his time on the farm in Virginia, raising horses and playing polo but also continuing to write. He and Lange took up fox hunting, although she got a little rattled after getting thrown from a horse and suffering a concussion. And Shepard loved reading aloud to the kids, Shura and Hannah and their pale blond brother Walker. "He's one gene short of an albino," Lange said. "We call him White Boy." The whole family spent holidays on Lange's 120-acre estate near Duluth, visiting with Lange's relatives.

If Shepard's acting and playwriting careers seemed on-again, off-again, Lange remained on Hollywood's short list of leading actresses and averaged at least one picture a year. She kept her star polished with a lucky mixture of projects. Costa-Gavras's *Music*

Box and Tony Richardson's *Blue Sky*, for which she received her fourth and fifth Oscar nominations in 1990 and 1995, gave her prestige. The swashbuckler *Rob Roy*, a Liam Neeson vehicle for which she rode shotgun, and Martin Scorsese's *Cape Fear*, which co-starred Robert De Niro and Nick Nolte and which was Lange's biggest hit since *Tootsie*, kept her commercially viable. She made her Broadway debut playing Blanche du Bois in a revival of *A Streetcar Named Desire* with Alec Baldwin as Stanley Kowalski; though she didn't erase anyone's memories of Jessica Tandy and Vivien Leigh, she didn't make a fool of herself either. The production was later filmed for television. These successful ventures balanced out the movies that made no particular impression: *Everybody's All-American, Men Don't Leave, Night and the City, Losing Isaiah.*

Like any artist with her intelligence and talent, Lange itched to expand her work beyond being an actor-for-hire. She optioned Darrah Cloud's play *The Stick Wife* with the idea of producing it as a film. While that project never happened, Lange did star in Cloud's adaptation of the Willa Cather novel *O, Pioneers!*, filmed for the public television series *American Playhouse* in 1992. For a moment she considered undertaking the role of Dorothy Dandridge, a black actress who passed for white in Hollywood, for a biographical film in development for HBO. But when the black press objected, Lange backed off. She bought the rights to Jayne Anne Philips' novel *Machine Dreams*, which she planned to adapt into a screenplay herself with the idea that she and Shepard would act in the film (playing brother and sister for a change). That project floated around for years without ever actually landing, which frustrated Lange.

Still, she had plenty to do juggling three kids and an active movie career, not to mention her relationship with someone as complicated and restless as Shepard. In an unusually frank and realistic 1991 interview with Nancy Collins in *Vanity Fair*, Lange dashed any fantasy that their household was all sunshine, lollipops, and rainbows. For one thing, she said Shepard felt hemmed in by the forest living in Virginia. "He gets 'horse eyes,'" she said, a condition somewhat alleviated by movie gigs in places like the Badlands of South Dakota, where he was currently shooting *Thunderheart*.

"The worst part [about living with Sam] is the separations," Lange said in the same interview. "He's not the kind of man who's going to follow a woman around. He'll come see us, but he's not going to pack his bags, sit on my location for three months, and twiddle with the kids." She admitted that "Sam would've been happy if I never made another movie, if we could've lived together in the wild, idyllic manner we had in the beginning. But I kept wanting to act. Those separations became sources of real, um, difficulty for us."

In 1991, Lange filmed *Blue Sky* on location in Texas and Alabama. It became a somewhat beleaguered film project. The director was Tony Richardson, who had introduced Shepard to the Royal Court Theatre when he moved to London in 1971 and almost directed his screenplay *The Bodyguard*. Sadly, Richardson died of AIDS shortly after *Blue Sky* finished shooting. Then the film's distributor, Orion Films, declared bankruptcy. *Blue Sky* was one of ten finished films that went into limbo and the last to be released. It finally hit the theaters in 1994.

Lange co-starred in *Blue Sky* with Tommy Lee Jones, with whom she'd done the 1985 TV production of *Cat on a Hot Tin Roof*. Jones plays an Army scientist assigned to a nuclear-testing project; his wife Carly is volatile, flirtatious, and prone to temper tantrums. "Lange plays Carly not as a monster but as a profoundly unhappy woman who simply has no idea how to make herself feel better," wrote Terrence Raffery in the *New Yorker*. "It's a stunning performance—maybe the best of Lange's remarkable career." The film as a whole didn't fare as well with the critics as Lange did, though Rafferty gave it some credit. "The movie is trying to explore the inexplicable affections that keep marriages from falling apart; it's about the rigors of constancy."

Her performance in *Blue Sky* earned Lange her second Academy Award, the Oscar for best actress in 1995. At the ceremonies in Los Angeles, Shepard was conspicuously missing from her side. Nor did she mention him in her acceptance speech. All of this led to intense speculation that the two of them had split up. Later in the year, however, Shepard and Lange closed up operations in Virginia and moved their entire household to Minnesota. Lange bought a four-bedroom, four-bath farmhouse for $415,000 in the small town of Stillwater (pop. 13,800) on the Wisconsin border, a 45-minute drive from Minneapolis-St. Paul. The main reason for the move was so Lange could be closer to her mother, who was getting on in years and feeling the absence of her husband.

Lange's father Al died of a stroke at age 76 in June 1989. Shepard dug his grave.

In interviews Shepard has steadfastly refused to answer personal questions about his family, his children, where they live, or his relationship with Lange. In the controlled setting of his writing, he frequently delves into his inner emotional life. It surfaces very rarely in his comments to the press, though, and then only obliquely. In 1984, when he was surrendering to the tidal wave of emotions sweeping him out of his marriage to O-Lan and into his partnership with Lange, a writer from the *Sunday Times* of London asked him why he thought country and western music is so invariably sad. "Because, more than any other art form I know of in America, country music speaks of the true relationship between the American male and the American female." And what, asked the reporter, is that? With a chuckle, Shepard said, "Terrible and impossible."

In a 1994 interview for the *New York Times*, Ben Brantley brought up this statement and asked Shepard if still believed it. "The whole thing between men and women is really the most amazing thing there is," he said after a thoughtful pause. "It's impossible the way people enter into it feeling they're going to be saved by the other one. And it seems like many, many times that quicksand happens in a relationship when you feel that somehow you can be saved. And of course that's going to be a disappointment." He laughed at that recognition. "In that sense, yeah, I think the illusions about it are impossible." Does he still have those illusions? "No, I don't."

The next time Shepard let it be known that he had a new play, in the fall of 1993, it sounded like a big splashy event: a three-act play called *Simpatico*, which he himself would direct. Lewis Allen, who produced *A Lie of the Mind*, wanted to do it on Broadway and had a couple of big names already lined up: Ed Harris and, making her Broadway debut, Jennifer Jason Leigh, who'd been burning up the screen with fierce, fascinating performances in *Last Exit to Brooklyn*, *Mrs. Parker and the Vicious Circle*, and *Georgia*, among other movies. Even with these actors committed and the prestige of its being Shepard's first Broadway show, Allen couldn't raise the $650,000 the production required. Switching gears, Allen decided to produce *Simpatico* at a smaller theater Off Broadway, which would have scaled back the budget to $400,000 ("gas money on a movie," as Shepard put it). But he couldn't find investors to put up that much, either. Finally, Shepard picked up the phone himself and called George C. Wolfe, who had taken over the direction of the New York Shakespeare Festival after the death of the festival's founder, Joseph Papp, with whom Shepard had famously feuded over the New York premiere of *True West*. Wolfe agreed to put the play on the schedule for the following season at the Public Theater. Lewis Allen donated $325,000 to the Shakespeare Festival, a not-for-profit institutional theater, with the understanding that if the play became a hit, he would have first dibs at transferring it to a commercial house.

Simpatico returns to the same kind of identity exchange that Shepard dramatized in *True West*, this time in the milieu of horse racing rather than moviemaking. Carter is the hotshot manager of a thoroughbred business in Kentucky. He wears expensive suits and alligator shoes, and he's never far from his cellular phone. He's summoned to the cruddy, low-rent apartment in Cucamonga, California, of his former partner Vinnie. Vinnie's gotten into some kind of trouble pretending to be a detective; he's the kind of guy who lies when it's easier to tell the truth. Fifteen years ago, the two of them pulled a scam involving switching lookalike horses in a race. When the local racing commissioner caught wind of it, they conspired to run him out of office by creating some kind of scandal with a floozy in a hotel room. Carter profited profession-ally from the scandal and then ran off with Vinnie's wife, Rosie, and his even more beloved Buick. Although Carter has been pay-ing him hush money all along, Vinnie now threatens to expose Carter's hand in these shenanigans unless he turns himself in.

According to Shepard, he started and abandoned eight or nine plays about these two characters, Vinnie and Carter, before he fi-nally finished *Simpatico*. "It's an old, old situation that I've been struggling with for years," he said. (One manifestation of this ma-terial shows up in *Cruising Paradise* as the 1989 story called "Thin Skin," about a guy named J.D. who tries to impress women by pretending to be a private eye.)

The three-act play is written in conventional two-character scenes, but it defies any literal-minded analysis. Carter tries to do Vinnie a favor by talking to his girlfriend Cecelia, who bags gro-ceries at Safeway. His task is to convince her that he's a harmless nut, not a dangerous criminal. In the same amount of time it takes for Carter to go to Cecelia's house, Vinnie travels to Kentucky bearing his box of "evidence" (pictures, negatives, incriminating letters) to Simms, the man whose career they ruined, hoping that Simms will pay him for the stuff and then expose Carter. But Simms doesn't care; the past is the past. Vinnie then takes the box to Rosie and tries to talk her into running off to Mexico with him. Carter sends Cecelia to buy back the negatives from Simms, promising to get her tickets to the Kentucky Derby for her troubles. She shows up at Simms' office dressed for the Derby in an absurd new outfit: flowered dress, straw hat, high heels, white gloves, and a purse stuffed with cash to hand over to Simms. He doesn't have the negatives, he doesn't care about the money, but he does offer to escort her to the Kentucky Derby, which he points out is seven months away. Back to California, Vinnie shows no signs of disappointment at his failed mission. In fact, he's ready to pick up where he left off, working as a private investigator. Carter, meanwhile, has taken to bed and can't seem to stand up. "I'm dying," he moans to Vinnie, who is only concerned that Carter has depleted his supply of bourbon. Cecelia walks in and dumps out her purseful of money in front of Carter, who's lying on the floor in his boxer shorts, wrapped in a blanket and shivering.

In an interview with the *New York Times* during rehearsals for *Simpatico*, Shepard was perhaps too candid in admitting that he writes while driving across the country. "On Highway 40 West or some of those big open highways, you can hold the wheel with one hand and write with the other. It's a good discipline, because sometimes you can only write two or three words at a time before you have to look back at the road, so those three words have to count. The problem is whether you can read the damn thing by the time you reach your destination." Many reviewers commented that *Simpatico* looked like it had been tossed off while the playwright's mind was on more important matters, like staying out of the path of speeding semis.

It's true that on all the most immediate levels, *Simpatico* seems like a lame effort from Shepard. The plot is ludicrous and inconsequential. The characters do wacky things with no apparent logical motivation. They sustain an easy and sometimes lively banter, but the dialogue never latches onto actions that propel the play from scene to scene. In fact, the play calls to mind the story *True West*'s Lee makes up and tries to sell to the movie producer, which Austin describes as "two lamebrains chasing each other across Texas." And the production Shepard directed at the Public Theater, which made no attempt to play against the dramatic slackness of the script, seemed theatrically inert.

Ed Harris was indeed the star of the show, in the central role of Carter. But by the time it got to the Public Theater, *Simpatico* had lost Jennifer Jason Leigh. Replacing her was Marcia Gay Harden, with whom Shepard had done *Safe Passage*, and who also had gotten excellent notices in Wolfe's Broadway production of Tony Kushner's Pulitzer prize-winning *Angels in America*. The rest of the cast were all fine actors: Fred Ward as Vinnie, James Gammon as Simms, and Beverly D'Angelo as Rosie. But the critics called it "rambling," "lazy," and "tired." *Simpatico* sold out its run at the Public Theater, but any talk about a commercial transfer dwindled and quietly died. The play was much better received at the Royal Court in London the following year. Michael Coveney in the *Observer* wrote, "*Simpatico* is long and hard to follow. But it's easily the best play in London. Uniquely, it combines spiritual writhing with an overpowering sense of 'out there'—a Shepard trademark. The lines sing, the jokes sting, the situations buzz with danger."

It's entirely possible, of course, that there's more life to the play than was evident in Shepard's rather leaden production. Reading the published text of *Simpatico* makes it clear that Shepard is primarily interested in something other than who does what to whom and why. For one thing, he's exploring something surprisingly tender that usually goes unspoken: men's paradoxical longing for and fear of intimacy with other men. (Perhaps Shepard was thinking of his former father-in-law Johnny Dark, whose friendship he still valued even after the breakup with O-Lan.) Vinnie needs a friend to share troubles-talk with. Carter, who only thinks in terms of business and money and staying out of jail, comes to him feeling scared and guilty, which Vinnie pronounces "the wrong motives." In some misguided idealistic way, Vinnie wants to air his and Carter's dirty secret so it no longer dominates the bond between them, so they can be friends again.

Under the surface, *Simpatico* also seems to want to examine the nature of identity—when is it fixed? when is it fluid? Carter is extremely attached to his money, to his status, to sticking with the narrative he's created to present himself to others. Most of the other characters are not. Both Simms and Rosie have changed their names and pretend not to remember the past when it's convenient. And Vinnie says, "That's the one question that always throws me. The question of 'occupation.' What I *do* for a living." He makes it up on the spot and doesn't think twice about lying. At the end of the play, he seems to thrive specifically because he doesn't cling to a set identity, and Carter appears to be "dying" because he does. "Say for instance you could put the past to death and start over," Simms says at one point. "How many lives do you think a man can live? How many lives within this *one*?"

"Identity is a question for everybody in the play," Shepard said. "Some of them are more firmly aligned with who they are, or who they think they are. To me, a strong sense of self isn't believing in a lot. Some people might define it that way, saying, 'He has a very strong sense of himself.' But it's a complete lie."

Simpatico contains traces of Shepard's familiar fixations, though he doesn't really push them into any new directions. As with *A Lie of the Mind*, the playwright plays tricks with time and space; the play tracks parallel stories in two different geographical locations but pretends that the distance between them is nonexistent. Act three begins with a long passage of Rosie talking to Vinnie from offstage—a favorite Shepard device. Cecelia reminisces about living in London, as Shepard did, in the early '70s—the rain, the dog races, drinking tea and watching Secretariat win at Belmont by thirty-one lengths. Of course, the setting of the play allows Shepard to linger lovingly over the language of horse love: sesamoids and cannon-bones, Native Dancer and Nasrullah, bloodstock agents and "honest-to-God true horsemen" like "Sonny-Jim" Fitzsimmons and "Bull Hancock." When Carter rhapsodizes to Cecelia about the Kentucky Derby, Shepard's love of words and his horse fetish almost orgasmically merge: "It's like no other horse race in the world. Impressions are stamped on you for life. Branded. The Twin Spires. The icy eyes of Laffit Pincay. The hands of Eddie Arcaro. The rippling muscle of Seattle Slew. These are things that never leave you, Cecelia! Things beyond seduction. Beyond lust!"

In the guise of horse talk, Shepard slips in some indication of what he's up to thematically. "The glaring truth," Simms tells Cecelia, "is that every single solitary thoroughbred horse in the world—living or dead—and all those foals yet to be born are, in one way or another, related by blood." As with *A Lie of the Mind*, perhaps Shepard means to suggest that all the characters are, in some dreamlike way, different aspects of a single human psyche:

male and female, wise and foolish, corrupt and pure. In any case, their fates are inextricably linked. An early version of the script included a Beckett epigraph: "You're on earth. There's no cure for that."

An angel speaks of being put on earth with a mission. The mission seems to have been a failure. The angel entertains the possibility that there are other good reasons for being on earth—music, fucking, the delicious yearning for God—but mostly he considers birth a mistake. "Take me back," he begs, growls, demands. *The War in Heaven*, subtitled "Angel's Monologue," is a brief poem for the theater that Shepard created in collaboration with Joseph Chaikin. Like Chaikin himself, the speaker in the play perches between life and death. Almost out the door. Beautiful, bitter, and Beckett-like, the language is close to prayer.

"Nowadays, it's very difficult to write a hero or to write a good person or a person pure of heart or a person with spiritual integrity or whatever you want to call it," Shepard said. "It's very difficult to write that and not have it be the corniest thing on earth. So the only way to take it was to this absolute extreme—the world of angels. And I thought it would be very risky to try the premise of an angel crashing to earth . . . I thought if any actor could play it, it would be Joe, because he has that amazing innocence about him."

From beginning to end, the collaboration on *The War in Heaven* lasted nearly ten years, beginning in 1981. Chaikin had finished working with Shirley Clarke on the video versions of *Tongues* and *Savage/Love*, and he wanted to keep the ball rolling with Shepard. One of the first ideas Chaikin had for *The War in Heaven* had to do with lying. "I would like to explore that whole area—it's slightly spooky but very interesting," Shepard wrote to Chaikin. "I don't understand it at all. Especially how the lie grows. How the part that originally knew the lie was a lie begins to forget and becomes a conspirator in the lie—becomes confused about notions of truth and false." At the time, though, the concept of lying remained too abstract for Shepard to sink his teeth into. "You have to begin somewhere, of course, but I need something very personal now to get me going. I don't know if this makes sense. I have no idea of aesthetics—I'm just finding certain experiences—certain states of mind very powerful lately, and I want to find a way to explore them without naming them—almost as though they're being discovered in the moment. I realize this is a very private kind of thing and lends itself to writing by oneself and not to collaboration."

Another suggestion of Chaikin's was that the play take the form of an interrogation, someone asking someone else questions. Shepard fretted that the interview format would stray too far into a superficial comedy format, like a Nichols and May routine. Chaikin's idea was more along the lines of "The Grand Inquisitor" section from *The Brothers Karamazov*. "What if the person asking questions was some kind of angel—to a person," Chaikin suggested. "Or the other way around."

The letters they wrote during their collaborations, published in 1989, reveal much about their working process. But they also add up to a moving and intimate portrait of the loving friendship between the two men. They started working together on *The War in Heaven* in the spring of 1984 at the American Repertory Theater in Boston. Shortly afterwards, Chaikin had the stroke that severely impaired his speaking. The minute he heard about Chaikin's stroke, Shepard sent a telegram from Los Angeles saying "MY HEART IS WITH YOU I'LL TRY TO BE THERE IF YOU NEED ME JUST LET ME KNOW TAKE STRENGTH FROM YOUR OWN BREATH I LOVE YOU SAM." During Chaikin's recovery, Shepard spent time with him in New York practicing some of the language-reconstruction exercises he had learned when O-Lan's mother Scarlett had her stroke in 1979. Instead of abandoning *The War in Heaven*, they continued to work on it, letting Chaikin's struggle to speak through his aphasia feed the piece, and vice versa.

In the fall of 1984, *The War in Heaven* was taped for radio broadcast on WBAI in New York, with Chaikin speaking and Shepard playing music. Chaikin did a staged reading of the monologue in San Diego the following December, directed by Steven Kent. He continued to give performances over the years in San Francisco, Toronto, Italy, and Poland. Robert Woodruff directed a new staging in Los Angeles in March 1988. In 1991, Chaikin performed the play at the American Place Theater, after he and Shepard had refined the text further to something almost skeletal.

The conversations and exchanges Shepard had with Chaikin about *The War in Heaven* stirred up ideas that would eventually find their way into other projects. "Something's been coming to me lately about this whole question of being *lost*," Shepard wrote to Chaikin in 1983, from the set of *Country* in Iowa. "It only makes sense to me in relation to an idea of one's identity being shattered under severe personal circumstances—in a state of crisis where everything that I've previously identified with in myself suddenly falls away. A shock state, I guess you might call it. I don't think it makes much difference what the shock itself is—whether it's a trauma to do with a loved one or a physical accident or whatever—the resulting emptiness or aloneness is what interests me. Particularly to do with questions like *home*? *family*? the identification of *others* over time? people I've known who are now lost to me even though still alive?" That one letter alone contains seeds that would eventually bear fruit in *A Lie of the Mind, States of Shock, Simpatico,* and their subsequent collaboration *When the World Was Green.*

Shepard's relationship to Bob Dylan over the years bears some resemblance to his friendship with Chaikin. Like Chaikin, Dylan is a soulful, charismatic Jewish poet slightly older than Shepard, whom he looks up to as an artistic and spiritual touchstone. (There are other connections, too. Both Dylan and Shepard invented themselves as full-blown artists, complete with made-up names. And Dylan grew up in Hibbing, Minnesota, not far from Jessica Lange's hometown, Cloquet.) Although Shepard's collaborations with Dylan haven't been as extensive as those with Chaikin, there are a lot of similarities.

In the spring of 1985, they got together to write a song. "It's like a saga!" Shepard told *Rolling Stone* interviewer Jonathan Cott. An eleven-minute version of this "saga" showed up on Dylan's 1986 album *Knocked Out Loaded.* "He talked about making a video out of it. I told him that we should extend it, make it an hour and a half or so, and perform it like an opera."

Shepard got a big kick out of working with Dylan. "He's so off the wall sometimes. We'd come up with a line, and I'd think that we were heading down one trail over here, and then suddenly he'd just throw in this other line, and we'd wind up following it off in some different direction. Sometimes it's frustrating to do that when you're trying to make a wholeness out of something, but it turned out okay."

Not long after that, *Esquire* magazine sent Shepard on an assignment to interview Dylan. What Shepard turned in was a one-act play that the magazine called *True Dylan* (a title that probably made Shepard groan). It's a fascinating piece of work. One thing that's especially touching is how Shepard captures the ideal relationship straight guys want to have with men they admire—hanging out, being together without much of an agenda, being slightly deferential to the guy who has the most wisdom in his heart. Dylan talks about visiting Woody Guthrie when he was dying, hanging out in his hospital room and playing his songs to him on the guitar. These "meetings with remarkable men" become an informal version of darshan, the Hindu concept of a one-on-one audience with a spiritual master in which the student receives a blessing, some private instruction, or simply a glimpse of himself in a very clear mirror.

The play revolves around a series of direct questions Shepard asks Dylan, which not surprisingly stick to his deep-seated obsessions:

"Do you ever think about angels?"

"What was the first music you can remember listening to?"

"Do you think it's possible to have a pact with someone?"

"Are you superstitious?"

Most intriguingly, Shepard says to Dylan, "I've heard this theory that women are rhythmically different from men. By nature. That the female rhythm is a side-to-side, horizontal movement and the male rhythm is vertical—up and down. Do you feel those two different kinds of rhythms in you?" To which Dylan replies, "Yeah, sure. We all do. There's that slinky, side-to-side thing and the jerky, up-and-down one. But they're a part of each other. One can't do without the other. Like God and the Devil."

The dialogue appears to be recorded verbatim, but Shepard has carefully shaped his encounter with Dylan into a piece of art, mainly through sound effects. At the beginning and end of the play, Shepard calls for the sound of waves crashing. Twice in the play he asks for the sound of screeching brakes and a car crash, which neither of the characters reacts to—representing, perhaps, all the personal tragedies and blown-up marriages in the men's past that they choose not to talk about. Shepard even works in his own ambivalence about this whole procedure of the celebrity interview. The first sound to be heard is a piano solo. It turns out to be coming from Shepard's portable recorder, a tape by jazz pianist Jimmy Yancey. After they've been talking for a while, Shepard rewinds the tape to make sure it's picking up their voices, but all that comes out is the Jimmy Yancey solo. The same thing happens at the end of the play—as if to say, "All this blah-blah-blah doesn't matter. What really matters is the art."

The interrogation format that Shepard explored with Chaikin in *The War in Heaven* and in *True Dylan* developed full-blown in his next collaboration with Chaikin, which began in 1993. Originally called *Edge of the World*, then *A Chef's Fable*, it finally became *When the World Was Green*. From the beginning, it was clear that this piece would be a departure from their earlier teamwork in two respects: it was definitely not a monologue, and Chaikin would not perform in it.

The two characters in the play are an old man on death row for murder and a young woman who comes to interview him for a newspaper story. "How did this all begin?" she asks. "There was an insult 200 years ago," he says. "In our country, it takes seven generations or 100 years for an insult to come to an end. And it has to be a woman who stops it." Because of the original insult—a poisoned mule—the old man's father pointed out to him when he was five years old the cousin it was his duty to kill. The old man tracked his cousin Carl for many years, became head chef of his favorite restaurant in New Orleans and finally poisoned his potatoes. According to the Interviewer, however, it wasn't the old man's cousin: he killed the wrong man, who may or may not have been the Interviewer's long-lost father. In addition to the two speaking roles, the play calls for an offstage piano player, who supplies underscoring for the play and perhaps represents Carl, who is said to play piano in saloons.

Much about the play is left purposely mysterious and open-ended. Where does this story take place? Some references are clearly American and some are not. The word "Bosnia" is never spoken, but a viewer in 1996 couldn't help thinking about the genocidal "ethnic cleansing" in the former Yugoslavia when watching a play about a generations-old conflict whose roots can only be described as mythological. The Beckett-like setting (a simple prison cell, a gray slate wall, a single high window) and the interrogatory format are recognizable trademarks from Chaikin's theater background. Meanwhile, the themes and imagery—that ancient curse, the male-female standoff, the search for the father, the echo of old folk ballads—seem like pure Shepard, maybe with a tip of the hat to Gabriel Garcia Marquez's *Chronicle of a Death Foretold.*

At the same time, the way the two characters' stories circle and intertwine recalls the estranged lovers in Shepard's *Fool for Love* and *Paris, Texas.* Is the play examining the origins of masculinity and femininity? On one hand, Shepard and Chaikin seem to be trafficking in stereotypes about men as killers, women as lovers. On the other hand, they also challenge those clichés by making the Interviewer the active truth-seeker rather than a passive female victim. And the Old Man is not some macho cowboy but a chef who extols the virutes of individual herbs and knows just how to peel a mango. Is their encounter a quest for inner reconciliation, the exhausted male psyche in dialogue with the less-developed female part of himself? The brief, elliptical play leaves ambiguous the question of whether the curse, the insult, has run its course. In the last moment of the play, the Old Man mourns that "the killings have never stopped" while behind him the young woman waves the white scarf of surrender.

When the World Was Green was officially commissioned for the 1996 Olympic Arts Festival in Atlanta, Georgia, and had its world premiere during the Olympic Games. The play was produced by Seven Stages, an Atlanta theater company where Chaikin had directed and performed in the past. In the early stages of making the piece, there was talk about creating the piece to be performed by Bill Irwin, the great clown whom Chaikin had directed in Beckett's *Texts for Nothing* and Shepard had directed in *Silent Tongue.* Ultimately, the play went in a different direction. In Atlanta, the Old Man was played by Alvin Epstein, an actor with a long history of performing in Beckett plays, including the American premieres of *Endgame and Waiting for Godot.* Chaikin's direction of the play gave it the simple flavor of a prayer for healing.

Once more, the play incorporates Shepard's ambivalence about one of the realities in the life of the contemporary artist: The Interview. Shepard himself seems to enjoy reading interviews with other artists. Apparently, he was quite taken with the last interview that misanthropic French novelist Louis-Ferdinand Céline gave in his life. The interviewer's final question was "What do you really want in this life?" Céline's reply: "I just want to be left alone." Shepard liked this Garboesque sentiment enough to quote it both in the story "Homage to Céline" (in *Cruising Paradise*) and in *When the World Was Green.* The play includes a couple of other jabs at journalists. "I don't understand this concern you have for me—you're from the press," the Old Man says, his voice dripping disgust. And later he tells her, "You're like the rest of the press. You fabricate stories."

Like many artists, Shepard questions himself enough in his work; having to field inquiries from journalists all the time gets downright tedious. However, for all his vaunted reclusiveness, Shepard made himself available in recent years for a hefty number of interviews with prestigious publications such as the *New York Times*, the *Village Voice, Esquire, Interview, Rolling Stone,* the *New Yorker*, and London's *Time Out.* And for the most part reporters and critics have treated him generously and respectfully. So after a while, his griping about journalists began to sound like unexamined shtick.

1996, the year *When the World Was Green* debuted at the Olympic Arts Festival, became a watershed year for Shepard. He rewrote two of his best-known plays for major revivals. He enjoyed retrospectives of his body of work in New York and London. And he published *Cruising Paradise*, the culmination of several years' worth of prose writing.

Shepard's friends and colleagues knew that he had been working on something that wasn't a play or a movie. In fact, he had started two different books. One was a collection of pieces he'd written during down time on movie sets, similar to *Motel Chronicles,* which had the working title *Slave of the Camera.* The other was a work of fiction, written both in prose and in dialogue, concerning the tempestuous relationship between a man and a woman that strayed not too far from Jessica Lange's description of her early days with Shepard ("drinking, getting into fights, walking down the freeway trying to get away—I mean, just really wild stuff"). Apparently, neither of these projects came together to his satisfaction. Still, he had a small mountain of manuscript pages that he somehow wanted to publish. The would-be novel, for instance, got up to 150 pages before he ran out of steam. Over a period of several years he and his book editor LuAnn Walther cooked up the volume that eventually bore the title *Cruising Paradise.*

Walther was concerned that the book might look too much like a collection of fragments. She suggested grouping the 40 stories thematically and in some cases chronologically. Shepard, however, preferred to go in exactly the opposite direction. Rather than making it easy for the reader to connect the dots, he created a more intuitive order for the stories. Among other things, he scattered the *Slave of the Camera* material ("Homage to Celine," "Spencer Tracy Is Not Dead," "Papantla," "The Real Gabby Hayes," and "Colorado Is Not a Coward," among others) throughout the book. And he broke the unfinished novel into several discrete chunks (including "Quick Stop," "Hail from Nowhere," "Just Space," and "Pure Accident"). He also made a couple of other somewhat perverse decisions: each story ends with the date and place it was completed, and the book includes no table of contents.

The reader proceeds through the book as if it were a novel, even though the chapters have individual titles and take sometimes wildly different forms. Unabashed first-person pieces mingle with less directly autobiographical stories in which the narrator calls himself Clayton Moss, juxtaposed with brief prose poems and stories that are completely invented. A short piece called "Synthetic Pink" puts together two speeches from *When the World Was Green*. An amusing dialogue with a stranger on a train exhausts the subject of why he refuses to fly, and the *Slave of the Camera* sections provide both amusing glimpses of life on and off a movie set and also Shepard's sharp eye for telling details. Some of these pieces recall the essays of Peter Handke, the Austrian-born writer whom Shepard admires, in their meditative cataloguing of everyday phenomena. The overall effect of the book is that of touring the many chambers of human consciousness and seeing how fluidly the mind moves from present to past, truth to fiction, interior voice to exterior voice.

Familiar Shepard themes resurface throughout *Cruising Paradise*, at times with unexpected new depth. The lover's reverie "You I Have No Distance From" is a reminder of the tenderness of which Shepard is capable. And in several pieces he addresses with remarkable honesty his simultaneous longing for and fear of male company—the unshakable legacy of growing up with Sam Sr. In the lengthy tale called "Dust," the central character, Price, takes a traumatic horse ride through rough terrain. When an older man places a hand on the back of his neck, to direct his gaze at something in the distance, "it made Price feel like he was about nine years old. He was afraid he might cry out again, for no reason, or break down in some terribly injured part of himself that was forever missing a father."

The New Yorker printed three of the stories in *Cruising Paradise*, a literary coup for Shepard. He celebrated the publication of the book with a reading ι. the New School for Social Research. Joe Chaikin gave a brief introduction, and then Shepard spent about an hour reading from the book as well as from his plays, frequently creating separate voices for characters in dialogue (including an amusing impersonation of Volker Schlondorff in the story "Winging It"). Random House put out an audio version of the book, read by Shepard himself. It was recorded in a studio in St. Paul, Minnesota, in January 1996 during a cold spell so intense that they had to keep stopping the tape because the mike picked up the sound of windows popping.

The publication date of *Cruising Paradise* coincided with an event so long in coming that it had acquired its own mythological significance: the first Broadway production of a Sam Shepard play. It had become part of the litany of curious facts that journalists and critics loved to cite about Shepard's background. Right up there with the avocado ranch, the crooked teeth, and the first play supposedly written on the back of Tootsie Roll wrappers, the legend of Sam Shepard included the fact that he'd written more than forty plays and become one of the most famous writers in the country (elected to the American Academy of Arts and Letters in 1986, inducted into the Theater Hall of Fame in 1994) without ever having a Broadway show. It's the mainstream sign of acceptance that all playwrights, no matter how radical or show-biz-allergic they may be, are secretly supposed to crave. Shepard always claimed he didn't. "I never figured anything I wrote would be legitimate," he told one reporter, roaring with laughter at the very idea. "I'm no longer able to figure out who the theater audience is, that's the trouble," he said. "In the sixties, an audience was real apparent. But I don't know who's gonna pay $150 a pop, who can afford that?" Besides, he'd had plenty of productions, not just in Off-Off-Broadway dives but at classy theaters all over the country and abroad with heavy-duty actors and plenty of attention.

At a certain point, though, it didn't matter if Shepard wanted a Broadway show. Enough other people wanted it to make it happen. The play was *Buried Child*, which had won the Pulitzer in 1978 but which still hadn't been seen by that many people in New

York. And the architects of the revival were Gary Sinise and the Steppenwolf Theater Company, whose spectacular 1983 production had reversed public opinion on *True West*.

Sinise's history with Shepard's work goes back to 1979, when Steppenwolf was still completely unknown outside of Chicago. On a break from the company, Sinise went out to Los Angeles where he auditioned for and got cast as Wesley in *Curse of the Starving Class* at the Met Theatre, L.A.'s unofficial Shepard Central. In that production, James Gammon played Weston. Back in Chicago, Sinise directed *Action* at Steppenwolf in 1981, followed by the famous production of *True West*, with which he and John Malkovich made their auspicious New York debuts. Steppenwolf continued to produce Shepard's plays—*A Lie of the Mind, Fool for Love, Curse of the Starving Class*—in Chicago.

Meanwhile, Sinise was forging his own multimedia career as a director of plays and movies (*Miles from Home, Of Mice and Men*). As an actor, he played the leading role of Tom Joad in Frank Galati's adaptation of John Steinbeck's *The Grapes of Wrath*, which originated in Chicago, developed further at the La Jolla Playhouse in California, and eventually won the Tony Award for Best Play on Broadway in 1990. And Sinise was nominated for an Academy Award for best supporting actor playing the legless Vietnam veteran in *Forrest Gump*. In addition to *The Grapes of Wrath*, Steppenwolf had been transferring other popular shows of theirs to commercial productions in New York, including *The Song of Jacob Zulu* (starring the South African vocal ensemble Ladysmith Black Mambazo) and Steve Martin's *Picasso at the Lapin Agile*.

It was a big deal, therefore, when Sinise and Steppenwolf decided to mount a major revival of *Buried Child* with a cast that included James Gammon as Dodge, Lois Smith (a terrific veteran actress who played Ma Joad in *Grapes of Wrath*) as Halie, and young film star Ethan Hawke as Vince. Sinise invited Shepard to be around for rehearsals, and damned if he didn't start handing the director rewrites. "I was never real happy with the play," Shepard said. "It was somewhat raggedy, areas of it were sloppy. When the Steppenwolf production started, a whole territory of the play became clear to me. I started tailor-making it for this production." The production got such good reviews that the Steppenwolf machinery went into gear to move the show to Broadway. Shepard went with it, still fiddling with the text. "What triggered a lot of the rewriting was that I saw these weird actors and a director who intuitively understood the humor that couches the tragedy, and I wanted to reinforce that," he said. "You can't possibly do this thing as a Eugene O'Neill play. I've seen it done over and over again in a macabre, stone-faced, methodical, quasi-tragic form, and it's deadly."

Sinise did an excellent job of directing the play. Robert Woodruff's original New York production started out in a tiny theater and moved twice to only slightly larger spaces. In a big Broadway theater, Sinise was able to give the play real visual style by referring to Edward Hopper's paintings of lonely people isolated in big empty spaces. Sinise was presumably responsible for adding two other visual bits to the play that created startling effects in the theater. The revolting scene at the end of act two where one-legged Bradley sticks his grimy paw in Shelley's mouth usually lasts a few seconds, long enough for the audience to gasp. Sinise had the actors hold the fingers-in-mouth tableau for an entire agonizing minute, maybe longer. It was the difference between an unwanted grope and a full-scale rape. Even more outrageously, Sinise had Halie dressed like a fairy-tale witch in act one, all in black with her gray hair pulled back in a bun. When she returned in act three, not only was she wearing a bright yellow dress and waving a flask, but her hair was dyed bright flaming red.

Buried Child got great reviews. "This fierce testimony to the theory that you really can't go home again (and if you try, be prepared for the consequences) actually appears to have grown more resonant, funnier and far more accessible in the seventeen years since it won the Pulitzer Prize," said Ben Brantley in the *New York Times*. "*Buried Child* operates successfuly on so many levels that you get dizzy watching it. It has the intangible spookiness of nightmares about home and disposession, yet it involves you in its tawdry, mystery-driven plot with the old-fashioned verve of an Erskine Caldwell novel."

The leading actors earned unanimous raves. *Newsday*'s Linda Winer said, "James Gammon, with a voice that sounds as if it is being forced up from the bottom of a cistern, is especially icky as Dodge, the invalid father on the couch, a drunk so far gone his head and hands seem to float as if on marionette strings." The *New York Times*'s Brantley said, "Lois Smith, a bizarre counterpoint of ladylike hand gestures and a lewd, wide-legged, pelvis-forward walk, is equally stunning. She shifts unflinchingly from pious homilies about the decline of manners to raucous physical slapstick." The large theater was hard on the actors, though. Both Gammon's and Smith's voices were frayed by opening night. The young actors playing Vince and Shelley weren't nearly as good. (Ethan Hawke did not move to Broadway with the production.) Leo Burmester was fine as creepy Bradley, though, and the best performance of all was by Terry Kinney, whose quiet, damaged Tilden was heartbreaking.

Buried Child opened at the end of the theater season, when Broadway is always in a tizzy about Tony Awards. Awards have become one of the major incentives for producing plays on Broadway, partly for the honor and partly for the boost in ticket sales they provide. It's almost impossible to have a commercial success producing plays on Broadway without awards and/or brand-name stars. *Buried Child* had no stars to speak of, and Shepard's Pulitzer was too distant to provide box office buzz. Theater people are nothing if not resourceful, though. Despite the fact that changes in the text were practically microscopic, Sinise managed to convince the Tony Award committee that Shepard had sufficiently rewritten the play so that *Buried Child* should be eligible to compete in the category of Best Play, which the producers felt would sell more tickets that a nomination for Best Revival. It happened to be an unusually strong year for plays on Broadway, though, and *Buried Child* didn't win any Tonys. Without awards, it didn't draw big enough audiences, so it closed after only two months.

The production definitely put Shepard back on the map, though, after the lukewarm reception he'd gotten for *States of Shock* and *Simpatico*. And he enjoyed the attention. At the opening night gala, hilariously held at the Harley Davidson Cafe, Shepard partied hard in the company of John Malkovich, Tom Waits, and T-Bone Burnett. He went back to see the show several times. At the closing performance, the actors even managed to drag him onstage for the curtain call to take a reluctant bow.

The groundswell of interest in reconsidering Shepard's plays as a body of work began to gather momentum. As *Buried Child* was closing on Broadway, the Battersea Arts Centre in London was mounting a month-long Shepard festival. This mini-retrospective included productions of *States of Shock, Killer's Head, A Lie of the Mind, Suicide in B Flat,* and *Curse of the Starving Class,* renamed *Weston's Tale.*

Shepard couldn't rest on his laurels too long, though. He had another old play to resurrect. Carole Rothman, artistic director of the Second Stage, a company founded on the idea of reconsidering neglected plays, had been after Shepard for years trying to get permission to do *The Tooth of Crime*. Rothman had been Richard Schechner's assistant director on the Performance Group's 1973 production, in which the actors created their own music, and she practically knew the play by heart. Shepard kept saying no because he felt the play needed a brand-new musical score and he couldn't decide who the composer should be. Suddenly in 1995 he called Rothman to say "Let's do it." He'd determined that the new music and lyrics should be created by T-Bone Burnett, who'd been in Bob Dylan's band for the Rolling Thunder Revue. "He's the only one on the tour I'm not sure has relative control over his violent dark side," Shepard said about Burnett in his *Rolling Thunder Logbook*. "He's not scary, he's just crazy."

Around the same time, Shepard accepted another long-standing invitation. The Signature Theater Company, another Off-Broadway company founded in 1991 by director James Houghton, had a policy of devoting each season to the works of a single playwright. Its first five seasons honored Romulus Linney, Lee Blessing, Edward Albee, Horton Foote, and Adrienne Kennedy. Houghton had been in conversation with Shepard about doing a whole season of his plays. He was definitely excited by the prospect of seeing his plays in the context of one another. He was worried, though, about Signature's requirement that the playwright be in residence for the whole season. Once Houghton assured him that didn't mean he'd have to be there for every rehearsal and every performance, he felt better.

Houghton flew down to Dallas to visit Shepard on the set of *Lily Dale*, the Horton Foote play he acted in for cable TV, to plan the season. Shepard and Joe Chaikin were looking for a venue in New York to produce *When the World Was Green* after its premiere at the Olympics in Atlanta, and the Signature season seemed like an ideal occasion. Chaikin had long expressed the desire to direct Shepard's old one-act *Chicago*, so those two pieces were programmed together as the Signature Theater's season opener. As he and Houghton went down the whole list of his works, Shepard indicated that *Action* was one of his plays that he felt really held up over time. To direct it, he recommended Darrell Larson, who'd staged a double bill of *Action* and *Killer's Head* at L.A.'s Met Theatre. Shepard and Houghton talked about adding *The Rock Garden*, one of his earliest plays, to the *Action* evening.

But Larson suggested, and the others agreed to, the odd half-hour musical Shepard wrote with Catherine Stone, *The Sad Lament of Pecos Bill on the Eve of Killing His Wife*. Of course, Houghton was interested in the new version of *The Tooth of Crime* Shepard was already working on and arranged to co-produce it with Carole Rothman.

In the winter of 1996, Houghton and Rothman flew to Minneapolis to meet with Shepard, Burnett, and Bill Hart, who signed on to direct *The Tooth of Crime*. Two weeks later, Shepard sent everyone a new version of the first act that drastically differed from the original, so much so that he'd given it a new name: *Tooth of Crime (Second Dance)*. He'd also changed the names of several of the characters. Hoss's sidekick Cheyenne had become Chaser, the jive DJ Galactic Jack was called Ruido Ran, and Star-Man was now Meera (a reference, perhaps, to the Indian-born spiritual teacher Mother Meera). Shepard had ruthlessly cut anything that made the play seem dated, including almost all references to sports cars and rock music idols (Dylan, Jagger, Townsend) as well as two of the most memorable set-pieces from the original play, Hoss's reminiscence of a high-school rumble as class warfare and Becky's rape-scene soliloquy. In a hundred large and small ways, he'd made the play "leaner and meaner," as Houghton put it. "The focus of the play has shifted," Rothman elaborated. "There was always a fine line between whether it was really about rock and roll or really about killing. Now it's gone over the line toward killing."

Ultimately, the new *Tooth of Crime* became more about dying than killing. Whereas the original play wielded its peculiar babel of pop-culture jargons as an attack on the contemporary fixation on style and media image, Shepard's rewrite pushed farther into the metaphysical realm. It became about the death of the Self, about transcending identity altogether. The climax of the play is still the second-act showdown between Hoss and Crow. But in this version, the referee bails after the first round, unable to make heads or tails of the strange moves he's witnessing. After the referee's exit, the duel suddenly shifts into almost mystical territory. It conjures up all of Shepard's alter-ego conflicts (Austin and Lee circling each other at the end of *True West*, Carter dying from the disease of identity while Vinny shrugs his off in *Simpatico*) with an added flavor of Faust and Mephistopheles. Crow holds out his arm and invites Hoss to slit his wrist, to make him bleed, to prove he's a human and not an alien (or demon). In that moment, Hoss recognizes in Crow a younger version of himself (a little like Vince's vision of seven generations of male ancestors reflecting back at him from his windshield in *Buried Child*). Hoss goes into a kind of shamanic trance in which he realizes that he's holding onto an image of himself that no longer serves him.

In the original version, Hoss's suicide is a defiant act, even noble, but undeniably an admission of defeat. His former colleagues rally around Crow as the new champion and prepare to play the game all over again. In *Tooth of Crime (Second Dance)*, Hoss dies from his own knife rather than a gunshot. And like the Samurai warrior's hara-kiri, it comes across as a spiritual triumph. It's a relief to leave behind the exhausting game of images. Hoss is liberated in the way that Buddhist philosophy defines liberation: recognition that nothing is permanent, that human experience leads to suffering, and that there is no individual self. Escaping from the cycle of death and rebirth, ignorance and illusion, what the Buddhists call *samsara*, leads to nirvana. Hoss collapses on the floor in the same outline that shows up on the floor in *Suicide in B-Flat* to represent the last earthly trace of Niles, who wanders through that play unseen, like a soul after death.

These elements may have lurked somewhere under the surface of the original *Tooth of Crime*. In his 1996 revision, Shepard succeeded in drawing out these philosophical concerns with identity and self-transcendence that place the play on a continuum with his other work rather than off in its own rock-musical corner. However, the new version acquired some new literary depth at the expense of its theatricality. Without the topical references to hook the audience and make the world of the play seem fun or at least dazzling to encounter, *Tooth of Crime* became heavier, more somber, certainly less of a crowd-pleaser. It opended at the Lucille Lortel Theatre (formerly the Theatre De Lys) on Christopher Street, the prime Off-Broadway theater in the Village where *Buried Child* had once played, under Bill Hart's direction with Vincent D'Onofrio as Hoss. T-Bone Burnett's score was a vast improvement over Shepard's original music: its grunge-rock flavor unavoidably linked Hoss to Eddie Vedder and Kurt Cobain, charistmatic icons of '90s rock. And while scrapping Shepard's original lyrics meant losing the lines from "Crow's Song" that seemed absolutely central to the play—"I believe in my mask/The man I made up is me"—Burnett supplied Crow with a new number that, at long last, put the title of the play into one of the character's mouths.

The rest of the Signature season took place at the Public Theater. In addition to the Chaikin evening and the three one-acts led by *Action*, Signature arranged screenings of both Shepard's films as well as readings from his plays and his prose writings. And Houghton gave him the option of producing, at the end of the season, a new play.

Conspicuously absent from the Signature season were any of the family plays with which Shepard had become almost exclusively identified by critics and theatergoers. The most significant achievement of the Signature season was to draw attention to the length and breadth of his playwriting career. No assessment of Sam Shepard can be complete, after all, without taking into consideration the free-form, theatrically adventurous plays that preceded his semi-autobiographical cycle of family dramas. It's not so easy to follow or explain the leaps Shepard has taken in his plays. But that's not a problem—if anything, that was the point of the Signature season: if you think it's easy to categorize Sam Shepard as a writer, you've got another think coming.

There's no question that Shepard's rate of output has steeply declined since his fertile youth. Perhaps he's slowed down because he has less to say. Shepard has indicated not only that he's aware of the reality of his decreased productivity but that he recognizes the folly of denying it. As he admitted to one journalist, "Seems like playwrights hit a certain place where they're either repeating past work or trying to invent new stuff that has nowhere near the impact of the earlier work."

On the other hand, in a recent reminiscence of his thirty-year friendship with Shepard, Joe Chaikin wrote, "Sam is an artist. His mind has extraordinary imagination. Sam is never sure what he will do next. But I know he will write another play, and another and another."

Epilogue:

END WITHOUT ENDING

Luckily I love to drive. I've learned to love to drive. I love long-distance driving. The farther the better. I love covering immense stretches in one leap: Memphis to New York City; Gallup to L.A.; Saint Paul to Richmond; Lexington to Baton Rouge; Bismarck to Cody. Leaps like these. Without a partner. Completely alone. Relentless driving. Driving until the body disappears, the legs fall off, the eyes bleed, the hands go numb, the mind shuts down, and then, suddenly, something new begins to appear.

"Falling Without End," Sam Shepard

Playwright and movie star, serious artist and pop-culture hero—these split identities and the tension between them fuel Shepard's work. His plays often focus on the bizarre events and strange feelings that can be found in commonplace settings. His movie-star persona is the familiar element that defuses the strange. The struggle between those two things is the story of Sam Shepard.

"I'm driven by a deep dissatisfaction," he says. "What you accomplish in your work always falls short of the possibilities you know are sneaking around. The work never gets easier. It gets harder and more provocative. And as it gets harder you are continually reminded there is more to accomplish. It's like digging for gold. And when you find the vein, you know there's a lot more where that came from."

SAM SHEPARD BIBLIOGRAPHY

Plays

Cowboys (1964)
Rock Garden (1964)
Up to Thursday (1964)
Three and Melons (1964)
Replacement for Eight (1964)
Dog (1964)
Rocking Chair (1964)
Chicago (1965; Obie award)
Icarus's Mother (1965; Obie award)
4-H Club (1965)
Fourteen Hundred Thousand (1966)
Red Cross (1966; Obie award)
La Turista (1966; Obie award)
Forensic and the Navigators (1967; Obie award)
Melodrama Play (1967; Obie award)
Cowboys #2 (1967)
Shaved Splits (1969)
The Unseen Hand (1970)
Operation Sidewinder (1970)
The Holy Ghostly (1970)
Back Bog Beast Bait (1971)
Mad Dog Blues (1971)
Cowboy Mouth (with Patti Smith; 1971)
The Tooth of Crime (1972; Obie award)
Blue Bitch (1973)
Little Ocean (1974)
Geography of a Horse Dreamer (1974)
Action (1974; Obie award)
Killer's Head (1974)
Inacoma (1975)
Manfly (1975)

Angel City (1976)
The Sad Lament of Pecos Bill on the Eve of Killing His Wife (1976)
Curse of the Starving Class (1976; Obie award)
Suicide in B-Flat (1976)
Jackson's Dance (1977)
Seduced (1978)
Buried Child (1979; Obie award; Pulitzer Prize)
Tongues (with Joseph Chaikin; 1978)
Savage/Love (with Joseph Chaikin; 1979)
True West (1980)
Fool for Love (1982; Obie award)
The War in Heaven (with Joseph Chaikin; 1985)
A Lie of the Mind (1985)
States of Shock (1991)
Simpatico (1994)
When the World Was Green (with Joseph Chaikin; 1996)

Other theater pieces
Nightwalk (with Megan Terry and Jean-Claude van Itallie, performed by the Open Theater, 1972)
Re-Arrangements (with others; performed by the Winter Project, 1979)
Jacaranda (performed by dancer Daniel Nagrin, 19793
Drum War (performed by the Overtone Theater, 1979)
Superstitions (performed by the Overtone Theater, 1981)

Books
Hawk Moon (New York: Performing Arts Journal Publications, 1972). Prose poems by Sam Shepard.
Motel Chronicles (San Francisco: City Lights Books, 1982). Short pieces by Shepard, largely autobiographical, in prose and poetry.
Cruising Paradise (New York: Alfred A. Knopf, 1996). "Tales" that mingle fiction with memoirs.

Commentary on Sam Shepard
Auerbach, Doris. *Shepard, Kopit, and the Off Broadway Theater* (Boston: Twayne, 1982). Literary criticism.
Daniels, Barry, ed. *Joseph Chaikin and Sam Shepard: Letters and Texts, 1972–1984* (New York: New American Library, 1989).

Hart, Lynda. *Sam Shepard's Metaphorical Stages* (Westport, CT: Greenwood Press, 1987). Critical study.

King, Kimball, ed. *Sam Shepard: A Casebook* (New York: Garland, 1988). Critical essays by several authors.

Marranca, Bonnie, ed. *American Dreams: The Imagination of Sam Shepard* (New York: Performing Arts Journal Publications, 1981). Commentary on Shepard and his work by Shepard and others.

Mottram, Ron. *Inner Landscapes: The Theater of Sam Shepard* (Columbia, MO: University of Missouri Press, 1984). Critical study.

Oumano, Ellen. *Sam Shepard: The Life and Work of an American Dreamer* (New York: St. Martin's Press, 1986). Biography.

Patraka, Vivian M., and Mark Siegel. *Sam Shepard* (Boise: Boise State University, 1985). Pamphlet-sized monograph of literary analysis.

Weber, Bruce. *Sam Shepard* (New York: Little Bear Press, 1990). Photographs with a brief personal reminiscence by Weber.

Screenplays
Zabriskie Point (Michelangelo Antonioni; 1970)
Maxagasm (unproduced)
The Bodyguard (unproduced)
Ringaleevio (unproduced)
Fractured (unproduced)
Seventh Son (unproduced)
Paris, Texas (Wim Wenders; 1984)
Fool for Love (Robert Altman; 1985)
Far North (also directed; 1988)
Silent Tongue (also directed; 1993)

Screen appearances
Brand X (1970)
Bronco Bullfrog (1970)
Renaldo and Clara (1978)
Days of Heaven (1978)
Resurrection (1980)
Raggedy Man (1981)
Frances (1982)
The Right Stuff (1983)
Country (1984)

Fool for Love (1985)
Crimes of the Heart (1986)
Baby Boom (1987)
Steel Magnolias (1989)
Bright Angel (1990)
Defenseless (1991)
Voyager (1991)
Thunderheart (1992)
The Pelican Brief (1993)
Safe Passage (1994)
Streets of Laredo (1995)
Lily Dale (1996)

Acknowledgments

The material for this book was gathered from numerous personal interviews, original research, and published articles dating back to 1964. I am greatly indebted to William Kleb for his generosity in sharing with me his scholarship, his files, and his friendship, as well as his comments on the final manuscript. I'd like to thank Joyce Aaron, Charles Mingus, and Bill Hart for providing helpful background material, and to those who shared their personal recollections of Sam Shepard I am grateful: Lewis Allen, Nestor Almendros, Ralf Bode, Jacob Brackman, Joseph Chaikin, Jan Geidt, Wynn Handman, James Houghton, Tom O'Horgan, Albert Poland, Carole Rothman, Stephen Schiff, Peter Stampfel, Edward Swift, and LuAnn Walther.

I'd like to thank the following writers, critics, and journalists whose articles and interviews proved extremely useful in writing this book: Jennifer Allen, David Ansen, Ben Brantley, Eileen Blumenthal, Blanche McCrary Boyd, Robert Brustein, L. M. Kit Carson, Brian Case, Kenneth Chubb and the editors of *Theatre Quarterly*, Robert Coe, Nancy Collins, Jonathan Cott, Johnny Dark, Roger Downey, Jennifer Dunning, Stephen Fay, Michael Feingold, Linda Bird Francke, Samuel G. Freedman, Graham Fuller, Elgy Gillespie, John Glore, Robert Goldberg, Mel Gussow, Pete Hamill, Harry Haun, Michiko Kakutani, Naseem Khan, Jack Kroll, Michael Kuchwara, James Leverett, Amy Lippman, John Lion, Charles Marowitz, Bonnie Marranca, Stewart McBride, Alfred Nordmann, Julius Novick, Irene Oppenheim and Victor Fascio, Chris Peachment, Carol Rosen, Ron Rosenbaum, David Rosenthal, Stephen Schiff, Kevin Sessums, Jim Sharman, George Stambolian, Richard Stayton, Ellin Stein, Ruthe Stein, Dan Sullivan, David Thomson, Michael ver Meulen, Bernard Weiner, Michael White, Hartmut Wickert, and Scott Wren.

Special thanks go to William Harris, Gwin Chin, Tom Wiener, Anne Thompson, Joan Cohen, Alfred Nordmann, Karen Schimmel, Judith Greitzer and the Special Collections staff at Boston University's Mugar Library, whose assistance made things easier. I was tickled by Cal Gough's willingness to accompany me on a wild-database-chase through the horse journals of Texas. I'd like to thank my friends Harry Kondoleon, Alice Playten, and Joe Martin for their constant support and encouragement, and thanks to Merle Ginsberg for recommending me in the first place. Big thanks go to Gary Luke, who originally ushered this book into print, and to my first agent, the late Luis Sanjurjo, for his invaluable help and friendship. I'm grateful to my agent Robert Cornfield for his excellent taste, timing, and good humor and to Yuval Taylor, whose enthusiasm inspired the second edition. All kinds of valuable life rewards came from the care and kindness of my good friends David Lida, Sarah Schulman, and especially Harvey Redding.

Finally, there's no way this book could have happened without the grace, humor, and love of my friend Stephen Holden.

Index

LaVergne, TN USA
25 November 2009
165225LV00003B/44/A